Democratic Theory
Naturalized

Democratic Theory Naturalized

The Foundations of Distilled Populism

Walter Horn

LEXINGTON BOOKS
Lanham • Boulder • New York • London

Published by Lexington Books
An imprint of The Rowman & Littlefield Publishing Group, Inc.
4501 Forbes Boulevard, Suite 200, Lanham, Maryland 20706
www.rowman.com

6 Tinworth Street, London SE11 5AL, United Kingdom

British Library Cataloguing in Publication Information Available

Library of Congress Cataloging-in-Publication Data Available
Library of Congress Control Number: 2020944652

ISBN 978-1-7936-2495-6 (cloth)
ISBN 978-1-7936-2497-0 (pbk)
ISBN 978-1-7936-2496-3 (electronic)

To all those who have been silenced or ignored

Contents

Contents

Introduction

This is a book about and supportive of a particular kind of populist democracy—"populism" for short. It may seem a little surprising to see a book of this type these days, because the term "populism" has become something of a dirty word over the last couple of decades.[1] Even one who is not made uncomfortable just by hearing the term "populism" uttered without disdain is likely to wonder which of the two main types of populism I am talking about. In his widely read work on the history of American populism, Michael Kazin (2017) distinguishes "left-wing" (or socialist) populism of the early-twentieth-century progressive movement, from the arguably nativist and xenophobic "right-wing" variety that has been credited with the rise to power of Donald Trump in the United States, Boris Johnson in England, and Jair Bolsonaro in Brazil. However, as I understand the term "populism," if we strain away most of the goals identified by its supporters and just concentrate on its democratic essence, while it may be susceptible to both left- and right-wing varieties, it is not particularly conducive to either one.

NATIVISM, PROGRESSIVISM, RANDY NEWMAN, AND FRANK CAPRA

It is worth noting that, while Kazin has traced the history of the two "common man" strains of American populism in an engaging fashion, it is doubtful whether they're cleanly separable. Consider, for example, Randy Newman's apt representation of a Huey Long supporter at the time of the New Deal:

Kingfish

Who built the highway to Baton Rouge?
Who put up the hospital and built your schools?
Who looks after shit-kickers like you?
The Kingfish do

Kingfish, Kingfish
Everybody sing
Kingfish, Kingfish
Every man a king
Who took on the Standard Oil men
And whipped their ass
Just like he promised he'd do?
Ain't no Standard Oil men gonna run this state
Gonna be run by little folks like me and you
Kingfish, Kingfish
Friend of the working man
Kingfish, Kingfish
The Kingfish gonna save this land

(Newman 1974a)

It cannot be doubted that the sentiment expressed here is quintessential socialist populism. But is the singer/narrator entirely separable from the "redneck" Lester Maddox supporter depicted in another Newman song from the same album when the spirit of the following Dixie generation is invoked?

Rednecks

Last night I saw Lester Maddox on a TV show
With some smart-ass New York Jew
And the Jew laughed at Lester Maddox
And the audience laughed at Lester Maddox too

Well he may be a fool but he's our fool
If they think they're better than him they're wrong
So I went to the park and I took some paper along
And that's where I made this song

We talk real funny down here
We drink too much and we laugh too loud

We're too dumb to make it in no Northern town
And we're keepin' the n*****s down

We're rednecks, we're rednecks
We don't know our ass from a hole in the ground
We're rednecks, we're rednecks
And we're keepin' the n*****s down

(Newman 1974b)[2]

The aspirations of these two narrators may be somewhat different, but the boundaries between their two spirits are undeniably fuzzy. The moral that may be taken from both songs is, roughly, *you don't get to tell us what to do just because we're not "bigshots" like you. In America, we get to tell You what to do.* That, as Kazin confirms, has always been the rough basis for American populism. And that is simply a democratic motif that needs to be explained and either justified or rebuked. But because populism has been thought of in the United States as more of a *movement* (or bunch of movements) than as a philosophy or theory of government, there has been what seems to me to be an excessive concentration on the ethos and not much analysis of the theoretical underpinnings. Naturally, if one looks at slogans rather than either axioms or what follows from them, one is likely to find goals rather than justifications. As Newman's songs show, the goals might be increased socialism just as easily as decreased racial diversity.

It is interesting to note how distasteful populist ideals are to both standard conservatives and standard liberals. One of the former asked me recently,

If we lock our doors against possible thieves, why should we think it would be perfectly fine if those same miscreants ran the country? Isn't it obvious that they would quickly repeal all the laws against burglary? Let's face it, a call for "radical democracy" is just fancy a way of handing over all the power to residents of the American megalopolis—and we know how rapacious that group is!

But liberals are no less suspicious. You might hear one of them say, "Although we may try with all our might, it is quite likely that there will always be more uneducated bigots than people who are actually capable of understanding the fine points of governance. If you let the uneducated run the country, policies will not only be shortsighted, but racist, xenophobic and gun-crazy."

It may be noted that even when neither socialism nor nativism has been particularly prevalent among those pushing for more democracy (or both incentives have been cleverly cloaked), one can often make out a kind of

sentimental patriotism combined with the glorification of "the little guy."
Many examples of that sort of vague populism can be found in the movies
of Frank Capra. Consider the following excerpt from *Meet John Doe* (Riskin
1941).

> I'm gonna talk about us, the average guys, the John Does. If anybody should
> ask you what the average John Doe is like, you couldn't tell him because he's a
> million and one things. . . .
>
> He's Joe Doakes, the world's greatest stooge and the world's greatest strength.
> Yessir, we're a great family, the John Does. We're the meek who are supposed
> to inherit the earth. You'll find us everywhere. We raise the crops, we dig the
> mines, work the factories, keep the books, fly the planes and drive the busses!
>
> We've existed since time began. We built the pyramids, we saw Christ crucified,
> pulled the oars for Roman emperors, sailed the boats for Columbus, retreated
> from Moscow with Napoleon and froze with Washington at Valley Forge!
>
> I know a lot of you are saying "What can I do? I'm just a little punk. I don't
> count." Well, you're dead wrong! The little punks have always counted because
> in the long run the character of a country is the sum total of the character of its
> little punks. (Riskin 628–629)[3]

Like Randy Newman's songs, Frank Capra's movies try to capture a feeling rather than a philosophy. And it is precisely that feeling that populist
movements have tried to sell in order to gain purchase among the big political
parties. Whether a particular version has been "left" or "right"—whether the
chant has been "Banks got bailed out, we got sold out!" or "The Jews will not
replace us!" the means to the end (redistributive or homogeneous) has clearly
involved a type of comradery that has this at its core: we little guys get to run
the country—not the banks, not the politicians, not the professors. Maybe it
is, as the socialist might think, because we're the ones who built the pyramids
and dug the mines; or maybe, as the nativist might think, it is because we're
the only ones who came from these parts (or from a country where people
tend to have the same skin color as Washington and Jefferson). Or perhaps it's
because we're the ones who have died in the wars—rather than the generals,
the Standard Oil millionaires, or the Wall Street financiers. In any case, to the
extent that the history of populism is a story of what has driven "popular movements," a kind of "People's History of the United States," Kazin has done a
creditable job telling it, and I won't have a great deal to add to that story here.[4]

As indicated, all the strains of populism have certain common entailments as well as a common *feel* or *motif*. There is a resentment of bigshots,
of *elites*. Whether it comes from a racial or ethnic group or from Nixon's

so-called silent majority, and whether it aims its fear and loathing at Wall Street bankers or Mexican immigrants, most populisms have the theme that *Someone is preventing us from getting a fair shake, an equal opportunity to get what We want.* I hope to show in this book that this complaint is actually defensible and needs no additional left- or right-wing *feel* or justification. There is, and always has been, not only in the United States, but in nearly every polity in the history of the world, a failure to guarantee the fair opportunity for people to indicate what they want and make their governments at least try to obtain it for them. What I attempt to show here is precisely how a democratic polity must be governed to provide such assurance. Furthermore, I believe that the "distilled populism" presented here—or something very much like it—can help answer the question of why anybody ought to be expected to follow a law he or she doesn't personally agree with. Either significant dilution or significant expansion of its principles may result in legitimate rebellions both big and small, because the reasonable expectation of deference to the majority may disappear if substantial alterations are made to the model.

Of course, many have argued that no version of populism *ought to* be allowed to come into being because every species of it poses real dangers to life, liberty, and property in any country in which it dominates. It is even claimed that every populist government can only devolve into fascism or other type of mob rule. How, after all, can a radical democracy *not* be tyrannical? Isn't that why Madison and the other Founding Fathers wisely gave us a representative republic instead? A major focus of this book is to respond to those claims, so that arguments according to which any democracy worthy of the name must provide a fair opportunity for group members to get what they want, can be heard without fear or loathing. In other words, whether the procedures advocated here produce governmental policies which we approve or abhor, a road is described to a contentment with the manner in which policies are arrived at that far exceeds what any feebler democracy can provide. And this attitude may extend even to those cases where we find the results of some less democratic "republic" more congenial. Thus, I will be writing about premises that all defensible populisms involve—whether or not their left- or right-wing supporters have always realized it. And I will attempt to describe in a neutral manner the sorts of procedures that can be expected to result from those premises. What I will not attempt, however, is to find some supposed *essence* of populism, a quest that has been sensibly derided by Margaret Canovan (1981). For "populism" is a term that applies to a wide family of actual and possible arrangements, and, even if they all have one or two characteristics in common, other non-populistic polities might share those characteristics as well. My goal is rather to uncover *foundations* that can be used to support a number of populist arrangements, reasons why such (perhaps ideal) polities and only such polities should be considered worthy democracies.[5]

"DEMOCRACY YES, POPULISM NO!"

Now, it cannot be denied that, during the same half-century that has produced the increasing dread of populism described earlier, there has also been a stream of literature urging the expansion of democracy. Huge numbers of works have been published calling for more frequent votes, more (and more carefully delineated) parliamentary deliberation, and more varied sorts of citizen participation. That current levels of democracy are regularly derided as obviously insufficient can be gleaned from the opening lines of Shapiro (2003, 1) when he tells us that "The democratic idea is close to non-negotiable in today's world." This is because, in his view, it is not only that every group wanting power claims to be more democratic than the system or leaders they want to replace, but also because apparently nondemocratic regimes tend to vacillate among (i) "We are actually much more democratic than we may seem"; (ii) "Any deficiencies are not our fault, but that of some intrusive foreign power(s)"; and (iii) "We'll get to it as soon as the population is ready for it." In other words, at the same time that additional democracy has been dreaded as a likely precursor to fascism, it has also been urged as being absolutely necessary to anything like a peaceful and prosperous nation. "Democracy"—whatever it may mean exactly—has thus come to have a sort of religious glow: no polity can be decent or "just" without displaying a lot of it.

Perhaps this sort of *"It's ruinous!" "It's indispensable!"* dialectic is unavoidable: surely it has been around since the Ancient Greeks argued about the value of popular input to governmental rule-making.[6] It is worth noting, however, that the idea that democracy is an intrinsic good that is beyond reproach has never been particularly widespread in the United States. There has always been a very substantial segment of the population, perhaps even a majority, who, since the time of John Adams and James Wilson, have been horrified by the idea of "government by the mob." While the radicals, the Tom Paines and early twentieth-century progressives, have popped up from time to time, they have rarely (if ever) ruled the roost, and are, like Presidents Teddy and Franklin Roosevelt, Andrew Jackson, Jimmy Carter, and (at least on some issues) Donald Trump, mostly admired or scorned for their aspirations and outcomes rather than for the theoretical underpinnings of their views.[7] This is, no doubt, partly because those underpinnings are items that these leaders may have been only dimly aware of themselves.

Here in the United States, as scary as *any* sort of popular sovereignty has generally seemed since the French Revolution, extreme versions of it have been even less respectable. There may be the occasional firebrands of the "right" or "left" who will dare mention the word "populism" in public,[8] but the academy has spoken against anything bearing that title with near unanimity. To give just one recent example, William Galston (2018, 4–5) has warned that

> Populists view themselves as arch-democrats who oppose what they regard as liberalism's class biases. Their majoritarianism puts pressure on the individual rights and the limits on public power at the heart of liberal democracy. More dangerous still is the populists' understanding of the "people" as homogeneous and unitary. . . . Faced with disagreement, populism responds with anathemas: the dissenters are self-interested, power-hungry elites who aren't part of the virtuous and united people. They are rather the enemies of the people and deserve to be treated as such.

I therefore want to emphasize at the outset that the distilled populism I promote here bears only limited connection to the populisms trenchantly criticized not only in Galston's work, but in a large number of other recent books and papers.[9]

Let me again stress that the defense of populist theory provided here comes from a perspective that would neither blame nor praise democratic procedures for outcomes we may or may not enjoy. I take no positions (at least not here) on redistribution of wealth, public ownership of utilities, open borders, the taxing of billionaires, gun ownership, NATO, or green energy. I believe instead that, whatever my own views on these subjects, the majority principle ought to apply and we mostly need to figure out how to find the majority will and implement it appropriately.

But how is it possible to remain aloof from all the pressing, sometimes existential problems facing contemporary polities? Furthermore, why *should* democratic theory shy away from what really matters—things like avoiding nuclear war and maintaining an environment our children will be able to live in? These are good questions, but the answers to them may be simpler than we think. When we "naturalize" democratic theory by eschewing Platonistic understandings of "the good," we will see the point of repositioning arguments for particular political goals. If we come to understand the connection between a prudential value—what it is that actually makes a single life or a group of lives better—and what people want, we may begin to embrace a democratic theory that is merely *consistent* with many of the particular political results listed earlier, but neither requires nor prohibits any of them. This will be possible with a theory that is indifferent to whether or not you or I happen to agree with this or that vision of desired political outcomes ourselves. Distilled populism allows us to conclude that many of our own views regarding public policy, justice, or morality have no special standing, that to the extent the redistribution or climate-change questions involve value judgments, what we must do first—*before* pushing our own particular values—is find out what the people actually want. So, what may seem like an aloofness to political outcomes in this book results from the belief that my own view on this or that issue is to a significant extent nothing more than that (unless I can get others to agree with it). In other words, populism, rightly construed, suggests that our first duty is to try to understand what would make our polity better off based solely on the aggregated desires of all constituents—regardless of what we might want ourselves. We are not foreclosed from pushing for this or that outcome—and, as we shall see, there are good reasons for seeking empirical support for the "value-free" portions of our positions—but the higher and first goal is always to ensure appropriate democratic mechanisms, so that every person's attitude will be given fair consideration.

Before we grasp the nature of prudential values and their relation to voting, we are likely to find this notion perplexing. But when we come to understand what democracy actually means and entails, we may find ourselves pressing our own views—other than those involving democratic procedures—with a bit more humility. It's not that they no longer matter to us: we may still be staunch socialists or Bible-revering evangelists. But we may come to understand that it is the democratic principles that must take priority in every polity that can claim to be self-governed.

In my view, those who give non-democracy-enhancing goals primacy not only get priorities wrong; they will not be able to make good cases for the positions they *do* exalt, because there will be no compelling first principles that they can rely on when others disagree with them. In fact, I will argue that to the extent to which theorists fail to rely on a naturalized theory of democracy of the sort propounded here, whatever species of liberalism or conservatism they happen to favor will likely be rootless as well as inconsistent with our most basic concepts of popular sovereignty. If we believe in democracy at all, we will have to come to terms with the fact that democratic governments must be by and for the people, institutions, that is, that endeavor to get for their members no more and no less than what those members want. Distilled populism by definition requires (and says little more than) this, but, simple as it seems, every form of traditional liberalism and conservatism is antithetical to it. I will not insist that both "liberal democracy" and "conservative democracy" are oxymorons; it may well be that the term "democracy" is now squishy enough that a government that isn't literally by and for the people can be called democratic or "a democratic republic" without contradiction. I do think, though, that the most basic sense of "government by the people" has been lost within most current and traditional arrangements.

Many will chafe at the idea that a new theory of democracy is of any use at all. The comments of one left-leaning friend of mine nicely exemplify that attitude. At the suggestion that further theoretical work may be needed on questions of appropriate democratic rule, he responded that we must rely on people's integrity, since without that, no procedural safeguards would be meaningful. He pointed out that when a dissident in China recently argued that he should not be prosecuted since the Chinese constitution guarantees free speech, the court simply replied that that protection applies only to utterances expressing praise of the Chinese Communist Party. My friend took this to imply that governments will provide the greatest good for the greatest number only when those in power want that, since no government will be praiseworthy if it's run by people mostly interested in retaining their power, prestige, or wealth. After all, he asked, didn't Kwame Nkrumah, the former prime minister and president of Ghana, once express bewilderment at the idea that those with the guns would voluntarily give up power to those without them? Isn't it just human nature to place loyalty to one's own religion, wealth, or tribe above any feelings for one's nation? In his skeptical view, governmental documents like constitutions and their apparently democratic institutions, for all their nice talk about freedom and security, will do absolutely nothing without the support of those in power, so analyzing problems with democratic mechanisms is a fool's errand.

These criticisms are understandable. There is certainly a limit to what any theory can do—even an attractive one. It cannot make dishonest people honest. It cannot guarantee that votes will be counted in accordance with its principles. It cannot promise that the electorate will study up on political issues or agree that democratic fairness is more important than religion, wealth, or power. But it does not follow from any of this that political theories are useless or impractical. We may be interested in how to set up a democratic government where no particular assumptions are made about the goodness or malevolence of the population or of the outcomes of their group decisions. I believe that naturalizing democracy does not require one to assume that people are inherently honest and noble rather than deceitful or power-hungry.[10] And I will argue that taking this tack will help us to answer Nkrumah's question of why one would ever peacefully cede power. In any case, I do not endorse my friend's pessimism. And I note that although a robust democracy tells us what choices we are absolutely required to make only on certain quite specific matters, it does not instruct us to hold ourselves above the fray on *any* political issue. It simply necessitates a reordering of priorities.

The hopelessness expressed to me by my friend will likely produce different reactions among different readers. For example, rather than just throw up their hands, some may respond to his concerns by saying that, while the skepticism is correct with respect to fancy democratic rules, it is not that we should do *nothing*. This group may instead suggest that we expend our efforts on teaching "decent values" to various populations. Such respondents may not realize that the position they are taking is itself an autocratic or elitist one. By its lights, what *ought to be done* in some polity is a strict function of what this group thinks it is *right* to do. As they believe they know what kinds of societal results are just or unjust, perhaps as a result of their religious or other moral instruction, they believe they can, like the missionaries of old, simply educate the populace to be more like them. A naturalized democracy does not take that route. It rather implies that what would make a society better off is understood in a different, more modest way that does not rely on any view from above regarding just outcomes.

But dropping what is morally good or just brings us back to the "dirty word" problem.[11] It is no secret that the positions of Le Pen, Trump, Johnson, and Bolsonaro have been characterized as populist, and have consequently been lumped with those of Mussolini and Hitler. Now, I do not deny, for example, that distilled populism is consistent with the walling off of unwanted minority groups. However, as I hope to show, the sort of democracy espoused herein simply cannot engender fascism (properly so-called), and entails a kind of self-adjusting mechanism for dealing with border walls. In fact, I will argue that claims of legitimacy for any worthy democracy require its absolute prohibition of certain sorts of discriminatory acts within any polity. It is equally true that any alliance between populism and traditional liberalism is necessarily constrained. But those who think the populism supported here must then be "illiberal" should remember that it is essentially plebiscitary: it leaves no openings either for mob rule or mystical identifications between a leader and "his people," and it takes no demagogue seriously who claims to simply *know* (without the necessity of polling) what some group wants (or what is best for them, whether they want it or not). In fact, a properly arranged populism will make it significantly easier to dismiss such "strong men" than it is for traditional liberalism to do so.

DISTILLED POPULISM

I am not the first person to attempt to naturalize democratic theory. Perhaps the first to try his hand at it was Jeremy Bentham (who, incidentally, may also have played a small role in W. V. O. Quine's attempt to naturalize epistemology). Unlike Bentham's utilitarianism, however, the naturalized theory proposed here neither relies on hedonism as an explanation of either personal or group success, nor attempts any explication at all of what is (morally) *good, just*, or *right*. But distilled populism does share at least two things with Bentham's approach. First, they are both attempts to reduce prudential values—what makes individuals and groups better *off* (if not *morally* better)—to some conception of "the people getting what they want" without reference to any Platonic verities. Second, they share a reliance on their own particular aggregative methods of determining both what a group wants and the prudential values they entail.[12]

I focus my attention on the United States almost exclusively because while I have extensive experience with government in the U.S. style (both in the executive and legislative branches in Massachusetts) I am much less qualified to opine on other sorts of governmental arrangements. But in spite of the fact that my specific recommendations for changes are limited to U.S. constitutions, I believe that the principles of naturalized democratic theory apply everywhere.[13]

So, it is the *democracy* aspect of populism that I focus upon. Margaret Canovan (1981, 173–174) has suggested that the supposition that populism and democracy are somehow separable may seem odd to some observers:

> "Populist democracy" sounds like a pleonasm. Since "democracy" is widely supposed to mean "government by the people," how could a genuine democracy be other than populist? But this minor linguistic oddity conceals an important point: for the ideals and devices of populist democracy arise precisely in political contexts where "democracy" in some sense is officially accepted as a norm, but where dissidents feel that democratic practice does not live up to the promise of the name. Populist democracy consists of attempts to realize that promise and to make "government by the people" a reality.

As my position is largely plebiscitary, making the fairness of election mechanisms essential to (and nearly sufficient for) the correct determination of what the people want, it must depend upon a theory of appropriate voting systems. I will advocate for the combination of two specific types of voting schemes: approval voting (AV) and the single-non-transferable vote (SNTV). The first is a manner of taking the temperature of an entire district or country-wide populace. The second provides for minority representation, but does not even suggest what the people-as-a-whole want.[14] Neither seems to me sufficient on its own. I take appropriate representation of voter interests to require both such mechanisms, as well as a specific manner of combining them. Why I think advocacy for the combination of these two methods of aggregating the wants of the populace should be considered majoritarian will be discussed in some detail.

Like nearly everything I have written in the last thirty-five years, this book has been at least partially inspired by the work of Everett Hall, an American

philosopher who died in 1960. Hall published only one short paper (1943) on
the subject matter focused on here, but also left a draft of a never-published
book that he completed just after World War II. That manuscript, *The Road
to Freedom: An Ethics for Today*, is an elaboration of the paper just mentioned.[15] Much of that work seems to me still relevant, and it has certainly
had its effect on this book.

   While many of the proposals formulated here may seem abstract and/or
impracticable, I'm happy to note that at least a couple have been recently
advocated on Capitol Hill by members of Congress and high-level bureaucrats or are currently being pushed by one or more active national pressure
groups.[16]

PLAN OF THE BOOK AND ACKNOWLEDGMENTS

The plan of the book is as follows: chapter 1 focuses on what "democracy"
means, notes several paradoxes that come up when we think about it, and
considers whether it is the case that there is need for democratic reform in
the United States. Chapters 2 and 3 set forth what I call Choice Voluntarism
(or "CHOICE"), a new, though Hallian, theory of prudential value according
to which both individual and social valuations are of items that are human-
created but nevertheless objective. These chapters present the fundamental
arguments for naturalizing democracy and for moving to a particular way of
utilizing a principle that we could follow Hall 1943 by designating "The more
good, the better." These chapters are, in places, somewhat more technical
than the others, since they engage in detail with the contemporary literature
on prudential value. Those who dislike analytic philosophy may wish to skip
them, but this can be done without loss only if it is understood that their main
conclusions, which involve the assertion that what makes the world better for
people is a function of the quantity and scope of successful free choosings,
are essential to my case for distilled populism.

   Chapter 4 is a discussion of the thorny issues surrounding the equality of
persons and their votes, and whether the equality of one necessarily implies
the inequality of the other. I argue that acceptance of the CHOICE standard
discussed in the two prior chapters leads to an understanding of how both
votes and voters may be considered equal, without contradiction.

   Chapters 5 and 6 center on what are sometimes called the boundary issues
of democratic theory. Once it is decided that each person is to get a vote
with a weight equal to everyone else's, we now need to figure out just who
these persons are that are to be enfranchised. Chapter 5 focuses on whether
it is affected interests or geographical placement that is most relevant to
the issuance of group voting rights and eventually argues for the latter.

Chapter 6 urges the reduction of the minimum voting age to sixteen and the enfranchisement of "permanent residents"–including those who may be incarcerated and those having what some would consider only the slightest "competency."

The following two chapters are largely devoted to voting mechanisms. Chapter 7 urges support for AV, an age-old system that was reintroduced and popularized in the twentieth century (mainly by Brams and Fishburn [2007] in their eponymous book on the subject). AV is claimed to have significant advantages over other electoral systems, including that of having a method for addressing the "problem of intensity," something which has been claimed to fatally infect all populist majoritarian theories. Chapter 8 advocates a particular sort of implementation of SNTV. It is argued that SNTV, would best provide (sizable) minorities with proportionate voice, and, if appropriately combined with AV, would produce a democracy that is both majoritarian and protective of minority political rights. In chapters 7 and 8, I also consider "majority cycles," the appropriate size of legislatures, the concept of fair apportionment, and what it means to be "majoritarian."

In chapters 9 through 12, I turn more particularly to U.S. governmental structures and procedures, sometimes offering quite specific recommendations for change.[17] Chapter 9 focuses more closely on the nature of both votes and the act of voting and considers what these should suggest to us about appropriate levels of "directness" in worthy democracies. The classic question of whether representatives should be considered delegates or trustees is there taken up. I also discuss the necessity of referendum, recall, and reversal provisions, and attempt to set forth their limitations.

Chapter 10 continues the discussion of representation, focusing on the value of deliberation within lawmaking assemblies and the appropriate mechanisms for making laws. It is contended there that "separation of powers" has been taken much too far in the United States and that bicamerality is one of the main defects that emerged from the "great compromise" that created the United States in 1787.

Chapter 11 makes the case that our Constitution is both too much and too little. By that I mean that it both contains various provisions that are not really fundamental and would thus be more appropriate for statutory law (if the people really want them), and also fails to contain a number of provisions needed to completely protect certain rights that must be exalted in any democracy—the political ones. For example, the Fairness (in broadcasting) Doctrine, something which largely disappeared during the Reagan administration, is claimed in this chapter to be a fitting constitutional solution to current campaign issues—and something that may be especially important subsequent to the *Citizens United* decision. Because populism is skeptical of a number of "rights" countenanced by other theories, it is seen by some to be a sure harbinger of dystopia. So, I consider two science-fiction scenarios involving genocide to help see where the populistic conception of rights would land us. I also talk about the approach naturalized democracy would take toward the real-world "pro-choice/pro-life" debate, and concede the theory's limited capacity to create concord there.

Chapter 12 provides responses to several objections to democracy recently brought by libertarians and others. Some of these critiques are based on the belief that the only value that can be claimed for democratic processes must be found in the outcomes of those processes. Others allege different sorts of defects that I claim are related to an incorrect, epistemic construal of voting. I attempt to show the extent to which all of the objections would be friendly to elite "guardians" being in charge of our country. I argue that Platonic, guardian-friendly theories are inconsistent with both popular sovereignty and any coherent derivation of "rights," and conclude by indicating the extent to which naturalized democracy produces a more positive, less fearful view of government than the conception espoused by Alexander Hamilton and his fellow Founders.

I am grateful to Richard Hall, Joanne Kaliontzis, Aaron Lisec, Larry Tapper, Kevin Zollman, Caleb Huntington, Steve D'Amato, Greg Dennis, Aaron Hamlin, Alan Linov, Carol Calliotte, John DeMouy, Bruce Switzer, and several anonymous contributors to the Skeptical Zone website for helpful conversations, expertise, or encouragement. Chapters 2 and 3 are essentially revisions (some substantial) of a paper appearing in *Philosophia* (Horn 2019). I am grateful for permission to reproduce that material here. But my deepest appreciation goes to the wonderful Carol, the amazing Emma and Chloe, and the extremely soft Dumbledore for putting up with their cantankerous husband, father, and favorite lap provider (respectively), throughout his long and mostly solitary struggle to understand what makes something a worthy democracy. They're the best.

NOTES

1. For two recent almost simultaneous examples of that sort of usage, see Yascha Mounk (2019) and Debora MacKenzie (2019).

2. These excerpts from "Kingfish" © 1974 (renewed) WB Music Corp. and Randy Newman Music, and "Rednecks" © 1974, 1975 (renewed) WB Music Corp. are used by permission of Alfred Music, Inc. All rights are reserved by the copyright holders.

3. This excerpt from the *Meet John Doe* screenplay is used by the generous permission of Pat McGilligan.

4. I will note, however, that I find it odd that in discussing the progressive variants of populism, Kazin makes no mention of the classic books of Herbert Croly, Walter Lippman, or Walter Weyl (the highly influential founders of *The New*

Republic) or of W. S. U'Ren, who was largely responsible for bringing the initiative petition and referendum to Oregon and who tried valiantly to establish proportional representation and the single tax there as well. He also cites no works by Charles Beard or J. Allen Smith, the greatest of the progressive historians. This is also true of Goodwyn's (1976) celebrated history of American populism, which does not even mention Teddy Roosevelt. In any case, those missing thinkers and ideas are among the main influences here.

5. It is illustrative to consider that Nadia Urbinati, a theorist I quite admire, would likely classify many of the mechanisms defended here as plebiscitarian rather than populistic. I note, however, that her take on the nature of a plebiscite is narrower than what I mean by that term.

6. This is a recurrent theme of Ernesto Laclau (2005).

7. For an excellent explanation of why Jimmy Carter makes this list, see Canovan (1991, 269–273).

8. See, e.g., Thomas Frank (2018).

9. See, e.g., Urbinati's body of work on the subject.

10. Just as I require no presuppositions according to which "the people" when left to their own devices, must be susceptible to Joe McCarthy-type demagogues, neither will I join President Andrew Jackson, in holding that "we may have an abiding confidence in the virtue, intelligence and full capacity for self-government of the great mass of the people, our industrious, honest, manly, intelligent, millions of freemen" (Canovan 1981, 176). The antipodal caricatures painted by those siding with the fearful and disdainful Tocqueville (and Edward Shils) and those who agree with the pandering Jackson (and William Jennings Bryan) will both be claimed to be largely beside the point.

11. One observer who is almost explicit about treating "populism" as a dirty word is Nadia Urbinati, although she is somewhat easier on American strains. She removes "Occupy Wall Street" from her list of populist groups—exonerates it, really—because, while a "popular movement" it has no leader and does not seek to take over the country or convince the current leaders to create a more autocratic system. The Tea Party, on the other hand, wins a populist designation from Urbinati because of its allegedly dastardly intentions—whether it is quite "popular" or not. I mean no criticism of Urbinati here: as will become clear, I not only admire her work, but share many of her views regarding representation. But I do not mean by "populism" what she does when, following Bobbio, she writes that its "outcome, if actualized, would not be an expansion of democracy, but the condensing of the majority opinion under a new political class" and goes on to conclude that "Its achievement would be an exit from representative and constitutional democracy" (Urbinati 2014, 133–134). Similarly, Jan-Werner Muller (2017, 3) calls populism a form of identity politics because, he claims, when its advocates are not only necessarily critical of elites, but are also anti-pluralist, in the sense of insisting that only populists sympathizers represent the people: "When running for office, populists portray their political competitors as part of the immoral, corrupt elite; when ruling, they refuse to recognize any opposition as legitimate. The populist logic also implies that whoever does not support populist parties might not be a proper part of

the people." It will be seen that such "logic" is inconsistent with the distillation of populism presented here.

12. A more recent approach than Bentham's that may be seen as an attempt to naturalize democratic theory can be found in the (very much *non*-hedonistic or consequentialist) work of John Rawls. As will likely become clear, I do not find Rawls's work particularly congenial, and, although I have great respect for the ambition and scope of his output, it seems to me largely an attempt to determine a number of matters I consider undeterminable. In any case, I will not discuss it in much detail here.

13. Naturally, the author of any work making specific proposals of the type scattered around this book must acknowledge two facts. First, there is the one so apparently exciting to Bentham (1872): "To the whole contents of this proposed code, one all-comprehensive objection will not fail to be opposed. In whatever political community, by which it were adopted, it would, to a greater or less extent, probably to a very large extent, involve the abolition of the existing institutions." Second, there is the (non-Benthamic) consequence: what value the work has is likely destined to be more theoretical than practical.

14. While AV has not been adopted by any significant governmental entity, SNTV has been used in several jurisdictions around the world. However, the manner in which I claim it must be implemented has never been adopted anywhere (in spite of apt suggestions by several American progressives in the early twentieth century).

15. As might be surmised from the title, Hall's book was, at least to a certain extent, intended to be a response to Hayek's *Road to Serfdom*. I am grateful for the assistance of Aaron Lisec at the Everett Hall Archives at the University of Southern Illinois and for the permission granted me by Everett's son, Dr. Richard Hall, to quote from his father's manuscript.

16. I'm thinking here of Barbara Boxer, John Dingell, Jamie Raskin, Nicholas Johnson, Elizabeth Warren, Pete Buttigieg, the Brennan Center for Justice, National Youth Rights Association, and the Center for Election Science.

17. Those interested in comparative government or critical theory may be disappointed at this American tilt, but I hope many of the arguments and morals found here will be amenable to translation.

Chapter 1

Axioms, Paradoxes, and Alleged Deficits of Democracy

There is a lot of talk these days about the way the U.S. Electoral College works or fails to work. Those who supported Al Gore or Hillary Clinton in their Presidential campaigns complain that it was antidemocratic for that system to prevent the victory of candidates who had received more votes. Similar arguments are brought against the requirement that each state in the United States gets exactly two senators—regardless of the population of the state. These two features of the U.S. Constitution seem explicitly designed to prevent the majority from getting what it wants. Naturally, it is currently Democrats who are most vocal about this. For if the more populous states had more senators, there would seem to be a much greater likelihood of enactment of policies now favored by Democrats. Similar grievances are brought against the Supreme Court of the United States (hereafter SCOTUS). "Why," it is asked, "should nine unelected individuals who may serve until they die get to decide whether people may carry automatic weapons or receive abortions in their third trimesters? Shouldn't it matter what large majorities of the citizenry want? Isn't that what democracy requires?"

Of course, not everyone would see additional democratic features as unvarnished governmental goods. Many Americans may be tired of reminding their more "progressive" friends of the many illiberal democracies around the world where governments seem to have no scruples about nationalizing hard-earned private property or throwing people in prison for expressing their opinions in public. "Sure, the majority may have elected these thugs," you may wish to tell them, "but that doesn't make their actions acceptable. The very idea that some governmental act is appropriate just because it was arrived it by democratic means is ridiculous! Have you never heard of the tyranny of the majority?"

17

FOUR POLITICAL DIMENSIONS

While many on the "right" today are likely to claim that any alleged anti-democratic elements in the U.S. Constitution are features rather than bugs, it is important to recognize that aligning the "left" with democratic tendencies and the "right" with-antidemocratic or libertarian thinking doesn't always work. It has not always been America's "left" that has clamored for more democracy and objected to what was considered a usurpation of the power of the people by some empowered minority. There have also been numerous instances in which conservative members of Congress have chafed at the failures of clear majorities in their states to get their way. For while "progressives" have pushed for abolition of slavery or for increased regulation of the economy based on claimed majority preferences, the same sorts of arguments have also been brought by those wanting to preserve some "state's right" to retain slavery or to ignore a Federal regulation considered too harsh. On both sides, there have been appeals to the fact that the majority of some jurisdiction's voters (if not always of all of its residents) *want* this or that. At present, "left" appeals to various "human rights"—say to universal health care, a "living wage," or transgender bathrooms—are claimed to trump the will of majorities in various jurisdictions, and where this is the case, it is generally "conservatives" who may clamor for more democracy. But, again, we see the opposite dynamic when the "right to life" is somewhere opposed to majority support for "a woman's right to choose."

Thus, it is normal to wonder if there are reasons that can be adduced for majority rule that are entirely independent of the results expected to be produced by it. We may just want to know generally whether it makes sense to support democracy even in those cases where we believe the majority is evil, stupid, uninformed, or uninterested. It is easy to find both affirmative and negative answers to these questions in the existing literature on this subject. Indeed, countless books on political theory have been devoted to this subject since Plato wrote the *Republic* in about 380 BC. But the innumerable discussions of vote aggregation, "epistocracy,"[1] natural rights, deliberation, participation, decision theory, general will, sovereignty, consensus, and polyarchy have largely managed to miss something that seems to me central. And this has been the case regardless of how brilliant those works have otherwise been. Anti-democrats, from Plato to John Adams, Edmund Burke, Voltaire, Joseph Schumpeter, Ayn Rand, Robert Nozick, William Riker, and Jason Brennan have scoffed at the very idea that "the ignorant mob" ought to be asked much more than whether the current bums should be kicked out (if even that!). Others, like John Lilburne, Tom Paine, Jean-Jacques Rousseau, Herbert Croly, Theodore Roosevelt, Jürgen Habermas, Robert Dahl, Amy Gutmann, and Gerry Mackie, have insisted that the "general will" must be consulted before governmental actions can be authorized. With all these first-rate minds dissecting these topics from nearly every conceivable angle, what could possibly have been missed?

To answer this, we must consider the nature of the disagreement. Is it that there are different conceptions of what a utopian society would consist in? Perhaps those who want more democracy and those who either want less or think the present level is fine simply have different visions of Eden. Couldn't that make it quite natural for them to disagree on the means—democratic or otherwise—for reaching their great societies? I think not. "Result-assessment" cannot be a sensible reason for supporting different levels of democracy because, as we have seen, there is nothing like unanimity of goals either among the democracy-doubters on the left or the right,[2] or among the democracy exponents to be found there. Consider a continuum moving from (A) antipathy to all governmental limitations on what citizens may or may not do on one end, to (Z) support for extreme governmental autocracy on the other. We may find at the "don't tread on me" (A) end such unlikely partners as left-wing communitarian anarchists and right-wing evangelical decentralists. While at the "it's good to do as the wise instruct" (Z) extremity, there will be a wide variety of different sorts of utopians: a collection including both those advocating the mandatory use of Skinner boxes and those who would require conformance to Sharia Law. The communitarians and the Skinnerians are thus at opposite ends of the autocracy continuum in spite of both arguably being "far left" (say, because of their support for high levels of "mandatory sharing") on the political spectrum. Similarly, Sharia Law proponents and devout Calvinist decentralists may, from one point of view, be said to take like political stances because they are both on the (perhaps theocratic) "right" on several issues, in spite of their likely differences regarding what they think are appropriate governmental powers. Paradoxically, libertarians may find themselves closer to the autocrats on this autonomy dimension than to those anarchists who may seem to them to be no better than the beast worshippers in *Lord of the Flies*. That is because libertarians are often quite insistent on the strict constraints they believe must be placed on any "infringements of essential freedoms." It should thus be evident that there is no easily derivable relation between the progressivism/conservatism dimension and the autonomy/autocracy dimension. The fact that median members of the large U.S. political parties may be found somewhere in the middle of both ranges should not suggest that the two dimensions are identical.

But there is another complication that should be added here. Both liberals and conservatives have argued for many years about whether personal goals should or should not be left entirely up to individuals. We have already seen that, for their part, small "d" democrats may be liberals, conservatives, centrists, socialists, anarchists, or states' rights nativists. But there is an additional difference of opinion that can be found among these groups regarding whether there are obligatory personal goals, like, for example, caring for one's children or service to Allah. In other words, we can zoom in on members of the various groups mentioned above, wherever they may be found on the autocracy or left-right dimensions, and ask whether they believe that the personal goals they have chosen—whether these involve improved video game skills, memorization of *Hamlet*, amply providing for one's family, increasing one's number of sexual conquests, or decreasing worldwide carbon emissions—ought to be left entirely up to them. Thus, we have a third dimension, this one specifying what might be called "the latitudinarian scale." Here, we are likely to find the libertarian at the highly latitudinarian end and the theocrats, Skinnerians, and communists on the other, dogmatic end. This dimension should not be confused with that involving autonomy/autocracy, because nothing prevents a latitudinarian on the personal level from being entirely pro-autocracy on the group level. A libertarian, for example, might have an extreme distaste for the idea that her personal goals may be set by anyone else—even the wisest guardian—but may feel that a benevolent, powerful dictator is the best way to produce the latitudinarian regime she desires. Thus, all of our three dimensions seem to be orthogonal with respect to one another.

These three continua (left/right, autonomic/autocratic, and latitudinarian/dogmatic) have been the focus of discussion by moralists, political theorists, and economists for hundreds of years, and these thinkers have burrowed more and more deeply into all that might be connected with the question of what constitutes the good life. The puzzles they've wrestled with are familiar: "Must desirable societies encourage goodness and frown on evil activities?" "Is the enjoyment of push-pin of less value than the enjoyment of poetry?" "How much of what we have should we share with the needy?" The answers given to such inquiries—both as to appropriate goals, and as to appropriate methods of obtaining them—are what primarily divide people into different political groups. For example, a classical liberal of the dogmatic variety, safe in her assurance that all people must be protected in their persons and property, may work out the details of what else (if anything) might be required to bring about heaven on earth; while a more community-minded person might concentrate on how far worker control of industry or protection of indigenous customs must be pressed to ensure a good society. Just as the classical liberal has somehow determined that freedom and security must be protected at all costs, the communitarian has come to what she takes to be a reasoned conclusion that, in a decent society, corporate greed cannot be allowed to result in the exploitation of children, gays, or the rainforest. These opposed groups often confront each other, sometimes to argue, sometimes to compromise, sometimes to protest; and over time a pendulum seems to swing back and forth between the traction gained by moderate and extreme views. The heroes of each group—scholars, novelists, saints, politicians, theologians—have provided copious arguments for every position on all the continua: from Chomskyan anarcho-syndicalism or Randian libertarianism to Marxian socialism, Amish primitivism, and Skinnerian utopianism.

When thinking about democracy, it is crucial to notice that the dimension stretching from perfectly distilled populism on one end to no-popular-control on the other is not identical with any of the three dimensions discussed so far—not even with the one stretching between (A) and (Z). On one end of the populism continuum, we will find people getting from their governments what and only what they want—whatever it might be; and at the other extreme we might find totalitarianism. But at that undemocratic terminus we also might find utter anarchy, constitutional libertarianism, theocracy, scientistic paternalism, or, paradoxically, even certain types of town-meeting-style communitarianism. Any arrangement that either systematically ignores the desires of the majority in favor of anything thought to be superior to that goal is essentially antidemocratic, whatever else it might be. The main feature of the populist perspective is its extreme resistance to every claim regarding what constitutes social good except for one: group self-governance. No other ostensible societal *good* is deemed fundamental by the distilled populist.

SEVEN POPULIST COMPLAINTS ABOUT THE UNITED STATES WITH MADISONIAN RESPONSES

It cannot be denied that the current situation is one of stalemate all across the board. It would therefore be pointless for me to take my own attitudes regarding what I take to be a shortage of democracy in the United States today as being likely to carry much weight with anyone else. To illustrate this, consider the ease with which a Madisonian (i.e., someone who mainly worries about the tyranny of the rapacious mob) can respond to a number of concerns that a populist might bring up about the present state of American government.

1. Something seems wrong about (e.g., presidential) elections in which a candidate receiving fewer votes than one of his/her opponents nevertheless wins the race.
   A. "The Great Compromise," whereby the several states agreed to enter the union only under certain conditions is a feature of our freedom. Our constitutional system is precisely what allows for protection of individual rights against a tyrannical majority. If there were too much democracy—such a majority could crush every minority group.

2. Something seems wrong about a small handful of unelected "supreme" jurists being able to overturn the evident will of a large majority—especially if such jurists cannot be removed by the citizenry based on the substance of their decisions.

   A. It is exactly this sort of judicial review that makes the United States a jurisdiction of "laws, not men." Justice Marshall understood that *something* had to be the last word on what the government may and may not do, and he made sure it was our Constitution.

3. Something seems wrong about the incredible influence of wealth in electoral politics. Doesn't a system that allows this violate some important principle guaranteeing the equality of political power among citizens?

   A. Shouldn't a guaranteed right to free speech, assembly, and association mean that no public entity may curtail anyone's right to unrestricted political activities? Only the right to unlimited use of money to advocate for particular candidates or issues can guarantee political freedom. Any limitation would be pure despotism.

4. Something seems wrong with a system that allows legislators to fail to enact laws that majorities want and provide no recourse to citizens until some subsequent election.

   A. Wouldn't systems allowing for the recall of authority figures or reversal of their actions simply make it impossible to govern? Shouldn't we insist that *representation* is not reduced to mere *delegation* so that capable, experienced office-holders may actually govern and not just take orders?

5. Something seems wrong about a system that provides majorities not only with 100 percent of "rule" but with 100 percent of representation.

   A. Proposals for proportional representation or "fair voting" schemes are really just hobby horses. There are an infinite number of such proposals, and all are inconsistent with each other. It is only simple, understandable federal systems, like the one the Founders gave us, that can be depended upon to ensure that minorities will have their fair say in government.

6. Something seems wrong when high school students who want additional gun controls (because so many of them are being shot in school) are given no right to vote on a matter that affects them so greatly.

   A. Obviously, children are insufficiently mature to vote—and what's more, they don't pay taxes. They are free to agitate on the matter (as they have), and their parents can certainly be expected to represent their interests. That is sufficient.

7. Something seems wrong about strange, result-oriented district shapes that are constructed precisely for the purpose of preventing fair representation.

A. Shouldn't states be allowed the latitude to do what *their* voters want? In any case, *all* forms of voting have been determined by the most important thinkers on this subject (from Condorcet to Arrow and Riker) to be riddled with paradoxes and contradictions. So, singling out gerrymanders is just political posturing.

I think this little colloquy between two discussants, one an advocate for additional democracy and the other a Madisonian supporter of republican constraints, provides a good illustration of the difficulties that must be faced by any theorist arguing for additional "people power." And consider how much more demanding this task would be if all the other theorists—the socialists, the theocrats, the anarchists, and the libertarians—also had their chances to respond to the seven populist complaints listed above! Why should any theory be given precedence? Can the populist seriously suggest that every position but hers is mistaken? That apparently arrogant standpoint is precisely the position of this book. As indicated earlier, I *do* think something has generally been missed or mistaken in discussions of these matters. And I believe that puzzle piece is the key to understanding which of the many voices on democracy should be heeded. The burden of this book will be to make a plausible case for this admittedly audacious claim.

It will help to see the case I am required to make here if we shift to another manner of looking at the panoply of political positions. The following list separates democratic theories according to their consistency with one or another of the following mutually exclusive and ostensibly exhaustive propositions:

(1) The proper goals of both persons and societies are objective items/truths that are either generally known or can be determined by religious, philosophical, or empirical investigations.

(2) The proper goals of both persons and society are objective items/truths that are not generally known, but may, on the societal level, be discovered by democratic means, since elections are "truth-tracking" activities: they provide evidence that this or that goal is the right one.

(3) The proper goals of both persons and societies are objective items/truths that are not generally known, but democratic procedures cannot help us discover them on the societal level, since elections are not truth-tracking.

(4) There are no "proper goals" of any society, because societies, like the individuals within them, have only subjective ends. But what the subjective goals happen to be within any society may be discovered on the societal level by democratic means, since elections are truth-tracking in the sense of helping us find the subjective ends actually subscribed to by the populace.

(5) There are no "proper goals" of any society, because societies, like the individuals within them, have only subjective ends. What the subjective goals happen to be within any society cannot be discovered by democratic means on the societal level since elections are not truth-tracking.[3]

It is thus clear that, in light of the large number of competing theories regarding the nature of social goals and choices, on the theoretical level the populist has a lot of work to do if anyone is to be convinced. In addition, there are empirical contentions requiring response. Populists must deal with the fact that anti-democrats may be able to produce numerous historical cases in support of their claim that significant reductions in governmental checks to democratic urges are quite likely to produce unpleasant results. Several ostensibly populist regimes (that which immediately followed the French Revolution is a favorite example) seem to bear out the fear that terror necessarily follows upon radical democracy. And it may well be that if we look to what has happened in the most democratic jurisdictions throughout history, we will find instability, extensive corruption, even beheadings and genocide. Who will want to defend that heritage? Although it is true that the autocracy camp has equally horrible precedents to explain, perhaps those can be attributed to insufficient protection of "natural rights" or to the fact that the wrong goals were sought or experts put in charge. It seems more difficult for the populist to reply that if there had only been more democracy in place, there would surely have been reduced guillotine use. And if the populist tries to make apparently democratic tyrannies a function of insufficient education among the democratic electorate, the response will surely be, "Well, then, we must presume that those electorates were not actually supportive of additional education, since they were democracies and could have done exactly what they wanted in that area too!" The moral seems to be that shifting the focus from philosophical arguments to empirical outcomes may not be too helpful to the populism advocate.

Returning to the theoretical side, it seems undeniable that societal goals must be either objective or subjective and that democratic procedures must be either conducive to the discovery of truths or not. What other possibilities could there be? Again, I will argue that the set of (1)–(5) is importantly misleading and incomplete. Obviously, that is a claim that requires ample support, and fulfilling that requirement is one of the principal tasks to be undertaken here.

But before we turn to what having and discovering goals consist in on personal and societal levels—the main topic of the book—it may be well to think about whether there is much point to this inquiry at all, whatever the right answers to those questions may be. For there is a Panglossian line of objections according to which there is nothing to worry or complain about with respect to the current level of democracy in the United States, because it is perfect right now. Of course, if what we have in the United States today is no less than the paradigm for which all democratic entities reach, there can hardly be any point to a lengthy inquiry into the nature of democratic procedures. Perhaps the list of supposed democratic shortages in the United States just reflects a bunch of characteristics that only some impossibly flawless and ideal democracy could exemplify. According to that objection, the fact that I (in common with "free speech warriors," "identity-mongering" deliberation advocates, and other allegedly utopian theorists) *wish* for something different does not mean there actually *could be* anything more democratic than what we have now.

That is a pretty line, no doubt, but it seems clearly false. If "democracy" means anything at all, it must mean doing what the people want, and, for good or ill, *that* standard can hardly be said to be met in the United States at present. Our system may indeed be better than many others in a large variety of ways, but solid contemporary research (Gilens and Page 2014, 564) demonstrates conclusively that "average citizens and mass-based interest groups have little or no independent influence" on the policies taken by our government. That extensive study demonstrates that, in reality, for over a decade, corporate interests, rich individuals, and powerful interest groups have, through monetary contributions and effective lobbying, been the prime movers of American policy. The desires of average citizens have been largely irrelevant. One may argue, of course, that these results have been good for the country, or even that they've made it better than any possible alternatives could have. But that would not make these practices democratic. We may even engage in a sort of "reflective equilibrium" (Rawls 1971) by revising our original definition of "democracy" in consideration of actual (arguably paradigmatic) practices we find around the world currently, or can find in historical records. Such a move would not help very much with respect to the U.S. system. For the reasons given, the United States simply cannot pass muster as a polity in which the people rule. When one finds oneself insisting that practices that allow nine unremovable individuals to have the final say in what shall be the laws of a country of 350 million are definitory of the concept of *democracy*, one is no longer making sense: and it does not matter whether those practices are or are not beneficial to those millions.

The above list of seven claimed democracy shortages in the United States may be useful in helping us to unearth the basic meaning of the term, for it is the concept of *democracy* that causes the disquieting impression that "something is wrong" with this or that present policymaking procedure. I believe that, as a first approximation, we can assert that these discomforts stem from apparent inconsistencies with one or another of two propositions. We might even dub those propositions axioms.

TWO AXIOMS OF DEMOCRATIC THEORY

A. A democratic polity must at least try to do what its citizens indicate that they want done: there is no "higher authority" to which one may appeal for better or more legitimate instructions regarding what must be done.
B. Each citizen in a democracy must be treated equally when it comes to the determination of what its citizens want their government to do.[4]

One may again resist these as ideal formulations, and insist that one is better off defining "democracy" extensionally by providing a list of polities one believes ought to be considered democracies or have been so described in political histories. If we proceed in that (arguably question-begging) manner, and the United States is among the examples on the list, it will, by definition, be an example of a democratic state in spite of falling afoul of what seems to be expressed by (A) and (B). To repeat, however, that approach is inappropriate because those two axioms seem to provide a fairly orthodox take on what it *means* to be a democratic institution. After all, there is nothing about the concept of democracy that requires that there has ever been a perfect—or even particularly good—one. What we *do* know is that any such entities must be ultimately controlled by their members—or at least by a majority of them. Why? Because it is essential to the concept that, in a democracy, the supreme power—the *sovereignty*—is vested in the people at large: it cannot have been turned over even to a subset of them. A citizenry may exercise this authority either directly or indirectly through elected representatives, but if that authority is entirely alienated by its complete conveyance to anything else—whether a person, a group, or a deity—democracy is no more. It must be the people rather than the kings, the oracles, or the riches that decide what public actions will take place. It will therefore not do to take every country whose name has ever been found within some list of ostensibly democratic states, and say "these and anything like them should be considered democracies just because their names are on this list."

While it cannot be sensibly doubted that there are serious deficiencies to be found in the current state of democracy in the United States, some might claim that it does not follow that such alleged shortcomings have not been good for the country. Whether that is so or not (and I think it is not), we should at least be willing to agree with this sentiment found in J. Allen Smith (1907):

> It is [the] conservative approval of the Constitution under the guise of sympathy with majority rule, which has perhaps more than anything else misled the

people as to the real spirit and purpose of that instrument. It was by constantly representing it as the indispensable means of attaining the ends of democracy, that it came to be so generally regarded as the source of all that is democratic in our system of government.

I will argue that it is *not* a good thing for a country to lack real democracy, and it is my hope that this book will aid in discovering some possible means of improvement. What I cannot provide, however, is a happy prognosis. For my medicines, like Bentham's, "would, to a greater or less extent, probably to a very large extent, involve the abolition of the existing institutions." I don't call for such abolition here (though I may wish for it occasionally): I simply say that without significant changes that may depend on the abolition of this or that system or practice and its replacement by something else, the United States cannot justly be called a democratic regime. And I hope to show that being a good democracy is something to which we should aspire.

Perhaps unsurprisingly, (A) and (B) are much trickier than they may appear at first glance. A correct understanding of them could be claimed to depend on which proposition we pick from our (1)–(5) list. For example, a good deal of the literature on democratic theory has focused on whether or not what citizens want in axiom (A) should be thought to be a function of enlightened consideration of such matters as the effects a course of action is likely to have on everyone, and so, perhaps, depend upon our conceptions of justice. Further, theorists have struggled even to answer questions regarding just which individuals should be taken to be the citizens in (B): Is anyone who stops by for a visit qualified as a relevant person, or must one pay taxes or own real estate where their wishes are to count? And what about the desires of the clearly insane or those of convicted felons? What of children or even newborn babies? Must their wishes also be included in the mix? If so, why should we consider it to be definitory of "democracy" that the vote of a young child be given equal weight with that of a constitutional scholar? As can be seen, our axioms might be few in number, but they are far from simple.

Let me repeat here that even if we were to sort out this matter of what "democracy" (or "good democracy" or "worthy democracy" or "populist democracy") calls for, that would not have gotten us anywhere near the point where we could claim that having such a system is beneficial or that getting closer to it in the United States would be good for U.S. citizens. At present we are only considering what democracy *is*. Obviously, justice cannot be done to any of these matters in this introductory chapter. But I can at least provide a sense of what is to come in the sequel. As a first illustration, let us consider for a moment some of the thorny problems surrounding (B).

LIBERALISM, REPUBLICANISM,
NATIVISM, AND CITIZENSHIP

In an insightful article that is essential reading for those interested in U.S. attitudes toward inclusivity and exclusivity since its founding, Rogers M. Smith (1988) distinguishes three basic attitudes: liberalism, republicanism, and ethnocultural Americanism. As Smith explains, the liberal outlook, taking all (property-owning white) males to be created equal, was the most inclusive of the three creeds. On that view, one is born with inalienable rights, and among them is being eligible to have one's votes counted upon reaching (male, white) adulthood—although, perhaps one might also be required to have a mite of freehold property to show sincerity and ability. Smith's point is that, for liberals during the colonial days, white, male adults were essentially indistinguishable "from the inside," so it seemed there could be no insurmountable bars to anyone's citizenship. One might need to reside somewhere for some period of time or show one's seriousness by the acquisition of real estate, but other characteristics, such as those involving language, culture, education, or the like, were considered incidental. If they don't matter to God—show up "under the hood" as it were—they should not bother registrars of voters.

As Smith sees it, a second strain, which he calls *republican*, has been more goal-oriented. Rather than taking citizenship privileges to be implied by natural rights, these colonial Republicans focused on what they took to be characteristics likely to promote the common good through self-governance. Since a homogeneous citizenry was seen by these Republicans as essential to the avoidance of intractable controversies, what liberals had taken to be unimportant, accidental characteristics, were viewed by the Republicans as essential to the welding together of a functioning community.

This strain of communitarianism was taken a step further by *ethnoculturalists*, who believed (and may still believe) that even homogeneity is insufficient to produce a decent society. In their view, "sameness at the core" is not enough: some races or genders are simply less competent. Indeed, even cultural and ethnic characteristics are thought to make crucial differences. On the more nativist strains of this position, only homogeneous groups of "real Americans" can be expected to produce a competent, limited government in the people's interest. Smith (1988, 233) writes,

> In the Jacksonian years, the scientific racialism of the "American school of ethnography" and the cultural nationalism of the European romantics gave these ideas intellectual credibility. They were subsequently reinforced by the racialist anthropology, history, and Social Darwinist sociology and political science influential in the late nineteenth and early twentieth centuries. Publicists,

professors and politicians worked these ideas into a general "political ideology" of "American racial Anglo-Saxonism."[5]

So, who are "the people"? Is it simply whoever the laws apply to? Such an answer is suggested by the American colonist chant, "No taxation without representation!" But analogous slogans could currently be shouted by long-time, noncitizen residents who must comply with numerous statutes—including tax laws—over which *they* have no say. And what was urged by women and African Americans in the not-so-distant past is sometimes heard today from advocates not only for resident aliens but for minors or felons. After all, those groups are also subject to the laws of the land. But, of course, it is equally true that various statutes apply to toddlers, babies, even pets! At what point does agitation for suffrage simply become ridiculous?

These issues are not new. Indeed, not only the Federal government but every state has regularly had to take them up since voting rules were first established among them. Are there any general principles we can now turn to for resolving these questions, or are we forced to take them on a case-by-case basis and acknowledge, in light of the widely different answers and approaches adopted throughout the country since colonial days, that there are no such principles to be found? These matters will be taken up in chapters 5 and 6.

FROM WHO MAY VOTE TO WHAT MAY BE VOTED UPON

Turning now to axiom (A), we will find that a number of "chicken-egg" issues pop up whenever one considers problems of democracy. For example, it is well known both that a large percentage of eligible voters fail to cast votes in U.S. elections and that many of those who do vote have little knowledge of the issues or people they are voting for. Suppose both of those assertions are correct. We might infer that voting is unimportant to a vast number of citizens, and that this is just as well, because American voters are ill-equipped to be involved in governance. But it might also be thought that the apparent disinterest is no more than a result of the way our system is set up. That is, some might say that in our large, winner-take-all elections there is no real reason for people to learn about the issues or even to care about voting at all. If I believe that my vote can't change anything, or if I don't like any of the candidates, or understand that, after I vote, elected officials will do whatever they want anyhow, there's a good chance that I won't bother to study the issues at hand or even make my way to a polling booth. The evidence suggests that a feeling of pointlessness is not unreasonable. The study by Gilens and Page (2014) looked at about 1,800 policy positions considered by Congress between 1981 and 2002, and found that the views of the majority of Americans on those issues were largely ignored in favor of the views espoused by powerful (mostly corporate) lobbyists. The recourse for that, of course, would seem to be to "throw the bums out" at the first opportunity, but not only may there be no election on the horizon, those same corporate interests may be very effective in preventing any bum-throwing. Thus, it seems reasonable to wonder whether the voters are to blame for their indifference or the system is to blame for making voters largely irrelevant. The more indifferent voters are, the more irrelevant they are bound to become, and the more irrelevant voters are, the more indifferent they are bound to become. So, chicken or egg?

Even if we stipulate that there are problems with the current system and ignore any concern that we would not be able to implement improvements even if we could find them, it is difficult to see how to progress. Chicken-egg problems seem to arise at every turn. As we have said in reference to (B), democracies require knowing the will of the people, since in self-governed jurisdictions the citizenry must always make the final determination on matters of public policy. But if we are to take the pulse of "the people," we need to know who they are—whom to ask. Like the old joke regarding one who has lost her glasses being unable to look for them until she finds them, it seems that "the people" must be asked in order for us to discover just who "the people" are!

Democratic paradoxes extend beyond *who* may vote to *what* may be voted on, whether there are items of law that must be placed beyond the voters' reach. Such limitations may be expected to be found in constitutions, particularly sections designated as "bills of rights." Smith (1988, 230) notes that "Enlightenment liberalism's 'natural' rights were fairly minimal: they did not include rights to any specific political membership, much less enfranchisement." But it is worth noting that, even if such provisions *had* been included, the limitation of "rights" to guarantees of protection against governmental incursions means that those provisions would not have been able to go terribly far in ensuring government by the people. Suppose, for example, that businesses began to offer desperately needed jobs only to those who would give up their right to vote. A constitution limited to protecting citizens against government actions could do nothing to stop that practice. In this way, even an ostensibly "democratic" constitution guaranteeing the political rights of free speech, assembly, association, suffrage, and the right to run for public office would seem to allow democracy to disappear. The question of whether one ought to be able to give up voting rights in return for employment is similar to the ancient puzzle of whether someone ought to be allowed to contract oneself into slavery. In that latter case, the alleged *inalienability* of personal freedoms is often thought to make any such contract invalid. However, a similar demonstration of inalienability for political rights might falter since individual liberties (including such "economic liberties" as "the right to choose one's vocation") have generally been thought to trump equal access to the mechanisms for obtaining and using the vote or for gaining public office. Although it is true that those wanting to liberalize suffrage have increasingly (if slowly) won numerous battles against various opponents in the United States, it is also the case that the national government has generally moved in the direction of stressing "private rights and commercial development over democratic participation" (Wood 1969, 562).

Perhaps, however, the widespread attitude that political rights should be discounted in favor of what may be considered the more "basic" claims to life, liberty, and the pursuit of happiness is misplaced. It is doubtful in any case that there has been unanimity on that ranking. At the Federal Convention of 1787, Pierce Butler of South Carolina claimed that "There is no right of which the people are more jealous than that of suffrage" (Kurland 1987, 49). Before concluding the discussion of this issue here I want to mention one populist attempt, by Herbert McClosky, to guarantee democracy (and overcome this democratic paradox of what may be voted on) by the exaltation of political rights above all others. It is a prototype of the approach that will be taken in this book. McClosky (1949, 653–654) writes, "It may appear a paradox, but democracy, though choice is of its essence, precludes one kind of choice: we cannot, under it, choose not to choose. We cannot, with democratic sanction, choose to cut ourselves off from those requirements that make all choice possible."

But how is this debacle to be prevented? According to McClosky (1949, 646) we must

distinguish political freedoms, such as the freedom to participate in the choice of rulers, from nonpolitical freedoms, like those often claimed for property or religion. The principle of majority rule recognizes no limitations on the power of the majority or its government except those that are essential to the attainment of freely arrived-at majorities and to the maintenance of political consent and accountability. Freedoms associated with property are of an entirely different order from the freedoms to speak and publish. The latter are political freedoms, without which a majority rule system is impossible; they cannot, therefore, be legitimately abridged. Freedom of contract, on the other hand, may, so far as the majority principle is concerned, be regulated and controlled in whatever fashion the majority or its government deems best. Whether industry shall be national-ized or privately owned; whether wages shall be set by government or by private contract; whether polygamy shall be permitted are matters that a democratic government can, if it likes, control. It cannot, however, properly determine whether political criticism will be tolerated or whether elections should be abolished, for the right to oppose and the right to elect are among those political freedoms from which its power derives.

This is an elegant resolution of the paradox, certainly, and it will come up again as we progress. But is there really a credible basis for accepting it? Why is it just those political rights mentioned by McClosky that are "inalienable," and not any others, like those of life, liberty, and property, set forth by Jefferson in the *Declaration of Independence*, protections which may seem even more fundamental? If democracy may be limited by one or two unbreakable principles, why not others? Is it just the convenience of paradox-smashing that causes McClosky to stop at the political axioms? Furthermore, how do we tell which ones actually *are* the political ones? For example, is *habeas corpus* political because its defiance could keep a political activist under wraps? And there is a more serious objection even than these: supposing we could precisely delimit the political principles, isn't disregarding the rights enumerated in the *Declaration* a very dangerous move? One acute critic of populism, Wilmoore Kendall, warned of what might be the result of trivializing all but those rights that McClosky characterizes as political. Kendall suggests, sarcastically, that, in McClosky's view, we would be required to rely on the people's good will with respect to all the other, "trivial" matters. For example,

[W]e can trust the majority to delimit itself, and so can leave it free *inter alia* to set up extermination camps for Jewish children (not Jewish adults, because that would evidently prevent majorities from being freely-arrived-at by silencing some electors)—and, presumably, to obligate the minority to pay tax-monies with which to defray their expenses. (Kendall 1950, 712)

In what follows, I will give what support I can to the strategy of exalting political rights, but it cannot be denied that the objections to this approach are quite serious, and finding plausible replies to them is among the most important *desiderata* with which I will be concerned. It is my view that that here too the correct responses require what I have called "naturalizing," not only of democratic theory, but of at least one segment of value theory. We have, then, at least two obstacles to a naturalized conception of democracy. First, there's the problem that while (1)–(5) seem mutually exclusive and exhaustive, none of them fits very well with any theory according to which we must design electoral mechanisms to tell us something objective about what would make a polity better off, but that should not be expected to be "truth-tracking" with regard to any such facts. Second, we must reply to the objections that populist democracy not only suffers from paradox, but is consistent with fascism. It is easy to see how an otherwise attractive theory might be sunk by the jutting rocks of either of these. I believe, however, that there is a safe passage that has been overlooked. I will begin to map it in chapter 2.

NOTES

1. Rule by the knowledgeable or wise.

2. It is notoriously difficult to get a consensus understanding of the left-right spectrum, and nothing particularly rides on agreement with my own conception, but the general idea should be clear: average members of the Democratic Party are currently to the left of average Republicans; doctrinaire theocrats are to the right of average Republicans; strict Marxists are to the left of average Democrats, etc.

3. Obviously, a similar assortment of views can be taken toward the "proper" (or most efficient) *methods* for reaching the goals specified in this list. These means may be thought to be objective truths that either can or cannot themselves be discovered through democratic procedures or they may be thought to be entirely subjective items that may or may not be found through elections or other participatory activities. And as one could take one view about the subjectivity/objectivity of the "proper goals" (and whether and how they may be discovered) and a different view about the subjectivity/objectivity of the "proper means" (and whether and how those might be discovered), the number of positional possibilities here could be significantly enlarged. It is also possible to hold that while individuals may have proper goals, societies do not, or vice versa.

4. As we shall see in chapters 5 and 6, the use of "citizen" here is somewhat misleading.

5. Perhaps when we consider the Emancipation Proclamation, women's suffrage, and the Voting Rights Act of 1964, it will seem that these issues have sorted themselves out through a steady increase of liberalism and an increasing disdain for nativism. But the renewed focus on and fear of immigrant crimes and "caravans of dangerous hordes" certainly suggest otherwise.

Chapter 2

Individual Values Naturalized I

Objective Voluntarism

When I claim that for democratic theory to be significantly improved it must be "naturalized," what do I mean? The term suggests that we can turn normative political theory into some kind of scientific endeavor, but if that is actually possible, it must surely be accomplished by political scientists and economists working in the area of social choice theory. (And, perhaps, some of that work has already been done by such theorists as Vilfredo Pareto, Lionel Robbins, Duncan Black, Kenneth Arrow, and Kenneth May.) But by "naturalization" I mean something a bit different from the claim that the study of democratic policy can or should be reduced either to decision theory or the empirical study of elections. As I use the term "naturalization," it simply requires the abandonment of both Platonic verities and any assumption of agreement on even basic truths regarding morality or well-being. And it is worth noting that, so understood, "naturalization" hasn't made as much of an incursion into democratic theory as one might think. Even the hardest-headed political scientists and economists have often let shared moral or prudential precepts drift in through a back window. In this chapter and the next I will explain what I mean by the abandonment of nonnatural precepts, starting with an attempt to explicate a concept of "objectivity" that does not require the existence of values—moral, prudential, or aesthetic—that have preexisted sentient beings. This will require explaining what it is about the world that can make value judgments true or false. I will also try to demarcate the sort of value judgments that are made when individuals or groups feel that getting some particular result will make them better off. We need to venture into these somewhat abstruse regions in order to provide justification for suggestions I have already made that getting what "the people" want is the ultimate goal, the summum bonum, of democracies.

THE NATURE OF VALUE-OBJECTIVITY

Whether some particular claim that is apparently made about the state of the world can be determined to be subjective or objective is among the signature questions of philosophy. Presumably, the most appropriate places for discussion of the general matter of what constitutes subjectivity and objectivity are epistemological studies, since the resolution of those issues is intimately tied up with what people do, or can, know. But the study of philosophy being what it is, this dispute regularly pops up in all the subfields, and wherever it arises it seems to dig in and stay. Although the nature of objectivity is a "heavyweight" matter and so not likely to be resolved in the foreseeable future (if ever), many—indeed, likely the majority of—philosophers have held that, when it comes to ordinary empirical assertions like "London is in England," not only can we know them, but they are in some important sense not entirely about the asserter. Neither of these claims can be proved, of course, but they do seem indispensable if one wants to avoid making joint inquiry entirely senseless.[1] In any case, leaving aside the question of whether we may know them, there is something like a consensus with respect to commonsense empirical propositions that they are objective in the sense that they say something not just about us but about the world outside us. Furthermore, we may often be wrong about them, and we realize that others are sometimes in a better position than we are to know when this is so.

While there has been no consensus on objectivity anywhere in axiology or democratic theory, favorable attitudes toward a story that includes objectivity have been more prevalent in the area of moral values than they have been with respect to values that are prudential (what makes lives or societies better or worse off) or aesthetic (what makes things beautiful or ugly).[2]

Views involving the complete subjectivity of all assertions regarding what is beautiful or what makes for improvements in a person's life have seemed easier to defend than have claims that, for example, what is morally right is no more than a matter of how or what someone (or some society) feels or believes at a particular time. Indeed, claims to the effect that when human beings make moral judgments, they can never do more than either assert descriptions or express feelings that are exhausted by their narrow, individual perspectives have been very harshly treated. So, it seems quite sensible for those with naturalist, empiricist, or subjectivist bents to try to restrict their claims to the often calmer waters of aesthetics and personal prudence, where an appeal to naturalist scruples is generally received with considerably less indignation than when expressed inside the angry, oceanic eddies of ethical theory. No doubt, subjectivism in the area of personal well-being may still be met with a response bearing the faint odor of righteousness—say when the matter involves an apparently self-destructive romance. But it is nothing compared to the accusatory glares likely to result from the assertion that it is purely a matter of personal taste whether or not it is ethical to preemptively raze a populous city. So, the move by naturalists away from moral issues and toward safer, prudential-only spaces is unsurprising. Nevertheless, most of the old disputes have reemerged in the study of well-being,[3] if with somewhat less *sturm* attached.

Interestingly, it seems possible to identify a divide among objectivists with respect to personal and societal well-being that is not common among epistemological realists. This split involves the manner in which allegedly objective truths come to be in the first place. While some phenomenalists have held that a complete description of the states of perceivers is all that makes "London is in England" true or false, realists of both commonsense and scientific varieties can be expected to deny that pretty uniformly. That is, in the area of empirical indicatives about the world, objectivists will generally deny that declarers *create* the truth makers; but in the area of axiology, we can separate out the *voluntaristic* objectivists, those who take *objective* values to be somehow created by valuations, from Platonic or nonnaturalist defenders of realism. The idea of voluntaristic objectivism may seem paradoxical: surely it is strange to suggest both that (i) we create prudential values by somehow "conferring" them upon items that are desired, enjoyed or otherwise honored, and also that (ii) we may be mistaken when making value judgments about what is good for our own lives, because such values are actually there to be discovered. That is a quandary on which I hope to shed some light in this chapter and the next, as I try to make a case for a new type of voluntaristic objectivism with respect to personal and societal well-being—a theory based on free choices. I concede at the outset, however, that, while I believe my construal of prudential value judgments should be no more frightening to naturalist types than the existence of physical laws, I can offer no *complete* escape from the nonempirical. The best I can hope to do is limit the intrusion of nonnatural propositions to one or two highly plausible axioms. This seems to me unobjectionable: it is my view that even the most "scientific" of philosophical and political theories—whether involving values or not—must include axioms of a nonnatural (i.e., philosophical) type. Even the hardest-headed empiricism cannot be "self-authenticating." It must begin *somewhere*.

"VOLUNTARISM" AND "SUBJECTIVISM" DEFINED

I have said earlier that I hope to illuminate—in a philosophically compelling way—what I take to be a somewhat paradoxical position: one that unites voluntarism with value-objectivity in the area of well-being assessments.

But actually there are ways to make such a marriage a very simple task. We might just say, "Well, values are like artifacts. Acts of valuation—like wanting, enjoying, or hating something—create values in the same way that acts of painting create pictures. Once created, both types of artifact endure." We could thus take valuations to "emit" values in much the same way that cartoon characters send out thoughts via thought bubbles: we might even take these value emissions to be objects that, once created, continue to exist forever. Surely this sort of voluntarism would be compatible with an objectivism according to which anybody may be wrong even about what is good for his or her own life. For there is no doubt that we can be mistaken about the characteristics of many items that we have created. Alternatively, we might define "objectivity" in such a way that "I like grapes" (or "Grapes are delicious") is objective; after all, that statement is true if and only if I exemplify the property of enjoying grapes, and that is something that can be taken to be a completely objective matter. Ignoring the fact that liking grapes is widely accepted to be a subjective judgment would again leave no difficulty in combining objectivity with voluntarism. However, there is no philosophical illumination to be found down either of those easy paths to a marriage of voluntarism and objectivity. We must rather try to retain the paradoxicality mentioned earlier by defining our terms so that they jibe with our pre-theoretic notions of both value creation and objectivity: whether or not one likes grapes must remain a subjective matter. Only then can an attempt to coherently unite the two—in spite of their apparent incompatibility—be philosophically fruitful.

Another thing we shall want to do is have the definitions of our key terms comport as far as possible with the ways in which prominent value theorists have classified their own positions. We must therefore begin with a quick survey of contemporary prudential value theories. The most popular are the objective-list theory (OL), desire-satisfactionism (D-S), and, though it is hard to see how it can manage not to be an example of OL, Hedonism (HED).[4] OL is a paradigm of what we shall certainly want to call an *objective* theory, one according to which values may generally be said to be out there in the world, whatever attitudes anyone has toward anything.[5] Objective lists of prudential values generally contain such components as loving relationships, significant knowledge, good health, happiness, and personal achievement, where each item is thought to be a well-being enhancer for anybody who gets it—whether they wanted it or not. D-S is an example of a popular value theory thought to be subjective, one according to which it is the favorable attitudes of individuals or groups toward items that are claimed to make those individuals better off. Thus, the fulfillment of a desire (or perhaps the enjoyment of this fulfillment, if those are thought to be different things) is claimed by D-S supporters to be a necessary condition of—if not actually identical to—a positive prudential value. Some have found HED more difficult to place on this map.

Although often considered a "monistic" OL theory, since it treats as an objective matter the claimed facts that (i) every pleasure is intrinsically welfare-enhancing and (ii) no other items have intrinsic prudential value, HED is also a position that makes each individual's pleasure quotient—a clear example of a "perspectival" and so allegedly subjective item—the sole determinant of what makes life go well for her. While what is pleasing may be so whether or not anyone wants to be pleased, it seems that to be a pleasure an experience must be valuable *to someone*.[6]

A quick look at the value literature regarding subjectivity makes it easy to see how slight variations in the definitions of our key terms can affect our assessment of this or that version of HED or D-S. Frank Chapman Sharp, an early-twentieth-century value theorist who took his own views as voluntaristic objectivism, held that a value judgment should be considered objective just in case it "may properly be denominated true or false [in the sense that] there is something more than the bare assertion of the presence of an emotion or desire in the . . . person judging" (Sharp 1941, 253–254). R. M. Hare (1963, 196) wrote that according to a subjective theory, a value statement is true "if and only if some state of mind or disposition of some person obtains." L. W. Sumner, a subjectivist, also focused on the "perspectival" or "relativity-to-a-particular-person" aspect when defining as "subjectivist" any theory that "make[s] our well-being logically dependent on our attitudes of favor and disfavor" (Sumner 1995, 768).

Finally, Christopher Heathwood is an example of a subjectivist who agrees with Sumner in denying the independence of positive attitudes from individual well-being, but who makes positive feelings toward things ("pro-attitudes") sufficient as well as necessary for the creation of prudential values:

> A theory is subjective just in case it implies the following: that something is intrinsically good for someone just in case either (i) she has a certain pro-attitude towards it, or (ii) it itself involves a certain pro-attitude of hers towards something. (Heathwood 2014, 205)[7]

The key divergence here is with regard to the nature of the dependence of truth or falsity of value statements upon valuations. Chapman Sharp, a self-styled objectivist, believed that value judgments are almost never "bare assertions" of judgers' attitudes and required that subjective claims include *nothing but* the description of such attitudes. He thus made the field of subjective judgments quite narrow. Sumner broadens it immensely by requiring only that subjective judgments somehow comprehend the attitudes of valuers. For him, *any* attitudinal involvement makes a self-directed prudential judgment subjective. Hare, like Sumner, takes every attitudinal involvement in a prudential value judgment to be a mark of subjectivity, but, like Heathwood, insists that all such value judgments necessarily *do* include this involvement. For Hare, the truth or falsity of value claims is determined by the existence or absence of some particular attitude. Heathwood goes even farther: he takes the existence of relevant attitudes not just to be necessary and sufficient to generate the truth or falsity of every prudential value judgment, but also claims that these attitudes are, at least sometimes, *identical* to the judgments in question.

Going the Heathwood route produces problems for our agenda. If we want to leave the logical space to distinguish subjectivist from voluntaristic theories, we must be careful not to define these concepts in such a way that the creation of values by acts of consciousness[8] necessarily makes particular value claims true. Voluntarists have been keen to understand the "conferring of value" as a matter of creating, rather than finding (or seeming to find) values that are somehow already present in the world. But making a truth-condition or truth-maker isn't the same thing as making a truth: for that, there must also be something to *be* true—an assertion, judgment, belief, proposition, or the like. I suppose one could hold that "conferring" value is essentially a matter *both* of creation of and belief in (or assertion of) the existence of a value, creating a position of subjective voluntarism in which it is hard to see how mistakes can be made. But I believe it is important not to define either "subjectivism" or "voluntarism" in such a way that voluntaristic theories are ipso facto subjective in the sense of requiring some (almost surely) true belief or assertion on the part of a "value-conferrer." While, as we shall see, the sempiternal "value-bubble" picture need not be retained, creating value should not be construed as a necessarily belief-involving or epistemic activity. While it is indisputable that voluntarists *may* be subjectivists, it is important for our purposes to allow at least the logical possibility of objective voluntarism.

Sumner's definitions seem clearly to make too many theories subjectivist.[9] It is not enough for someone's perspective to be *involved* in the claim in some manner or other. As indicated earlier, to be legitimately subjective, we shall want value claims to be tied to attitudes in much the way that, for phenomenalists, the truth or falsity of physical object statements is a function of experiences of "sense-data." While I don't say that value subjectivists must endorse a position according to which no prudential value claim can ever be mistaken when made with respect to one's own well-being, I do think that subjectivists must at least claim, along with Heathwood, Hare, and Keller, that there is nothing to what makes a statement about S's well-being true or false at t that is not in some manner a function of S's attitudes at t. For a subjectivist, to be wrong about a self-directed prudential value claim must be analogous to being wrong about "I enjoy pasta," "That looks red to me," or "I am sad." No doubt, strong cases have been made that assertions of all those kinds actually *may* be mistaken, due, perhaps, to language malfunctions, conceptual confusions, or the like (see Bertrand Russell, Charles Sanders Peirce, Wilfrid Sellars, and other fallibilists on this matter). But perhaps we may be allowed to say that assertions of that type can be wrong only in peculiar ways that I shall call "passing strange." They are not, certainly, the sorts of claims that can be shown to be false by scientific investigation. I will take this difficulty of controversion to be one mark of legitimately subjective propositions—including those involving self-directed prudential value claims.

Let me try to capture this conception of subjectivity/objectivity (and also impose the commonsense requirement that objective judgments be unbiased) with the following definitions:

J is an objective judgment of some person S that P = df. J is a judgment by S that some proposition P is true (or legitimate) and J is not a subjective judgment.

J is a subjective judgment of some person S that P = df. (i) J is a judgment by S that some contingent proposition P is true (or legitimate); (ii) neither the truth nor the falsity of P is derivable from the existence of J; and (iii) either (a) S judges that P because (or largely because) she wants P to be true or S judges that P is false because (or largely because) she wants P to be false; or (b) it would be passing strange if J were incorrect.[10]

The idea is that, when S makes a value judgment like "Sewing machines are evil," rather than try to directly determine its subjectivity status by investigating whether it is tacitly perspectival (i.e., really about S without showing it), we test the matter by asking whether either (a) it reflects bias or (b) it would be odd in a particular fashion if S were wrong. If it is clear both that S is unbiased and that she could be wrong about her sewing machine contention without what we have dubbed "passing strangeness," it must be an objective judgment—though, of course, one that could be false. In fact, S might have no evidence whatsoever for her claim.[11]

It could be objected that we may, because of doubts or internal conflicts, just be unsure whether we do or do not like something. There may also be instances in which someone both loves and hates something at the same time. But it should be remembered that these definitions contain no requirement either that any of S's judgments—objective or subjective—be doubt-free or that the entire batch of them be internally consistent. There may even be cases in which both P's truth/legitimacy and its falsity/illegitimacy would be passing strange for S. As already indicated, the "strangeness" is intended to be the (itself undefined) sign of the peculiarly intimate relationship S has with certain propositions, a relationship that need not entail either certainty or self-consistency. The strangeness of being wrong about such "subjective" claims as "This looks green to me" (or "Scallops taste good to me") is a function of a "psycho-epistemic" principle that makes some types of knowledge even "easier" than such G. E. Moorean achievements as "This is a chair."[12]

Let us now turn to voluntarism. To recap, this view maintains that values are created only through acts of valuation; that is, something can be valuable or "disvaluable" only if it is (or perhaps has been or will be) valued (desired, eschewed, liked, disliked, enjoyed, hated, dreaded, etc.) by somebody.[13] Thus, nutriment, beauty, knowledge, friendship, courage, and so on can be goods only if somebody values (or, perhaps has valued or will value) them.[14] For voluntarists, in a world eternally without sentient individuals—or a world consisting only of individuals who are completely indifferent to everything— there would be no value.[15] On the other hand, nonvoluntaristic positions may be said to include every theory according to which at least one thing, event, property, or state of affairs—actual or merely imaginable—has positive or negative value, whether or not anybody has ever valued it.[16]

OL theories are realist (rather than voluntaristic) so long as they deny any requirement that people must have some attitude toward, say, friendship or pleasure in order for friendship or pleasure to be good for anyone. On the other hand, D-S would seem to be necessarily voluntaristic since it makes desires (or approval or enjoyment of their fulfillments) necessary for values to exist, and all such attitudes should be considered valuative acts.

With this in mind, let me now propose the following definition of "voluntarism":

Voluntarism = df. Any theory of value according to which an item or state of affairs X is valuable (or perhaps partakes of some particular type of value) only if, and during only such times as, someone approves of (is averse to), would choose (decline), or enjoys (suffers from) X.[17]

The point I want to make here is that, pursuant to my definitions, even if all nonvoluntaristic values are objective, we cannot infer that all voluntaristic values must be subjective.

I hope it is clear that the "value-bubble" picture I outlined earlier is quintessentially voluntarist, and that on such a primitively causal conception of value creation, anyone, including the bubble-making "conferrer," could still be wrong (without strangeness) when making a judgment about her own well-being—so long as conferring is not seen as an essentially epistemic activity. In any case, the attractions of voluntarism, about which I will have more to say later, seem to me to be largely contrary to the primitive, value-bubble conception, so it is fortunate that the definition does not require that conception. Our question is, rather, whether—if we move beyond value-bubbles—we can still leave open the possibility of a plausible objective voluntarism. For it could be argued that any "scientific" version of voluntarism will not only limit the existence of values to the durations during which some state of affairs is valued but also make the conferring activity essentially epistemic. After all, it may be urged by the empiricist that all we really have the power to do when we value something is believe that it is good or that it is bad, so that *must* be the sum and substance of valuing. But if we make the truth conditions for valuations a (near) function of the nature of such epistemic properties of the valuer as what they believe at some time or other, won't we just have to concede that voluntarism entails subjectivity?

To answer this, let us consider a simple valuation story. Say Oona, a woman with no death wish, has a desire for an entire wheel of Camembert at t. That at least seems like the assignment of a prudential value to the wheel. And, in fact, a simple D-S theory[18] might take Oona's receipt of a wheel of Camembert at t to be prudentially valuable for her, just because she wants it at t. Suppose, however, that in spite of her desire, Oona also *believes* at t that what she wants is only a small wedge of cheese, perhaps because she has been repeatedly told by a cardiologist friend that eating a lot of cheese in one sitting is never good for anybody's health. We can imagine an objective voluntarist saying the following about this case:

1. The goodness of any amount of Camembert for Oona at t requires her to like (want, hate, etc.) it.
2. Yet Oona is mistaken (in an "unstrange" way) when she judges at t that she'd like (only) a wedge of cheese, because, in reality, her taste runs somewhat, let's say, more expansively.

If 1 and 2 are true and our definitions are acceptable, this theorist would have a case for the claim that Oona makes an objective (yet false) value judgment at t. But if that claim is correct, surely it could not be Oona's overly optimistic belief that has somehow made objective what would have otherwise been a subjective valuation of a portion of cheese at t. For it is not the *existence* of errors that make some value judgments objective, it is the *possibility* of a non-strange mistake. Such possibilities arise with respect to items that are not of an essentially epistemic nature. And I note that such mistakes are even easier to come by if we move to a more complex view, one according to which there are only certain types of desires that create values, or only certain types of desired items that are ever valuable.[19] On some of these more refined versions of D-S, Oona can be wrong in her prudential judgment (without "passing strangeness") even when she simultaneously desires the wheel of Camembert *and* thinks that getting it would be a good thing for her life.

So, whether or not the position is true, it seems that one may coherently subscribe to voluntaristic objectivism with respect to well-being. On its own, this compatibility should trouble neither Platonists nor scientific naturalists. In fact, the case for a non-entailment relationship between naturalism and subjectivism was nicely made by A. C. Ewing—a foe of both—when he pointed out that strictly naturalistic theories might consistently push such assertions as "'X is good' entails that most people like X"; or "X is good just in case the existence of X tends to the satisfaction of most people's desires" (Ewing 1948, 36–77). Clearly, there need be nothing at all subjective about either of those theories; in fact, proponents of either could attempt to make ethics a branch of empirical science.

While our definitions allow voluntarist theories to be either subjective or objective, all voluntaristic theories seem naturalist—at least if all acts of valuation take place in nature. (Of course, if there *are* supernatural valuative acts, as divine command voluntarists claim, we would not have a natural-ist view.) It should also be noted that in spite of the "voluntarist" moniker, valuations need not be strictly *voluntary*. What matters is that, according to all voluntaristic theories of value, a desire for or aversion to something—or the enjoyment or displeasure resulting from it in some way—is required for anything to be valuable or disvaluable.[20] In sum, for voluntarism to be true, valuation attitudes need not be rational, well informed, or even voluntary. But they must be essentially "affective" (involve liking/disliking) or "conative" (involve moving toward/away from) even if judgments involving them also contain elements of cognition/intellection.

SOME ATTRACTIONS OF VOLUNTARISM

As suggested earlier, value theorists have not always been careful to dis-tinguish (or to put it more charitably, *have not always been particularly interested in distinguishing*) objectivist from subjectivist versions of vol-untarism. As a result, it is not always clear from which species the various alleged merits of some particular theory arise. Henry Sidgwick (1901, 112), for example, took it to be a virtue of D-S that it makes values "entirely interpretable in terms of fact . . . and [does not] introduce any judgment of value fundamentally distinct from judgments relating to existence; still less any 'dictate of Reason.'" David Lewis (1989, 113) concurred. He liked the fact that a theory of well-being according to which values are what we are disposed to value "invokes only such entities and distinctions as we need to believe in anyway, and needs nothing extra before it can deliver the val-ues. It reduces facts about value to facts about our psychology."[21] Thomas Scanlon (1975, 657) also applauded the fact that D-S theories give "theo-retical primacy" to empirical valuations, and added that they recognize "the sovereignty of individual choice."[22] Dorsey (2012, 410) has made this last alleged virtue explicitly a function of subjectivity, rather than of value creation:

> Subjectivism is able to explain the seemingly plausible connection between what a person values for her own sake and what is valuable for her for its own sake. As noted by Richard Arneson, subjectivism is characterized, and in part motivated, by the plausible thought that a person should be sovereign over her good—her evaluative perspective (at least under the right conditions) should determine her well-being.[23]

Whether stemming from value creation or subjectivity, I will call these two alleged philosophical virtues "value-naturalism" and "anti-paternalism."

Another benefit that has been identified with D-S is a sort of explanatory depth that it seems nearly impossible for OL to provide. While OL theorists might tell us that, say, meaningful knowledge, loving relationships, and personal autonomy are on their lists of what makes someone's life go well for her, they are almost forbidden to say why this is so, since it cannot be, for example, that any item made their list because it is, say, something desired by many people (or everyone) or that it makes people happy or gives them pleasure. It seems the nonnaturalist must be content to determine whether some item is indeed a prudential good by contemplating either the property or ordinary talk about it. One then simply *sees*.[24] Sumner (1995, 769) has put concerns commonly brought forth with respect to enumerative "theories" of alleged objective goods this way:

> It would be a . . . plain mistake for a theory to confuse the conditions which constitute someone's being benefited by something . . . with any of the particular things capable of being beneficial. . . . A theory therefore must offer us . . . not merely a list of the ingredients of the good life but an account of what qualifies something . . . to appear on that list.

A related merit that may seem to inure only to D-S, but that I will argue can apply to another sort of voluntarist theory as well, is what might be called "availability of a plausible axiom of value." As Mill famously (if confusingly) pointed out, there seems to be at least *some* sort of necessary connection between being desirable and being desired—even if it is not an analytic one.[25] It is hard to see how the claim that, for example, loving relationships are intrinsically valuable can be taken as a nearly self-explanatory first premise of any theory of prudential value: it is simply insufficiently intuitive. I will have more to say about this matter in the next chapter.

The last batch of virtues that might be suggested for certain types of voluntaristic theories is that they may be claimed to provide benefits for democratic theory. Empirical theories of value, even those that have not relied on Benthamic hedonism, have seemed to provide welfare economists, political scientists, and legal theorists a promise of what might be called "calculationism"—the hope of one day being able to calculate both individual and societal welfare by such means as counting revealed preferences and estimating the probabilities of various consequences.[26] Such a hope may be based on the belief that things like desire-fulfillments or chosen items might be coherently more aggregable—or at least have more promise of one day being so—than either degrees of the instantiation of some nonnatural goods or amounts/intensities of pleasure/displeasure can ever be. And if votes are analogous to choices, we may have a model for democratic procedures. Such dreams as these may seem far-fetched, but I believe they have been motivating factors for a number of theorists and may continue to motivate others. In any case, whatever one may think of the welfarist and democratic prospects for objective, dichotomous voluntarism, it is clear that various voluntaristic proposals have remained popular among value theorists at least since Duns Scotus.

NOTES

1. This is the subject of Horn 2018.

2. Although it may not be obvious at first glance, there is good reason to distinguish prudential from moral judgments. Frank Jackson (1991, 461) has explained that

> Our lives are given shape, meaning and value by what we hold dear, by those persons and life projects to which we are especially committed. This implies that when we act we must give a special place to those persons (typically our family and friends) and those projects. But, according to consequentialism classically conceived, the rightness and wrongness of an action is determined by the action's consequences considered impartially, without reference to the agent whose actions they are consequences of. . . . It seems then that consequentialism is in conflict with what makes life worth living. . . . One way to reply . . . would be to break the implicit connection between acting morally and living a life worth living. Doing what is morally right or morally required is one thing; doing what makes life worth living is another.

See also Scanlon (1981).

3. As well as in aesthetics. See, e.g., Horn (2015).

4. These three basic positions are set forth very cogently in the opening pages of Keller (2009), although HED is there called "the mental state theory."

5. This is stated a bit too categorically, since nothing prevents an OL from containing elements, like happiness, that seem to require positive attitudes.

6. A good discussion of the proper placement of various styles of hedonic theories may be found in Dorsey (2011).

7. Similarly, Keller (2009) makes the objectivity/subjectivity characterization a function of whether the item being considered is deemed valuable because of, or independently of the valuation.

8. Or, I suppose, "unconsciousness." See, e.g., Perry (1926), particularly chapters 8 and 9.

9. Sobel (1997, 506–507) makes the same point.

10. The first conjunct of (ii) is there to handle such judgments as that there are people. That counter-example (suggested to me by Keith S.) is evidently objective, in spite of being passing strange if false, but (at least supposing that we mean "sentient beings" by "people") the judgment cannot actually occur if it is false. It is an interesting and perplexing question whether, if it is the case that for some judgment J by S, it would be passing strange if J were false, that this must be necessarily so—i.e., be the case in every possible world in which S exists and makes that judgment. It does not seem to me to be relevant to the argument being made here, however, so I will not pursue it.

11. The contingency requirement rules out the subjectivity of any judgment that must be correct solely because of the meanings of the terms involved or is otherwise axiomatic.

12. I discuss this in Horn (2018).

13. Note, however, that while voluntarism takes valuative acts to be necessary for the existence of prudential values, it does not suggest that they are sufficient. More may be needed.

14. Voluntarism is thus unsympathetic to Moore's (1903) disgust with uninhabited, never-seen ugly worlds and his paeon to the intrinsic value of never-to-be-experienced beautiful ones.

15. See, however, endnote 17 in chapter 3.

16. Thus, divine command theories are voluntaristic, as are some versions of theories according to which there is nothing to value judgments but autobiographical commentary or expressions of emotion. But neither divine command theories nor anything like emotivism is necessary to voluntarism; all that is required is, roughly, that for all states of affairs P, without some act of valuation regarding P, P could be neither valuable nor "disvaluable."

17. I note that Sobel (1997) and (2009) take a somewhat different view of the nature of subjectivity. It may be found objectionable by some that my definition stops at necessary conditions. I hope to remedy this matter in the next chapter when I propose a standard of value.

18. For descriptions of simple desire-satisfactionism, see Parfit (1984, 439–502) and Murphy (1999).

19. These elaborations of D-S will be discussed later.

20. Additional argument would be required to show that all naturalist positions are voluntarist. Perfectionists may claim that human flourishing is both naturally value-enhancing and nonvoluntaristic.

21. Dorsey (2012, 436) also suggests that "D-S is most consonant with our naturalist, scientistic worldview."

22. Adams (1999, 86) has also singled out these two characteristics of D-S.

23. Dorsey (2012, 410). His citation is to Arneson (1999). Sumner (1996) and Keller (2009) also give subjectivism the credit for making essential the ties between what is good for one's life and one's personal perspectives.

24. This criticism is made by Bradley (2007). OL defenders have seemed largely untroubled by charges of explanatory failure, however. Rice (2013) tries to handle the objection that OL theories are merely enumerative mostly by noting that the word "because" can be found in such sentences as "Friendships are constituents of a person's well-being *because* they involve friendship, an intrinsic prudential good." Perhaps others will join me in failing to find that terribly illuminating.

25. See Hall (1949) and Millgram (2000).

26. For extensive bibliographies of political and welfare economists working in this area in the twentieth century, see Mishan (1960) and Brock (1973). Of course, much of the work of such well-known observers as Arrow, Barry, Baumol, Beitz, Bergson, Braybrooke, Buchanan, Dahl, Downs, Dworkin, Fishburn, Hansson, Harsanyi, Hayek, Hausman, Hicks, Little, May, Nozick, Posner, Rawls, Riker, Samuelson, Sen, and Waldron is devoted to—though in some cases critical of—claimed connections between choice (individual or social) and individual or general welfare. I will briefly discuss a couple of the principal criticisms in the next chapter.

Chapter 3

Individual Values Naturalized II
The More Good, the Better

For all of the virtues claimed for voluntarism in the preceding chapter, there have long been plentiful and powerful criticisms too. There seem to be biological facts, for example, that make certain things good for us, whatever anybody may think, enjoy, or desire. Surely, if Oona should eat that entire wheel of Camembert in a half-hour, it may well not be good for her life—whatever she may have desired at any time. It is also said, for example, that the obtaining of a mutual, loving relationship cannot really be bad for one's life even if it is unwanted and might sometimes make things more troublesome. And the age-old questions persist: Can a malevolent person—or an entirely deluded one—have a life loaded with well-being if the pleasure she is swamped with is sadistic or delusive? Must physical injuries be intrinsically bad—even for those who seem to enjoy pain? Let us look at these matters more closely.

SOME OBJECTIONS TO VOLUNTARISM

Roger Crisp (2006) has identified the two most common and long-standing criticisms of HED as concerns about "swinish" behavior and the pseudo-satisfactions provided by delusions or "experience machines."[1] And subjective theories that are not explicitly pleasure-based (like many D-S theories) have also been subjected to these critiques. Taking "swinishness" first, the objections run along the following lines: "How can an addict's or suicide's acquisition of a dangerous drug be good for her, even if and when it is desired? And is the satisfaction of a purely malicious desire to gratuitously punch a stranger on a train ever prudentially valuable if nothing is gained but that malevolent pleasure?" The intuitive answers, "It can't" and "No" have long been seen as support for OL theories of prudential value. Another basic intuition that seems to conflict with subjectivism (and thus, certain voluntarist positions) is reflected in what might be called "Parfitian pointlessness."[2] For example, one may ask the D-S theorist: "How can the fulfillment of your desire for it to be discovered, exactly ten years subsequent to the date of your death, that there are precisely 343 hickory trees in the state of Louisiana having the same number of leaves that the tree on your front lawn had on November 11, 2011, somehow make (or have made) your life go better for you?"

There have been two main strategies taken by voluntarists—hedonistic or otherwise—to allegations of swinishness, non-veridicality, or pointlessness. They have been to either (i) bite the bullet or (ii) idealize our valuations or their consequences in some manner.

Biting the bullet on swinishness or Parfitian pointlessness[3] involves responding with something like "I'm sorry, but those fulfillments just *are* good for the addict (suicide, sadist, hickory leaf obsessive), regardless of how it might seem to them later, or anybody else ever. After all, nothing but my attitudes can determine what is good for me: it is *my* enjoyment/the fulfillment of my desires/and so on that are the sole determinants of that." Such a response suggests a basic clash of intuitions, indeed an end to any useful discussion. Rather than make this move, let us simply agree that intuitions supporting perfectionism and other OL theories are too deeply ingrained to simply be scoffed at or ignored by voluntarists.

The idealization response to accusations of both swinishness and pointlessness involves some sort of "making sure" process. For example, a number of D-S theorists[4] have made the value-conferring capacity of desires more limited (or eliminated it entirely), unless the desire is for something an individual wants herself to want; or for something still sought-after psychoanalysis sufficient to have eliminated relevant confusions; or is such that it would be retained by individuals in possession of "full information" regarding the consequences of that desire's fulfillment. Dorsey (2012) has done an admirable job refuting claims of success for these methods of handling the traditional objections, and I will not repeat his arguments here. I will only add the remark that to the extent that "idealization" is required, it seems difficult to maintain that one's position is strictly voluntarist. That is, if an increase in value resulting from additional information makes some desire prudentially valuable (or more so than it would otherwise have been), then, according to voluntarist principles, it seems that this increment must itself have been created by one or more valuations, and it is hard to see what arguments might be used to defend that highly counterintuitive claim.[5]

When we move to the second item in Crisp's catalog of long-standing objections to hedonistic theories, concern over non-veridicality, we will see the same strategies utilized by respondents. Some HED theorists again simply bite the bullet.[6] "How," they ask, "can anyone insist that a machine-simulated 'pet pony' is in any respect worse for any pony-desirer's life than a real pet pony, or that a faithful marriage is any better for a cuckold's life than one that only *seems* to him permanently and in every way committed? For purposes of our personal well-being," they may go on, "it is enough that we *believe* we have gotten what we want when there is no way to verify the real truth." This again seems insufficient to me. At least since Bishop Butler pointed out that it is not really the case that what we generally desire is our own pleasure, value, and welfare theorists have managed to find their way out of the confusions of psychological egoism.[7] Most have come to understand that conflating belief or evidence with truth is as deleterious in the area of value theory as it is in other corners of philosophy. I understand full well that there are no proofs to be had here.[8] But whoever may be right about this matter, intuitions suggesting a categorial difference between truth and mere facsimiles thereof are again too widespread and deeply ingrained to be either disregarded or gainsaid; the voluntarist will have to do more than insist or ignore.

Responses to the experience machine challenge that go beyond shrugging have also been proposed. For example, Fred Feldman has suggested that we specifically allow for "truth-adjustments" to valuations.[9] On this view, a satisfaction is simply "worth more" (perhaps even by a specific, quantifiable amount) if the enjoyment is veridical. Of course, such a move would again seem to commit one to a value enhancement that somehow manages *not* to be a strict function of the value-creating activity.[10] Such enhancements are evidently consistent with a voluntaristic theory only if they are at least partly a function of exogenous factors, like, for example, association with an increase in the production of *other* value-creating activities (by oneself or others). Although that is not an approach that Feldman considers, I think there is something to it and will say more about it later.

Generally, the strategies taken to find passage between the Scylla of biting the bullet on swinish delights or delusive fulfillments and the Charybdis of appeals to apparently non-voluntaristically created values have involved attempts either to find special *objects* of valuative acts or to distinguish special valuative *acts* that produce all and only the changes in prudential value that appeal to the theorist. Mark Overvold (1982) takes the first tack; Dorsey (2012) takes the second. On Dorsey's proposal, which he calls "Judgment Subjectivism," what a person prudentially values is precisely what she believes is good for her—only given certain conditions. While Dorsey allows someone might be wrong in these self-assessments, he says this can no longer happen once the beliefs are "rendered coherent." With that elaboration, his position allows for no mistakes in our beliefs about what is good for us, because, as Dorsey (2012, 423) puts it, "I cannot coherently believe that it is good for me to be worse-off." Thus, if true (rather than simulated) friendship increases someone's well-being, it is not because of list-membership, or because anybody *desires* true friendship (or even desires to desire it). It is because the person in question (coherently) *judges* of true friendship that it is welfare-enhancing for her.

It is hard to believe that a large number of value theorists—voluntarists or not—will be moved by this strategy for handling objections to subjectivism. First, while it attempts an analysis of "what we prudentially value" via error correction, it gives no help regarding what is good for the lives of those with no beliefs at all about the matter, such as babies. Second, as long ago as 1932, Ralph Barton Perry (1932, 66) responded to a suggestion by Orlie Pell that since, for voluntarists like Perry, something must be valued in *some* manner to be valuable, such theorists ought to insist that items must be *judged valuable* to be valuable, since such judgments themselves seem to be valuations. Perry's response to this seems to me dispositive:

> In my view the fact of value consists in an interest-in-something. The judgment which refers to this fact, that is, the judgment of value, can be disputed only on the ground that there is no such interest. Such a judgment is not infallible in the sense that what is judged valuable is ipso facto valuable, for the interest (like anything else) may be judged falsely; nor [has the judgment been shown not to exist] by the discovery that the object of the interest is not what it is judged to be. (Perry 1932, 66)[11]

The crucial point being made by Perry here is that it is a mistake to try to convert a largely conative process into a primarily epistemic one. That valuations are objective does not mean either that they are true or that they are justified.

OBJECTIVE VOLUNTARISM WITHOUT DESIRE-SATISFACTIONISM

Before attending to any of the specific criticisms of naturalist theories brought earlier, it may be wise to question the reasonability of the entire project attempted herein. I have argued that there may be benefits to pursuing voluntarism while eschewing subjectivism. But is this even remotely plausible? If values are created by valuations and last only so long as do these acts or the dispositions to have them, how can it be that values are objective in the way that empirical statements like "London is in England" are? Surely in the latter case, no one's judgment is involved in the "creation" of the truth, which would survive the death of all sentient creatures. Even if we have cleared logical space for an objective voluntarism, doesn't every good theory of prudential value at least have to display some minimum level of initial credibility?

One thing I hope can be accepted by value theorists of all stripes is that in order for a theory of value T (prudential or otherwise) to be found congenial by someone S,

(a) T commits to (or provides a clear path to the commitment to) all and only the values that S, on reflection, believes to be in the world (if any); and
(b) T has what S takes to be a sufficient batch of the characteristics required of any good philosophical theory and none (or not too many) of what S takes to be the characteristics of inadequate or otherwise defective philosophical theories.

Perhaps a few readers will join me in taking the position that any granting of congeniality to a theory of value also requires something like:

(c) T provides what S takes to be a plausible "standard of value."
    Since, however, the inclusion of (c) may be thought to unfairly rule out the completeness of some styles of philosophical theorizing by insisting that any good theory of prudential value must be of a type that goes beyond the simple enumeration of a list of allegedly objective prudential goods, let us bracket (c) for the moment and take (a) and (b) alone to be our congeniality requirements.

Both (a) and (b) seem entirely uncontroversial. For example, for any rational S subscribing to OL, every OL theory will completely satisfy criterion (a) for her: that is because S can simply add to her list all and only those items she finds intuitively welfare-enhancing. And if S believes that the list may change over time, she can add the conditions under which each list-eligible entity becomes an actual prudential value. If S is an OL theorist who is drawn to hedonism, the list of values will be quite short, but there may be a benefit to a pleasure theory with respect to criterion (b), for the hedonist can claim to be attempting to provide an explanation as well as a list, and many philosophers believe that good theories ought to be illuminating. For the hedonist, but not the OL theorist claiming a variety of list items, the explanation can be expected to be, roughly, that *there is something we all understand to be unique about pleasure and those things that tend to increase it.*

Unfortunately for the hedonist, claims about the alleged "specialness" of pleasure—or any other natural property—have been credibly attacked for committing the naturalist fallacy—the attempt to derive the existence of a *value* from items that are purely descriptive (physical or psychological facts about the world). Even many who are sympathetic to naturalism have been forced to admit that none of the following can be true of *being pleasing, being the fulfillment of a desire*, or any other natural or empirical property N:

- *N* is identical to being valuable.
- "*N*" and "good" are synonymous terms.
- *N* (or items that exemplify *N*) is (are) the only thing(s) we ever seek.
- *N* is the only thing we seek "for its own sake."
- *N* is itself the only intrinsically valuable item.
- Every exemplification of *N* (or occurrence of an *N* item) is intrinsically good.

I will not here rehearse the arguments showing that none of these passes philosophical muster, but simply refer doubtful readers to the works of Moore, Ross, and Ewing.

It may seem that the forfeiture of these six propositions with respect to any natural property that one might name must result in a victory for a non-hedonistic OL over all other theories, precisely because it leaves precious little ground for explanatory vigor in *any* theory of value. I don't believe the situation is quite as dire as that, however. In a series of mid-twentieth-century works, the American value theorist Everett Hall (1947, 1949, and 1952) explained how, given a proper understanding of the need for axioms in any philosophical theory, one can render unto Mooreans the falsity of all the naturalistic reductions listed earlier in this chapter without giving up one's empirical scruples. For example, Hall (1949, 10) suggested that those volun-tarists with a hedonistic bent can endorse something like the following as the first premise of their value theories:

HED-1. Things experienced as pleasant, and they alone, are good. Indeed, only things experienced as pleasant are desired for their own sakes.

It should be noted that this standard, which those wanting to add criterion (c) to (a) and (b) will welcome, continues to tie values to valuative acts. But it is not violative of any of the six prohibitions. There is no claim of synonymy, for example, or that the property of *being pleasing* is itself good, let alone the only thing people ever seek. As we have seen, however, there are other objections to naturalist theories besides accusations of committing the naturalist fallacy. And when we look to see how HED-1 handles the classic objections involving experience machines and swinishness, it seems quite unpromising. True, it offers only necessary (not sufficient) conditions for welfare enhancers; but how does knowing that only what is experienced as pleasant is both good and desired for its own sake help us distinguish values emanating from the enjoyment of merely ostensible ponies from the receipt of real ones? And HED-1 doesn't seem to do any better with respect to swinishness. Since we have already conceded the intuitiveness of objec-tions from OL backers on those issues, HED-1 seems an inadequate theory.

Without referring to these problems, and perhaps with other goals in mind, Hall went on to suggest an alternative manner of fashioning a hedonic standard of value, one that, by baking in an objective consequentialism and utilizing the concept of lawlike regularity, seems to fare better against the objections highlighted by Crisp. Hall's proposals suggest a move to something like[12] the following standard:

HED-2. For any property N and person S (or society Y or world W), an exemplification of N is intrinsically (prudentially) good for S (or Y or W), if and only if such exemplification would causally contribute, pursuant to one or more physical laws, to a subsequent increase in the ratio of total pleasure over displeasure in S's life (or in Y or W).

Thus, according to HED-2, that and only that which is generally conducive to overall pleasure (for some person or group) is good. While traditional versions of utilitarianism, whether ideal or otherwise, have separated the chosen utils (the intrinsic goods) from their consequential aggregation, according to HED-2, intrinsic goodness itself requires *conduciveness to overall pleasure*.[13] HED-2 handles the experience machine objections roughly by saying that it is only in those cases in which a simulation produces more pleasure in the overall scheme of things that it can be intrinsically good for anyone (or any society or world): delusive fulfillments may or may not be valuable, depending on their predictable consequences. The same response can be made to charges of endorsing swinishness. According to HED-2 what matters is whether the swinish behavior is conducive to a greater net ratio of pleasure to displeasure.

To what extent these rejoinders to the two traditional objections identified by Crisp are successful, and to what extent they simply rely on the existence of a (merely dreamed-of) Benthamic calculus are interesting and difficult questions. Presumably, many OL theorists would insist that the making of a machine that, pursuant to physical laws, would give *everyone* continuous, everlasting pleasure is no more intrinsically valuable than a single, fleeting non-veridical pleasure induced by such a machine. And, surely, with respect to swinishness, it is hard to know what evil lurks in the hearts of *most* men and women as it is to know what lurks in *any of them*. Furthermore, even if the voluntarist responses to these objections were deemed entirely adequate, there would remain the complaint that neither HED-1 nor HED-2 seems a plausible candidate for a first premise of axiology, simply because of an insufficient conceptual connection between pleasure and (even prudential) goodness. That is, one can argue that HED-1 and HED-2 are implausible axioms of value theory just because pleasure and goodness are, apparently, worlds apart. Thus, while HED-1 and HED-2 were proposed to provide a theory that would fare better on criterion (b) than OL theories do, the nonnaturalist is likely to simply counter with "But why should what is pleasing be thought to be valuable in the first place?" It is not that the HED defender is required to claim an analytic connection between pleasure and goodness, it is simply that no satisfactory theory of value ought to rely on axioms that have so little initial conceptual attractiveness. If the response is, "It is just obvious that what is pleasing is good for us" it's not clear that the proposal offers anything in the area of explanatory value that OL does not.

This impasse naturally leads to D-S, for it seems clear that the popularity of D-S is to a great extent a function of the close conceptual connection noted by Mill—whether or not he explained it satisfactorily—between what is desired and what is desirable. Along with anti-paternalism and value-naturalism, it has been this intuitive connection between satisfaction of desire and prudential value that has made D-S attractive to so many philosophers. So, even if HED-2 *did* successfully respond to the Crispian objections to naturalistic value theories, it would still seem to make sense to convert it into a D-S standard.

CHOICE

Rather than consider the prospects for either HED or D-S further, however, I propose to offer an alternative standard of value, one suggested by Hall (1943, 1945). I believe it reflects a voluntarist perspective that, like D-S, can provide a more plausible (if still unavoidably unempirical) first premise of axiology than can any hedonic standard.[14] And this proposal also provides insight into the relationship of well-being to personal autonomy to an extent that neither HED nor D-S standards can.

> CHOICE. For all possible states of affairs S and persons P, S is intrinsically prudentially good for P at t if and only if (i) S is freely chosen by P at t; and (ii) pursuant to one or more physical laws, the obtaining of S will, under ordinary conditions, causally contribute to the subsequent increase either in P's ability to make successful choices or to an increase in the alternatives[15] available to be freely chosen by P.[16]

On this standard, only that which is freely chosen can be intrinsically good for anyone, although it does not preclude the possibility that a needed rain shower, a baby's impulsive reach for a bottle, or the passage of a budget bill is instrumentally good to the extent that it predictably engenders subsequent successful free choices.[17] Note again that CHOICE must not be taken to imply that either "goodness" or "intrinsic goodness" means the same thing as "being freely chosen" or that every free choice or every freely chosen item must be good for the chooser.[18] Furthermore, an act can be intrinsically good for someone under CHOICE even if it provides less in the way of prudential value than any number of other actions she might have taken.[19] But a "success" and an increase in the capacity for more of them are, together, sufficient.

There is a line of objection that I think it is important to anticipate here. It is that I have provided no analysis either of *freedom* or of *success*. Those are complex and multifaceted issues, making the nature of human autonomy a heavyweight philosophical question. I will attempt no contribution to that debate. I simply depend on the commonsense view that to the extent one is "forced" to take something one doesn't actually find attractive (or "really want"), one is to that same extent denied autonomy. And that is because *success* requires that the acquired item is something one approves of (ex ante).[20] As this book is largely about voting, and voting is a matter of expressing ex ante approvals, I will have more to say about success in upcoming chapters. I want to stress now, however, that value theorists, whether pushing standards according to which prudential values are a function of the level of happiness, the intensity of desire-satisfactions or the number of successful events, should not automatically be expected to provide a complete theory of happiness, satisfaction, or success. Each of those subjects presents its own complexities.[21] So, while I will say what little I can about what these terms mean as we proceed, there is no doubt that it will not be nearly enough.

As indicated earlier, CHOICE shares with D-S standards the appealing feature of promoting a first premise of axiology that is highly intuitive. For, just as it seems clear that there is a close conceptual connection between what is desired by people and what is desirable for them, it is hard to deny that there is an analogous tie between what is chosen by people and what they deem valuable (i.e., what are, in common parlance, "choice items"). But CHOICE has advantages over its sister theory. CHOICE makes autonomy (whatever that is, precisely) fundamental to the consideration of what makes a life go well for someone, while the other proposed axioms do not. Because of the inclusion of "free" in CHOICE (however this term may be unpacked by compatibilists or libertarians), there need be no concerns about the insufficient autonomy of an otherwise value-creating act, as there might be pursuant to a D-S standard. Coercion and addiction issues are thus avoided. In addition, CHOICE waives away Parfitian pointlessness, for although such weird desires do seem to be capable of "success" in some sense, no choices are actually made in those scenarios. Nothing is acquired. Thus, regardless of how intensely such confections might be desired—there is no "acquisition" to be intrinsically welfare-enhancing for anyone. And again, unlike both pleasant or unpleasant experiences, desires, or aversions, choices are dichotomous in the sense that they do not vary by intensity or duration. Either they happen or they don't. While pleasure, happiness, desire, and satisfaction all are intensive qualities that may come in greater or lesser amounts, choices can only be counted. This simplicity makes the CHOICE standard potentially more amenable to any theory interested in vote aggregation.

The question of how anyone could think it is reasonable to completely ignore the apparent intrinsic differences of choices and note only whether or not they are "successful" will be put off until chapter 4. But I want to note now that, as suggested by the second conjunct of the CHOICE definition, there are other ways to prioritize choices besides focusing on their intensity or any other intrinsic characteristic. Hall (1945, Ch. 3) noted that

> [D]esires frequently conflict. This indeterminateness can be resolved if there is a choice of, or preference for, one of these goods. The chosen or preferred good is then better than the non-chosen. Choices, however, conflict in this ranking of goods. Taken by themselves, conflicting choices are to be considered equal. Hence, those choices that are in the majority are to take precedence; their ranking is to be accepted. We must not confine our attention to intrinsic goods, objects as themselves desired. We must also consider the extrinsic good of these same things. That is, we must consider what happens to other objects of desire if they are actualized. The highest good for any situation then is that which would, if achieved, actualize the largest number of preferred desires, where desires of consequences as well as of things for their own sake are included. Some of these desires however are only potential. In any case, they may or may not be actually present in the given choice.[22]

The idea is that those choices that have the *extrinsic* characteristics of leading to more successes or increasing the number of obtainable items are to be considered preferable to those with fewer such causal qualities.[23]

When we look at the obviously objective second prong of CHOICE, we can see that it clearly makes expertise of certain kinds important for assessments, but we must also recognize that getting a reasonable estimate of future successes is a function not only of knowledge of the relevant physical/psychological laws and antecedent conditions but also of what will actually be wanted in the future—and that remains a subjective matter. The best way to determine what people want must, for good or ill, always be to ask them or see what they actually do—both now and later. Certainly, we should hunt for the most appropriate mechanisms and the best people for estimating what people now want and what they are most likely to want in the future, but both the mechanisms and the experts face a basic limitation. Because the subjective nature of the "success" aspects of the CHOICE definition is ineliminable in both of its conjuncts,[24] it can never be appropriate to rely exclusively on substituted "expert" judgments, even in the apparently scientific matter of fecundity.

What do I mean by "scientific matter"? Take Oona. In order for the satisfaction of her cheese craving to be intrinsically good for her, it must not result from or be likely to cause addiction and must do her no great physical harm or deplete her finances or future earning capacity to an extent that her opportunities for future successful choices will be constricted either in number or in scope. Experts of various types are very likely to know more about all those matters than Oona does. It is the same for assessment of the value of so-called useless pleasures.[25] If a dour, joyless life is shorter or leads to fewer free choices than one filled with video game adventures, then additional game-playing may be welfare-enhancing, but if the practice ends up significantly reducing earning capacity or healthy exercise, it cannot be.[26] The value of bouts on experience machines must be gauged in a like fashion.

It may be objected that we are all familiar with instances in which individuals at least seem to be made better off when we restrict their ability to choose. After all, some people are irrational and all of us are always suffering from incomplete information. According to CHOICE, however, while the freedom of a child or an irrational or confused adult may be advantageously constrained or even prohibited, it cannot be the case that a net loss in autonomy over the long term is ever good for an individual. I cannot, of course, "prove" the correctness of any such claim,[27] but I believe that its attraction is closely connected to our intuitive revulsion of pleasure machines and brain-in-vat scenarios.

To repeat, CHOICE is both objective[28] and voluntaristic. Although there would be no values without the occurrence of choosings or the existence of dispositions to choose, whether or not a particular state of affairs is welfare-enhancing is as objective as any Moorean might demand. And, surely, CHOICE is explanatory in a way that no OL theory can ever be: if personal achievements or the attaining of significant knowledge are said to improve someone's life, CHOICE tells us why and OL does not. It also provides more hope for calculationists.[29]

Hopes, of course, may be vain. And in addition to objections related to the CHOICE theory's avoidance of issues regarding morality/justice and intensities, I would expect it to generate complaints regarding the impossibility of its proposed calculations. Even if one drops any grievances involving the need for political theories to advise us on what tax policy is *right*, what labor laws are *fair* to businesses, or, generally, what sort of society everyone *ought* to strive for, the requirement that we count successful choices will be claimed by some to doom the theory at the outset. This point can be made by considering a famous passage from J. L. Austin (1956, 5) and noting how similar "making a choice" is to "doing an action":

> Is to sneeze to do an action? Or is to breathe, or to see, or to checkmate, or each one of countless others? In short, for what range of verbs, as used on what

occasions, is "doing an action" a stand-in? What have they in common, and what do those excluded severally lack? Again we need to ask how we decide what is the correct name for "the" action that somebody did-and what, indeed, are the rules for the use of "the" action, "an" action, "one" action, a "part" or "phase" of an action and the like. Further, we need to realise that even the "simplest" named actions are not so simple.

Suppose that Helen purchases a new car. Does this somehow include the following choices, items that might be needed to bring this primary choice to fruition?—the buying of the new car, the going to the dealership, the getting on the bus to the dealership, the getting out of bed, the moving her left leg toward the side of the bed, and so on. Each choice seems to break down into littler and littler wants, decisions and actions, ad infinitum. So, if it is the case that the more successes we have, the better, we must know how to count these choices/successes. Do the "big ones" (like obtaining a new car) include the "smaller ones" (like getting out of bed) or is each to be separately counted?[30] To generalize this line of complaint, it would seem we cannot count choices without identity criteria for them.[31]

These sorts of objections strike me as being less serious than one might at first think. I see no reason why we may not elect either to count the obtaining of a new car as one item or as many, so long as the same convention is consistently used. And, presumably, the conventions we decide upon will depend on the particulars of the policies we are interested in. For example, if we are concerned with the utilities created by the addition of more bus routes, we may wish to count Helen's choice to get on the bus to the dealership. If we are wondering about the good provided by prosthetic devices, counting walking to the bus stop might also be relevant. If we have questions about the value of one more day of life, successes as fine-grained as the successful moving of one's leg may be important. Even if, as Austin suggests, "overall" counts of utilities may involve a wide variety of sums depending on how we choose to bundle successful choices, so long as we are careful to parse such items in the same manner everywhere, there seems to me no great harm resulting from the fact that different counting conventions are available.

NOTES

1. See Robert Nozick (1974, 28–53). I will say objections related to delusions or simulations are due to "non-veridicality."
2. See Parfit (1984, 511).
3. For two examples, see Heathwood (2006) and Bronsteen, Buccafusco et al. (2010).

4. These include Sidgwick, Brandt, Lewis, Railton, Griffin, Kagan, and Sobel.

5. Keller (2009) makes a similar point, and David Enoch (2005) provides a thorough-going critique of claims for the consistency of idealization techniques with value-subjectivity.

6. For good examples, see, again, Heathwood (2006) and Bronsteen, Buccafusco et al. (2010).

7. See Butler (1827).

8. See Horn 2013.

9. This tack is taken by Feldman (2006), which also allows for adjustments based on desert.

10. Sumner (1988, 178) takes Feldman to task on this matter by questioning the consistency of consequentialism with a position that takes value enhancements to be based on desert or veridicality, because such enhancements appear to "violate the traditional assumption that the good is prior to the right." On Sumner's view, Feldman "abandons the traditional utilitarian project by rejecting the idea that principles about desert (and fairness, justice, etc.) are to be derived from the maximization of the good, [since] they are somehow or other (how?) determined independently and then used to partially define the good to be maximized." Keller (2009, 679) makes a similar criticism.

11. See also Kubala (2017).

12. For his original versions, see Hall (1947, 342–343 and 1952, 185–187).

13. Note again here that the pleasure does not constitute the value, even if production of it is the *reason* why the exemplification of N is a good thing.

14. Thus, it does well on theory congeniality criterion (c).

15. "Alternatives" must be understood to be limited to those that are *attractive* to the person(s) in question. For example, it is obvious that the beef items at a restaurant will be irrelevant to a vegan diner and that the availability of jobs in philosophy departments will be of no interest to those who are interested exclusively in careers in plumbing.

16. Here we give sufficient as well as necessary conditions for intrinsic value creation. It will be noted that the standard will usually be quite difficult to apply with confidence. There might be, to give just one example among many, an expected increase in successful choices along with an expected decrease in attractive future options. It will further complicate assessments when we recognize—and this will be stressed later—that since the tastes of choosers may change over time, estimating future successes requires predicting what will be *taken* as attractive options and successful apprehendings at later dates. Obviously, estimates of net changes in prudential value in such situations are unlikely to be simple. I believe, however, that one should expect nothing else from such standards. The absence of explicit guidance is—and should be—consistent with the limitations of human intuitions in these areas.

17. The voluntarism endorsed here refers exclusively to what is valuable for persons. Of course, Aristotelians often make much of the fact that it is reasonable to claim that things can be made better or worse for non-sentient entities: see Kraut (2007). I don't deny that sunlight is in some sense "good for" clover (as is oxygen for cancer cells and erosion for canyons) and that this would be so even if there had

never been sentient entities. But while it seems absurd to claim that what is good for clover, cancer, or canyons is, all else equal, intrinsically good simpliciter (i.e., good for the world as a whole), it seems to me at least plausible that a net increase in what is good for sentient entities over the long term makes the universe a better place ceteris paribus. In any case, I consider it basic that for something to be intrinsically good, its occurrence or instantiation must, if all else is unchanged, make the world a better place.

18. For an excellent discussion of the error in claiming that the existence of a successful choice or satisfied want is sufficient to produce a social or political good, see Barry (1973).

19. And, again, an intrinsically (prudentially) good act may also be immoral: I make no attempt in this book to explicate moral values.

20. These considerations show the close relationship between D-S and CHOICE. The differences between the two positions remain important, however. Unlike D-S, CHOICE (i) ignores intensity of desires and/or satisfactions; (ii) requires freedom/autonomy in relevant events; and (iii) bakes in consequentialism.

21. Indeed, at least one has an entire journal devoted to it.

22. Quotations from *The Road to Freedom* are used by the kind permission of Professor Richard J. Hall, the dedicatee of that work.

23. Again, the variance in the "fecundity" of a success as understood here does not imply any sort of *intrinsic* inequality in choices. The theory does not countenance the idea of some choice being "qualitatively grander" than another, perhaps to an extent that could make up for its comparative quantitative sterility. Fecundity is strictly a matter of causal connections with other successes, whether considered "big" or "little."

24. Note that our definition of "objective judgment," like Chapman Sharp's, is consistent with objective items containing such subjective constituents.

25. See Arneson (1999, 120) on "cheap thrills."

26. It is generally agreed that it is worse to have unsatisfied wants than to have no wants at all (assuming one remains alive, sentient, and autonomous). We may thus need to confront (perhaps Vedantist- or Buddhist-tinged) claims that truly good societies will not only contain the fewest individuals with unsatisfied desires, but the fewest individuals with any desires at all, and consequently, the fewest possible satisfactions or successes. Given such a perspective, CHOICE, with its focus on *more*, may seem to bestow its blessings on the most horrendous "wheel" of *craving—getting—craving* that one can imagine. I think, however, that genuine autonomy is inconsistent with the complete absence of striving and *getting*. I therefore think we should handle this concern by construing desires and satisfactions broadly enough to consider "going *beyond* wanting" something that itself could be a successful choice. While it may seem that we are perversely attempting to call the absence of desire something that may be sought, it cannot be denied that a sort of bliss is often promised to those who succeed in attempts at asceticism. If exalting *sadhana* is considered somehow exempt from rebukes stemming from the necessity of giving up desires, it seems acceptable to count the obtaining of this promised state of bliss a success. In any event, it seems to me that an autonomous person can't "just *be*."

One may also compare here the observations of Schwartz (2016). He complains therein that we may be "paralyzed" by, e.g., having too many sizes and styles of jeans to choose from. As explained earlier, however, "options" that are not attractive may be considered irrelevant to our analysis. Furthermore, Schwartz accepts without argument a standard of well-being involving happiness that he seems to take to be indisputably derivable from survey results. That the happiest people are the best-off does not seem to me to be an analytic truth.

27. Furthermore, I understand that not everyone agrees with this stance. For a defense of paternalism, see Hanna (2018).

28. CHOICE allows for two responses to the Socratic objection that the good being pronounced here is nothing but "that in which the beast delights," and the evil is nothing but "that which he dislikes." First, it is about prudential values only and makes no attempt to explicate what is "the just or noble." Second, no amount of delight is alone sufficient to produce an increase in intrinsic prudential value according to CHOICE. It must be the case that future successful choices will be multiplied.

29. I believe CHOICE is significantly different from what has previously been proposed in social choice theory, but it is true that use of "revealed preferences" has been suggested as a means of dispensing with preference orderings in economics and decision theory since the 1930s. (See, e.g., Samuelson 1938.) Unsurprisingly, such proposals have not been universally accepted. (See, e.g., Sen [1973], Sumner [1996], Broome [1978], and Hausman [2000].) I do not have space for a detailed discussion of the similarities and differences between former proposals and what I am up to here, but will note that some prior critiques do not apply to CHOICE. For example, John Broome (1978) takes what he calls the "Choice-Value Thesis" and the "Liberal Defense Proof" to be typical of social choice theories, and subjects each to acute criticism. But neither the thesis nor any premises in the proof entails or is entailed by CHOICE. Similarly, Sen's (1970) claim of a paradox resulting from the fact that a consistent liberal (as he defines one) cannot endorse Pareto optimality does no damage to CHOICE. To be specific, Sen requires of liberalism that it take the fact of X being chosen over Y by everyone in some group to entail that it would be good for that group for X to be chosen over Y. But CHOICE does not countenance that Paretian entailment. Not only does CHOICE's essential reference to the probability of future successes immunize it from Sen's criticisms, but the position makes no claim to liberalism anyhow. Finally, since CHOICE involves no attempt to define "preference" in terms of behavior, market, or otherwise, it is safe from objections that have been brought against those sorts of reductions.

30. A similar worry for D-S theorists could arise regarding whether to count desire tokens or desire types. That is, if I desire something each day for a week, is that a bigger deal than "still" (maybe subconsciously) wanting it (once) over the entire period? Indeed, should we count occurrent desires or dispositions to give affirmative answers to questions of the type, "Do you want so and so?"

31. There's an interesting discussion of this subject in Murphy (1999).

Chapter 4

Equal People or Equal Votes?

Now that I have concluded my lengthy (and perhaps numbing) discourse on prudential value theory, I am in a position to make at least partial payment on my promise in chapter 1 to set forth a political theory that describes a solution to various puzzles that many other theorists seem to me to have missed. Recall my array of propositions that I claimed covered the positions one can find in this field:

(1) The proper goals of both persons and societies are objective items/truths that are either generally known or can be determined by religious, philosophical, or empirical investigations.
(2) The proper goals of both persons and society are objective items/truths that are not generally known, but may, on the societal level, be discovered by democratic means, since elections are "truth-tracking" activities: they provide evidence that this or that goal is the right one.
(3) The proper goals of both persons and societies are objective items/truths that are not generally known, but democratic procedures cannot help us discover them on the societal level, since elections are not truth-tracking.
(4) There are no "proper goals" of any society, because societies, like the individuals within them, have only subjective ends. But what the subjective goals happen to be within any society may be discovered on the societal level by democratic means, since elections are truth-tracking in the sense of helping us find the subjective ends actually subscribed to by the populace.
(5) There are no "proper goals" of any society, because societies, like the individuals within them, have only subjective ends. What the subjective goals happen to be within any society cannot be discovered by democratic means on the societal level since elections are not truth-tracking.

Propositions (1)–(5) do seem to make up an exhaustive list, especially if we include all the complications implied by endnote 3 of chapter 1. Surely, the goals must be either objective or subjective, and democratic procedures must be either conducive to truth-discovering or not. What other possibilities are there? One notable thing about the CHOICE standard discussed in the previous chapters is that the understanding of electoral activities that it suggests is not correctly depicted by any of these categories. By its lights, it is the choices themselves that are at least partly responsible for the creation of (objective) values. And if votes are seen as conglomerations of individual choices, they too will not just be value-indicating, but be playing their roles in (objective) value creation. But on this view, votes are not beliefs, judgments, or propositions—items which may be true or false, justificatory or misleading. According to CHOICE, some proposition or person—winner or also-ran—is "in the people's interest" only if, and to the extent to which this proposition or person is reasonably estimated to be productive of more successful choices, where what are "successes" are a strict function of what these people approve of, ex ante. But the approval or vote is not an epistemic item like a belief—something that may be more or less justified. The goals are a strict function of the choosings, and any prudential value associated with reaching them involves both the two-part character of choices (approving and obtaining), and the two prongs of prudential value creation: subjective success and objective fecundity. We might set forth this understanding of prudential value and its consequences for democratic theory by adding the following proposition to our list:

(6) The goals of a person or society are items that are both produced and reached through autonomous choices made by that person or society, and the prudential values they create are objective. On the societal level goals can be created and obtained by democratic means if elections are accurate aggregations of autonomous individual choices. No part of choosing is truth-tracking (provides *evidence* that this or that goal is "a good one" or "the right one") because choices are predominantly affective/conative, not epistemic. Thus, neither personal nor societal goals can be "wrong," even when their being reached fails to increase net prudential values.

If (6) is correct, we can say that Rousseau (1762, Bk. II, Ch. 3) was close to the truth when he wrote that "the general will is always right and tends to the public advantage; but it does not follow that the deliberations of the people are always equally correct." Perhaps he might better have said that this composite will can never be *wrong* because what is wanted is not the sort of thing that is ever either right *or* wrong. Nevertheless, the "deliberations of the people" may be said to be unwise (i.e., imprudent) to the extent that they result in choosings that are unproductive of additional successful choices or attractive options (or are less productive than other available and feasible choices might have been).[1]

EQUALITY

In chapter 1, I proposed what might be called the equality axiom of democracy. It was this:

(B) Each citizen in a democracy must be treated equally when it comes to the determination of what its citizens want their government to do.

But when it comes to voting and votes, what is "equal treatment"? And is ensuring the fair and equal treatment of voters enough to ensure the fair and equal treatment of votes? Robert Dahl (1989, 348) writes, "To some . . . intrinsic equality means that all human beings are of equal intrinsic worth. . . . To others, intrinsic equality means that the good or interests of each person must be given equal consideration."

Most Americans have been taught in school that "all men are created equal." We know it is in the Declaration of Independence and we may have heard that that document's author, Thomas Jefferson, got the idea mainly from John Locke. Presumably, it is this supposed equality that is the basis for the claim that when there is a dispute about some matter, it is the majority that should win the day. After all, if everyone is basically equal, nobody's position ought to be allowed precedence over anybody else's. So, we can get majoritarianism from Locke, right? Unfortunately, matters aren't quite so simple.

Jefferson is said to have been a deist, but the "created" in the language of *Declaration* suggests that the asserted equality had its origin in a more particularly Christian conception regarding how God relates to His "children." This Protestant picture is spelled out in detail in Lindsay (1947, 77):

> All men are equal in the sight of God—not because they are indistinguishable, "the very hairs of their head are numbered," but because each in his separate individual existence is dear to God. Any one of them is at any rate "the least of these my brethren." In Puritan theology every believer is a priest because he has been called by God. That fact, common to all believers, is so all-important that it overshadows and renders relatively unimportant the differences which it does not deny. The equality of the elect is therefore the equality of a society in which all count, and in which all are recognized to have different gifts.

Of course, not everyone is a devout Calvinist, and some doubters are not even deists. A more scientific sort might rely on a different basis for an equality claim. This person might take each human being as a hunk of protoplasm with the same sort of DNA, and, as such, deserving of no greater or lesser intrinsic rank or consideration than any other similar blob. However, even a suitably scientific agnostic need not hop on board the equal-treatment-of-votes-express. He or she might rather take the position that, if persons are in some sense "equal," it is sensible to vary the individual weights assigned to each person's judgment regarding what a group should do at any given time. The idea behind that might be that if Jones has more intelligent ideas, stronger wants, or better goals than Smith does, we ought to take Jones's votes more seriously—give them more weight—since Smith cannot make up for such discrepancies by somehow being a more valuable *person*. One might in this way infer from an assumption of equal person-weights that we should weigh votes based on the disparity of passions, virtues, intelligences, and the like.

It may not be right to move so quickly from the assumption of equal weights of persons to a conclusion of variable weights of votes, however, at least where the votes are for *representatives*. This is because representation is, presumably, of *persons*, rather than of either total vote counts or aggregated vote weights. So, for example, if we were to ignore the Jeffersonian "created equal" tenet and decide that "smart people" must get three votes while others get only one, we would need to figure out what to do in a federal polity constituted by two states, one having 10,000 voters (one-tenth of them smart) and the other having 5,000 voters (half of them smart). In this scenario, perhaps, one might argue that the less populous state ought to be allowed to cast more votes than the more populous one. But we might not agree that it should therefore be entitled to more governmental authority— say in the form of a greater number of representatives (or Electoral College members). We might rather insist that we must utilize some sort of "equalization" process so that at least each *person* is entitled to "equal treatment" by the government, even if their votes aren't. That is, the recognition that elected officials represent people rather than votes may suggest that we implement some sort of procedure that would apportion representative authority to the number of people being represented, even if we believe that weighing constituent votes on the basis of "smartness" is of the highest importance. For without that step, assignments of "smartness" could entitle one to more than additional vote power: it could actually produce the authority to, for example, keep all nuclear waste in somebody else's district or ensure that other district residents pay the penalties for crimes committed by those living in one's own jurisdiction. On the other hand, if people are thought to be equal in no sense whatever, perhaps we need not ensure equal treatment of persons either inside *or* outside of voting booths. Why, it might be asked, should we just not agree that "more valuable" folks ought to be given additional representation?

These differences of opinion show that taking a position on the vote-weight question does not relieve us of an obligation to answer the person-weight question too.

These issues are tricky. When voting theorists consider how choices ought to be aggregated, they must face the dilemma that either there are good reasons and feasible methods to weigh the importance of one approval against others, or they will need to treat every choice as equal to every other one. But both horns may seem objectionable. On the one hand, interpersonal measures of the intensity of desires, satisfactions, and talents seem unavailable, but on the other hand, treating a whimsical urge for a lollipop as no different from a hope that one's child will not succumb to a dread disease seems heartless as well as blind.

There is an almost visceral tension here. Robert Dahl (1989, 99) has noted that even if every person is assigned the same basic worth as all others, such intrinsic equality of individuals would not imply that

> we are all entitled to equal shares, whether in votes, civil rights, medical care, or anything else. While [such equality] would rule out some allocations, it would allow an immense range. If my neighbor has defective kidneys and needs dialysis in order to survive, equal shares would require that both of us, or neither of us, would be entitled to it.

Looked at in this light, it may seem simply wrong, perhaps even a clear example of *unequal treatment*, to make each vote equal. For if it is wrong for a wealthy person's wish for one more piece of cake to be equated with a mother's hope that her child be cured of cancer, it seems that it must also be wrong for all votes on minimum welfare protections to be equal, even though some may be cast as a matter of life and death and others made only because of a mild aversion to paying an addition $20 per year in taxes.

The confusing moral here may seem to be that any assumed intrinsic equality of individuals could be claimed to absolutely forbid the equality of wants or votes, since the latter seems to require that my mere curiosity about what it would be like to have an extra kidney in the house must be given the same weight as your desire for a kidney transplant in order to avoid dying within the week! How can such a result not be antithetical to treating people with "equal respect"? Surely it is nothing like what Lindsay would say an omniscient and benevolent God would do! And this point need not be seen as a religious matter. Hayden (2003, 216) has made it this way:

> If . . . I have a box of cookies and a box of crackers to distribute to my two children at the start of a long drive, I would want to know the relative strength of each child's preferences with respect to those treats in order to choose the

distribution of cookies and crackers with the largest aggregate utility (or lowest decibel level).

Equality-of-vote advocates have not been silenced by these critiques, however. In this passage from their investigation of these issues, Richard Pildes and Elizabeth Anderson (1990, 2133–2134) object to the idea of weighting votes by listing a number of pragmatic justifications for equalization:

> Three reasons, at least, have been offered for believing that intensity of feelings or beliefs ought to be excluded from democratic processes. One is a moral consideration, based on a particular egalitarian conception of the one person, one vote ideal: when democratic choices concern matters of principle or collective destiny, preference intensities should not be relevant. In cases such as decision to go to war or to pass a bill recognizing fundamental rights, individual judgments about what is right, rather than individual desires, are at stake; each person's judgment should count equally. . . . A second reason for excluding intensity information focuses instead on a practical concern that should not be linked to these moral ones: no noncontroversial, objective way to gauge such intensities has been found. . . . In the absence of an objective measure of preference intensities, a neutral collective decision-making process must exclude such information. Finally, if intensity information is included, possibilities for manipulating democratic politics increase, because individuals can readily feign intensity of their preferences and no voting system can be designed that would be invulnerable to such strategic manipulation.

To that batch of practical considerations, Hayden (2003, 248) mentions an additional reason one might give for dispensing with the search for interpersonal intensity measures: "[A]warding votes or voting weight based on strength of preference is . . . a good way to reward hotheads or those easily dissatisfied." Hayden also points out that SCOTUS has relied on "one person, one vote" in a variety of apportionment and gerrymandering cases at least since the 1960s, largely because the principle is "objective in that it prevents the judiciary from imposing its own subjective political beliefs in redistricting cases." And it is not only "objective" to do this but also quite simple. So elementary in fact, that according to Justice Stewart, taking the tack requires no more than sixth-grade arithmetic to apply (Hayden 2003, 227).

CHOICE may seem weirdly sanguinary with respect to these problems. According to Everett Hall, the correct construal of this matter is to take both the votes and the persons as equal. But how is that possible? He writes,

> Human wants are equal as creators of value. This implies that individuals are equal in a basic sense—ethically equal as sources of value. Furthermore, the

various desires of a given individual are equal to one another as creators of value. I cannot rate my coveting of the latest book by Bertrand Russell above my appetite for a good steak on the ground that somehow the former desire is more noble than, or inherently superior to, the latter. Things are of different value, however, as they are objects of different numbers of desires. . . . This is not to say that men should have equal amounts of choice. It means rather that free choices are equal as bases of ranking conflicting goods, so that the more our social conflicts are resolved in accordance with majority preference the better. (Hall 1945, Ch. 3)

But what defense can be given for the apparent callousness toward the person who desperately needs the kidney transplant? The answer is partly a matter of admitting the incapacity of human beings to obtain certain types of knowledge. This is an old story. Jevons (1888) was surely not the first to note that, "Every mind is inscrutable to every other mind and no common denominator of feeling is possible." It has been hard for any thoughtful observer to deny this epistemic limitation. But with the stakes so high, many will think we have given up too early on the possibility of ranking wants and satisfactions on the individual level by limiting ourselves to counting "successes." After all, when considering expected future costs, no insurance company would look only at the frequency of claims and ignore their severity. What sense could there be in equating the costs of a scratched bumper with those connected with a vehicle that has been totally destroyed, or a broken finger with a broken back? How can it make sense for a democratic theory to commit the same sort of error? Would it not be more sensible to find a proxy for importance? Could we not, for example, let the money one would be willing to expend to get or keep something determine the relative importance of choices? Can't individuals be trusted to price their own desires based on how important they seem to them? The information loss resulting from simply declaring all successes to be of equal value seems both colossal and unnecessary.

Let me again put the CHOICE standard (this time explicitly indicating its applicability to groups) in order to see if a closer examination of it may yield any additional insights into this quandary.

CHOICE. For all possible states of affairs S, and polities P, S is intrinsically prudentially good for P at t if and only if (i) S is freely chosen by P at t; and (ii) pursuant to one or more physical laws, the obtaining of S will, under ordinary conditions, causally contribute to the subsequent increase either of the total capacity for successful free choices among the constituents of P or of the alternatives that will be available to be freely chosen by those constituents.

We have said that one response to the intensity advocate is to plead a reluctance to make judgments in areas where we must admit insurmountable ignorance and frequent irrationality. The second conjunct of the CHOICE standard may seem more courageous on that front, since it allows for third-party knowledge of a type obviously not available with respect to the first conjunct. But there are limitations to the availability of empirical knowledge with respect to both conjuncts, and the inclusion of preference scales would not help matters. A number of studies have shown that our preferences are not always rational. But even more important is the fact that our choosings don't always follow our orderings—rational or not. In a fascinating work, Harry Eckstein (1991) distinguishes actions that reflect actual preferences of the actor (those that are "goal conscious") from behaviors that are better described as "impulsive." We can suppose that the reflection of preferences is to be anticipated in goal-conscious behaviors, but we should not be expected to correctly predict activities that are functions of impulse.[2] And when impulses are likely to predominate over goal-direction is itself impossible to predict. This puts limits on the "science" that can be used to make second-conjunct estimates of net successes. We need not suppose that there are no causes at all for such behaviors, that they are completely random in any metaphysical sense. But to the extent that their origins are unknown either to the executor or observers, they cannot inform our calculations. Perhaps an expert will expect marked changes in behavior resulting from a future windfall or unforeseen wipeout even when the affected parties are unable to make any such predictions themselves. But what is purely impulsive is that which is, by definition, "out of the blue," that is, unpredictable, either by scientific observers or the agents themselves. Thus, our situation is one in which preference orderings (i) cannot be used interpersonally; (ii) are sometimes irrational on the individual level; and (iii) may, in any case, be ignored by agents in favor of impulses. While an ordinal ranking is not even a reliable guide to the revelation of actual preferences, an actual choice is more than a revealed *preference*: it is a revealed *success*. So, we conclude that we are better off omitting the rankings and their false promise of useful information.

I hope it will be admitted that individual preference orderings are largely incompetent to provide proxies for interpersonal comparative measures.[3] The arguments on this matter have been compelling at least since Robbins and Pareto. Neither the psychologist, the economist, the neurophysiologist, nor the philosopher can measure anything like variable "utils" in any way that would allow us to add or subtract levels of mine to or from those of yours.[4] That doesn't make subjective importance irrelevant. On both the individual and social levels, even in the absence of intensity measures, we will obviously work harder, give more of what we have, to obtain those things that seem most important to us at any given moment. And, at least on the social level, the resentment when governmental powers ignore apparent intensity differences among sizable groups can erupt in civil unrest. That is called "the problem of intensity," and it can threaten the sustainability of any democratic polity. We shall see that voting mechanisms that remain sensitive to the intensity of wants without importing traditional ordinal rankings can be helpful in this area. In a word, to the extent that our electoral and representative systems are competent to reflect felt importance in desires, they can defuse the counterintuitiveness of equal vote weights. And "equal treatment" is something that has long been at least claimed to be an important political goal in the United States and elsewhere. Such mechanisms must not, however, either assume cardinal differences where we have no access to them, or take personal orderings to have more significance than they actually have.

We should also note that the belief that it would be *wrong* to take the two desires mentioned earlier as intrinsically equal can result only from either switching to a moral plane or (if one is sticking with prudential values) hold- ing true some version of the objective-list theory that was criticized in previ- ous chapters. If we ignore the CHOICE-based assessment that a cancer cure is likely to have a much greater effect on the number of future successes than is a brief napkin possession, it will only be nonempirical premises that will allow us to derive that Jones not having her desire to be cured of cancer satis- fied is (all other things equal) worse than Smith not getting the napkin passed to him. I don't deny the existence of intuitions distinguishing the intrinsic importance of these desires, but for the reasons set forth previously—involv- ing epistemic limitations, the common irrationality of preference orderings, paternalism, the mysteriousness of anti-naturalism, and the apparent advan- tages of simple counting for calculationism—I believe it is better to deny both the Platonic and hedonistic pictures in their entirety, and just rely on fecundity. However, as said earlier, once we remember that the cancer cure is quite likely to be a more fruitful success than the napkin receipt, we may see that the intuition leading to the revulsion of equal treatment of desires in this case has not been entirely ignored by CHOICE.

Turning from intensity to variable voter capacities, how can it be appropriate to assent to our equality axiom when it seems so obvious that, due to differences in voter intellect or virtue, votes ought to be differentially weighted? I think it will be easier to address that nagging intuition if we consider more carefully what votes actually are: what they can and cannot do. The notion that, because Jones is smarter than Smith, her votes should be given more weight seems to require the assumption that votes can help us get to *the truth* in some disputed area. But, even if it were the case (and I deny it) that votes are essentially the expression of beliefs and that finding truths is the purpose of elections, can it really be sensibly insisted that, for example, Jones's belief that the town needs a new bridge is more likely to be *true* than Smith's belief that the old bridge will do? Suppose Jones is correct in thinking that the old bridge has only a few weeks left before it will collapse; it may be that Smith's vote reflects no view as to durability at all, but simply manifests utter indifference regarding whether the bridge will collapse or not. Or maybe she thinks that town aesthetics would be much improved without the bridge, or that people will be healthier if they are forced to walk around the mill creek, or that it is simply too expensive to fix the bridge, whatever else may be true about its condition. With all of those possible interpretations of Yea and Nay votes, it is utterly implausible that choices or votes could be truth-tracking.

THE INTENSITY PROBLEM OF MAJORITY RULE

As mentioned earlier, supporters of variable vote weighting need not rely either on an epistemic conception of elections or on their moral intuitions. For "the intensity problem" has also been claimed to be the main obstacle to stable polities, given populist majoritarianism. To recap the matter, according to populists, simple majority rule requires that a 51 percent portion of an electorate that doesn't really care that much one way or the other about what they are voting on will always defeat a 49 percent segment that cares a lot. Two of the leading Madisonians of the twentieth century (Kendall and Carey 1968) argued that a failure to accommodate the fact that a minority might care much more about some matter than the majority does, must result in either an unstable or despotic state. They do not deny that, because of the absolutely unbridgeable gulf between individual souls, we will never find an objective interpersonal measure of intensity. But they do not infer from this epistemic limitation that wants ought to be declared equal. Instead, they take our permanent inability to objectively measure interpersonal intensities to show that populist theories must fail. For, in their view, it is absolutely crucial that every polity take intensity into account. They write of the sort of populism I defend here, that

> Its bets are on the notion that . . . the majority must get its way. Its (and its theorists') only possible answer to the question, *Suppose the majority doesn't much care, while the minority cares "intensely"?* is: "So much the worse for the minority. If it feels so strongly about the matter, let it get out and win a majority over to its side." (Kendall and Carey 1968, 10; emphasis added)

This is a ruinous obstacle on the Kendall/Carey view because no government can ignore matters that are most important to its people without inviting revolution. Indeed, it is a problem that they believe no populist theory can solve.[5]

Others have agreed that intensity is a central problem for populism:

> The Populist theory, with its emphasis on the normative significance of one man-one vote majority rule, essentially ignores the problem [of intensity] or implicitly assumes it away. Madisonian theory has as its greatest virtue the preservation of minority interests through the various "checks and balances" created in the constitution by the separation of the government into three branches, the separation of the legislature into two branches, and the decentralization of government into a federalist system. (Mueller, Tollison, and Willett 1975, 143–144)

We have already faced the fact that the refusal of our voluntaristic conception of value to accommodate inferences that rely on nonnatural information subjects it to accusations of wanton cruelty when, for example, it allots the gratification of some glutton's desire for a third helping equal weight with a mother's distress of having her child conveyed to a gas oven. Now, we find it is subject to Madisonian anti-populist arguments as well. In response to the accusation of indifference to murdering children, we have suggested that fecundity measures within the CHOICE standard of prudential value may block the accusation of equality (and more will be said about this matter in later chapters). But we should also repeat that, even if this attempt fails, CHOICE is neither intended nor claims to provide an analysis of ethical values, so it is unsurprising when some moral intuition suggests that additional conditions are necessary for "permissible" social actions.[6]

The present difficulty is that, even in the unlikely event that the CHOICE critic were to agree that we can provide effective means with which to handle moral objections to CHOICE, there would remain the additional concern that any democratic theory that ignores intensity differences in its electorate must be unstable or despotic or both. One may look at "the problem of intensity" as a dilemma. Either we can find a way to assign different "importance values" to wants based on the degree to which they are wanted, or there will be civil unrest. Distilled populism (which requires majority rule and takes all voters as equal) would countenance only scientific measures for distinguishing votes based on their intensities. But as there is no scientific way of attributing intensity values to wants, it seems that either populism must be dropped or there will be civil unrest.

This dilemma is surmountable. I will try to show in chapter 7 how a majoritarian theory can dismiss preference orderings and declare all votes to be of equal weight without ignoring subjective voter intensities. And in chapter 8 I will describe what I take to be the best method of giving minority voices their appropriate say in a polity where majorities are allowed to rule. I believe those will constitute a comprehensive response to this objection to distilled populism.

Keeping all this in mind, let me summarize where I think we have gotten on the matter of vote/person equality. We have offered a view that dispenses with both capacities of voters and intensities of desires as bases for assigning differential vote weights. We have also suggested that both moral realism and OL theories of prudential value may be seen as mystery mongering. Abandonment of moral verities and ethereal "lists" leaves us with two independent sorts of justification that may be proffered for treating desires equally. One is pragmatic and consequentialist: it adduces the sorts of defense for such an attitude as can be found in the Pildes/Anderson and Hayden quotations earlier. That approach cites basic support for majoritarianism, fear of manipulation, concerns that electoral hopelessness might create a catch-22, the promise of less political manipulation, fears about giving too much power to hotheads, and an interest in simplicity/calculability. The other route simply takes the equal treatment of successes within CHOICE as axiomatic. I suggest we do not disparage either road.

It will be recalled that I earlier expressed a concern that if we start with vote equality, we may end up with person *in*equality. It is true that some persons likely make *more* choices than others, but there is no reason to suppose that persons are nothing but conglomerations of choices, so it does not follow from the fact that Smith makes more (equal-valued) choices than Jones, that Smith must be "better" or "more worthy of respect" than Jones. I suppose one might claim that, even without any assertions of "intrinsic worth," Smith is in some sense "more important" than Jones if she makes more choices, because the choices themselves have been claimed to be of equal importance. I myself find it hard to make out a coherent sense of "importance" on the personal level, but it would certainly be true on the social level that if each choice of Smith's and Jones's were to be counted, Smith could reasonably be assigned more aggregate "importance" in social decision making. If people are concerned about achieving that sort of importance, they may be encouraged not to miss any voting opportunities. Generally, however, election procedures are indifferent to the number of choices one makes outside of plebiscites. Within them, it is usually the case that each person is given precisely one vote on each ballot item. It doesn't matter how many other desires he or she may have "at the ready," since a voter's having wants or approvals handy does not magically produce ballot questions. Furthermore, as discussed earlier, representation must be of voters, not votes, so Smith's alleged "superiority" in terms of want-production cannot be allowed to make her a "super person" with respect to governmental treatment (though she may be a more vociferous—and "more consequential"—constituent) in any case.

Before leaving the matter of vote weights, I want to mention one additional objection to the proposal that each vote ought to be taken as equal. According to this view, it makes sense to assign differential weight to votes in the sorts of elections in which there are specific kinds of issues or authority involved: those where we can easily partition those voters with greater, smaller, or no interest at all in the matters at hand. Hayden (2003) gives as examples (i) a school district election where some have children or will pay school taxes and some don't or won't, and (ii) a "lake basin water storage" election in which the results of the vote would seem to affect only certain landowners (and that group in direct proportion to the assessed value of their land). This may seem a reasonable suggestion and it is one that should be addressed by any theory of democracy that declares votes equal, but I shall leave it to the next chapter.[7]

MORE ON "EQUAL WORTH" AND "EQUAL TREATMENT"

In his critique of secular egalitarianism, Louis Pojman considers offerings of libertarians (Nozick and Machan), liberals (Rawls and Dworkin), utilitarians (Bentham and Singer), a Marxist (Nielson), and several others (Gewirth, Vlastos, Hare, and Feinberg). In Pojman's view, none of the arguments these philosophers have proposed either for (i) treating everyone with equal respect or (ii) assuming (even for practical purposes) that each person has equal worth is any good. While I doubt Pojman would have much more use for my own ideas on this matter, it may be worthwhile to set them down with a bit more clarity than I have to this point.

Pojman objects when this or that philosopher proposes that we simply assume that people have equal "moral worth" because, he complains, we might just as easily have started with the assumption that some people have more worth than others. For my own part, however, I make no assumptions about "moral worth": the equality that people are here claimed to have is either taken as an axiom or as derivative from the combination of (i) the assumed equality of individual approvals; (ii) the nature of a plebiscite, which necessitates the aggregation of approval/no approval results on particular questions; and (iii) the fact that it is *representatives* that one is generally voting for. I have taken it as axiomatic that one *choosing* is as "good" as any other, except to the extent that one may be productive of more successful choosings than another, though I have offered other means for getting to that position as well.[8] And I have noted that if choices are treated equally, the people will have to be treated equally as well, at least in most respects.[9] According to distilled populism, which elevates only political rights, people are entitled to equal treatment, not for moral reasons, but because their votes must be counted fairly in order that each may take its rightful place within the jigsaw puzzle of the general will. Each of us has at least a general understanding of what it is to make an autonomous personal selection, so we have an inherent sense that if a group is to treat non-coerced member choices analogously, each chooser must be treated with respect and all the choices must be fairly counted and aggregated. Therefore, voters must receive certain protections and guarantees. When I claim there is a right to association or free speech or to equal protection under the law, I mean to suggest that such rights can be derived from the basic proposition that we must attempt to discover what people want, if they are to authentically govern themselves. These derivative "rights" are needed to reach that goal.

What distinguishes my approach from those criticized by Pojman is that it has a sort of compositional aspect that it shares with Locke's corporeal argument for majority rule, something that will be discussed in more detail in a later chapter. The people's will is taken as a kind of composite made up of individual choices. No desire may be left out on grounds of epistemic defect because, as we all know from our own personal experience, to want something is not to have a true or competently justified idea. Choices are largely *affective* and *conative* items, *there or not there, effective or ineffective, fecund or sterile.* While some may be deemed wild or foolish and some are so trifling as to approach indifference, it does no good to pretend the nonexistence of some choice based on its exemplification (or lack) of those characteristics. Pojman asks, roughly, "Why does it not make as much sense to treat some people as worthless as it does to assign them equal worth?" On the view advocated here, that question is tantamount to asking someone who is weighing a barrow full of stones, why she thinks it is necessary to include the darker or rounder ones. Just as we must count all the votes fairly to understand what is wanted, we must also treat all the voters with equal respect, for disparate treatment of voters can also distort our aggregations.

WHAT, EXACTLY, ARE "EQUAL VOTES"?

We have settled on the requirement that if there is to be real democracy, votes must be equal. But that is an incomplete specification. Surely, saying that votes must be equally weighted comes with the obligation to set forth precisely what is meant by that imprecation. Let us therefore take a moment to consider more carefully what a jurisdiction must do if it is to "treat each vote equally." It turns out that it could mean any number of different things. In a helpful summary of this issue, Jonathan Still (1981) distinguishes six different criteria that might be suggested by the expression "equal vote":

(1) Universal Equal Suffrage: Everyone is allowed to vote, and everyone gets the same number of votes.
(2) Equal Shares: Each voter has the same "share" in the election, defined as what that voter voted on divided by the number of voters who voted on it.
(3) Equal Probabilities: Each voter has the same statistical probability of casting a vote which decides the election (under certain assumptions).

(4) Anonymity: The result of the election is the same under all possible distributions of the voters among the positions in the structure of the election system.

(5) Majority Rule: An alternative favored by a majority of the voters will be chosen by the election system.

(6) Proportional Group Representation: Each group of voters receives the same proportion of the seats in the legislative body as the number of voters in the group is of the total electorate.

These six criteria are taken by Still (rightly, I think) to generally impose increasingly high bars that electoral procedures might be required to meet in order to be considered fair. So, without (1), Smith could be allowed two votes while Jones gets only one. Without (2), the existence of districts of various populations might allow for quantitative vote dilution. Without (3), winner-take-all mechanisms within different districts could allow for inter-district majorities to be thwarted. Without (4), gerrymandering could make for qualitative vote dilution. Without (5), the favorite candidate in a multiply represented district might be denied a seat because of an at-large system. Without (6), majorities might receive not only all the power to rule but also all the representation.

I have argued that fair democracies require equal votes. Let me now suggest that this means that there must be electoral provisions sufficient to prevent each of the six defects that could result from ignoring any of Still's six criteria. In my own proposals to handle these, I will not be overly meticulous about guaranteeing equal probabilities, except to the extent that this is dealt with by eliminating single-member, winner-take-all districts. Furthermore, the method I will propose for ensuring minority representation, to be discussed in chapter 8, will not manage the concern expressed in Still's (6) by utilizing an "equal number of seats" provision.

It is my view, however, that, while something like each of these six principles is necessary, they remain jointly insufficient to ensure fair elections. More is required. On the other hand, I do not agree with those theorists who have insisted that the remaining deficiencies must be cured by considering the *outcomes* of democratic events. In their view, even the strictest democratic procedures cannot guarantee the fair treatment of all citizens, so election *results* must be checked to see whether a democracy is pure. I make no attempt to reach beyond procedural fairness myself[10] though, as will be seen, I take that expression more broadly than many others do. But as an advocate of CHOICE, I can make no appeal to any supposed standard of "the good society" other than a requirement that, to the extent possible, it reflects what is wanted by its members when each is guaranteed a fair opportunity to express his or her wants and have such expressions correctly counted.[11]

The first step in giving Still's list due consideration is to look at what "universal suffrage" means, so that we can be sure we are meeting the basic requirement in (1). That will be the burden of the next two chapters.

NOTES

1. Rousseau goes on to say, "Our will is always for our own good, but we do not always see what that is; the people is never corrupted, but it is often deceived, and on such occasions only does it seem to will what is bad." This, too, is quite illuminating and, I believe, closely related to the view advocated here. While their choices cannot be *wrong*, the people will be deceived if they draw improper inferences regarding what is prudentially best solely from the existence of successful acquisitions.

2. The classic discussions of the distinction between impulses and desire-producing activities are Russell (1917, 1955), which note that impulsive actions may seem no more than madness to observers. See also Eckstein's (1980) discussion of contingency versus inherency; Schulz (1992); and Simon (1985). It is interesting that while Eckstein focused on the frustration found in impulsive acts, particularly among the poor, Russell concentrated on their role in play and spontaneous joy.

3. In chapter 7, however, I provide some non-ordinal distinctions that I believe can be used to objectively "score" individual attitudes without the adoption of interpersonal intensity measures.

4. Jean Hampton (1997) is particularly good on this issue.

5. The somewhat less Madisonian Dahl (1989) agrees with that conclusion. The Kendall/Carey view is that the correct way to handle this matter is to accept Madisonian constraints on popular elections and let the representatives handle the intensity matters through lengthy deliberation and bargaining. As will be seen in coming chapters, I'm sympathetic to the idea that extensive deliberation by representatives is salutary—in fact, I'd require it. But I don't think the Madisonians are right that a populist approach has no answers of its own.

6. My own view of ethical values is that that where they seem to diverge from the prudential considerations circumscribed by CHOICE, they become almost random, there being no coherent scheme one can depend upon. As I do not suggest that CHOICE be considered a standard of all types of value, I leave open the possibility that some application of CHOICE will produce a result that many people in some society would declare to be evil. I believe, though, that such conflicts are unlikely to be as common or inevitable as one may at first think. The combination of CHOICE's exaltation of personal autonomy and liberty with its manner of estimating the successful choices of current and future possible individuals makes such any tensions difficult because, to the extent that our moral values are intelligible, they resemble prudential values in also being intimately tied up with autonomy, liberty, and success. Where there remain apparent conflicts between moral and prudential values, I believe the moralist is obligated to admit that her injunctions may well make everyone worse off. These issues are largely beyond the scope of this book, but I will discuss a couple of instances of possible conflicts between CHOICE and community moral standards in later chapters.

7. The main intent of Hayden's paper is to question the current strict doctrinal and legal separations among the ostensible rights to (i) vote, (ii) quantitative equality in district apportionment, and (iii) group protections against qualitative dilution by, for example, gerrymandering. He believes that voting rights should be generally broader, but that they should always be based on the level of group or individual "interest." Unfortunately, an equivocation between two meanings of the term "interest" infects much of his analysis. It is not the case either that one must have strong preferences one way or the other regarding some issue that clearly affects one's (e.g., property) "interests," or, alternatively, that one cannot have intense feelings about an issue that does not seem to touch one's "objective interests" in the slightest. Thus, one cannot use the single term and swerve back and forth between these two connotations as Hayden does without creating confusion.

8. It may be worth repeating here that if we did not treat choices as intrinsically equal, it would not be correct to say that the more fecund successes were in any sense of greater net "importance," since one "crucial" choice might be thought to swamp twenty "vapid" choices in intrinsic significance. It's not that the more fecund choices are worthier or entitled to more weight: it's simply that, because of the laws of nature, they will produce more future successes than other choosings will.

9. There are qualifications that must be made to this assertion which will be discussed later.

10. This may be put not too misleadingly by saying that the CHOICE standard can be understood, as Rae (1981) puts it, as "lot-based," rather than as reaching for a finer-grained, "person-based" or "stakes-based" analysis. (I will discuss a particular "stakes-based" approach (Brighouse and Fleurbaey 2010) in the next chapter). Rae might categorize CHOICE as "lot-based" because of its eschewal of Platonic notions of "good results" and of interpersonal measures of intensities, preferences, capacities, or interests. It is my view, in any case, that result-oriented understandings of democratic virtues require either Platonism or some variant of a calculus that can only be little different from Bentham's hedonic monstrosity. As indicated above, while CHOICE is sympathetic to calculationism, it is significantly more modest about what sorts of items can be calculated than its common consequentialist rivals.

11. There is an excellent discussion in Hampton (1997) of the battles between "competing conceptions of justice"—e.g., with Rawlsians supporting a maximin principle, Nozickians defending Wilt Chamberlain rights, and egalitarians pushing for a Salingeresque world of identical outcomes. While this dispute is certainly fascinating, it is bypassed by distilled populism. Once naturalized, democracy allows only such "primary goods" as are needed to make authentic self-government possible.

Chapter 5

Who May Vote I
Interest or Inhabitancy?

The previous chapter urged that when there is an election, the vote of each elector should be equally weighed. Let us now assume at least temporary assent to the answers we have given above to both the question of why any sort of right exists "to have one's expressed interests given equal weight in the determination of policy" (Beitz 1989, 7) and the question of what "equal weighting" of votes ought to mean. What does this entail for "equal treatment of interests" under the law? Here in the United States, SCOTUS has argued persuasively in a number of cases that a requirement of equal weighting means, at a minimum, that different constituencies must have roughly the same number of people who are allowed to vote, if those constituencies are to be given an equal say in the making of laws.[1] But if equal treatment of a particular kind may be required of each member of some bunch of people, which bunch? Who get to be the electors? One thing seems clear: we can't settle *that* problem by taking a vote. This is one member of what are called "boundary problems," and as Brian Barry (1979, 167) has written,

> [T]he majority principle has no way of solving them, either in practice or in theory. In practice, the majority principle, so far from alleviating conflicts over boundaries, greatly exacerbates them. . . . On a theoretical level, any use of the majority principle in order to establish boundaries must involve begging the question.

That is why it is natural to turn to properties that are independent of majority desires—perhaps things like *relevant interests*—to make these determinations. In the paper by Grant Hayden (2003) discussed earlier, various arguments are given for a decision procedure according to which there must be enough of the right kind of "interest connection" present between all those who might be allowed to vote on any issue and entrée to the booth. As indicated previously, however, Hayden isn't clear about what constitutes an interest, sometimes meaning by it a preference (or, perhaps, a "legitimate preference") and sometimes meaning a reasonably expected *effect* on a person. As I hope is clear by now, attempting to use voter preferences to determine who may vote creates a vicious circle. But no such circle infects the "predictable effect" connotation of the term "interest." But circumscribing those sorts of interests can be tricky too. Let us therefore open this chapter by looking at the matter more closely, and do so by hypothesizing a vote that is to be taken by a nongovernmental institution, a club.

WHO CAN CLAIM A LEGITIMATE INTEREST IN AN ELECTION RESULT?

Imagine there is a group called "The A-town Athletes," a voluntary organization that has arranged for time on a weekly A-town field to play various games, like soccer, football, and ultimate frisbee. Suppose Jack, a long-time member of the Athletes, has recently returned from a year in Glasgow where he had become familiar with a game that had just been invented there and is now all the rage in Scotland—*Sandieball* (Sandie for short). Sandie is a game that can be played on the A-town field, and Jack brought back all the equipment needed to do so. Others in the group begin to read up and watch videos of a Sandie league that has grown up in Edinburgh, and there begin to be arguments as to whether the game ought to be played with metal or rubber cleats; whether iron sticks may be used; whether "digging" is to be allowed; the penalties that ought to be assessed for "jam crashing," "vicious allotments," and other rule violations; the length of the periods; and so on. As they have long done when other disputes of this nature have arisen, the Athletes have scheduled a vote whereby all the difficulties can be resolved by a majority of its dues-paying members.

Word that a vote is to be taken on these issues begins to spread, and it isn't just local A-towners who are taking notice. In fact, for the first time in the hallowed history of the Athletes, a lot of unaffiliated people want to vote in this election. Here are eleven groups that have expressed this desire to participate and the main reason(s) they've given for thinking they ought to be allowed to do so:

(1) They live in the town and pay for the maintenance of the field. It is clear that passage of some of the rules would result in a type of play that would be extremely harmful to the turf and, thus, increase their taxes significantly for repairs.

(2) They live near the field and they don't want their children to be watching any "sport" that is brutal or dangerous. Some kids may be horrified at the injuries expected to result from some of the proposed rules, while others may be encouraged to take up that sort of "play" themselves. On the other hand, acceptance of gentler rules might result in these same children getting interested in an engaging new physical activity.

(3) They are members of the same health and accident insurance plan as many of the players and believe that if certain of these rules pass, their premiums will go up.

(4) They live in A-town and have been thinking of becoming members of the Athletes themselves, so the rules that are decided upon may well affect their lives.

(5) They are interested in televising the first season of American Sandie games and know well that some sets of rules will attract more viewers than others.

(6) They are located in another state, but are forming a national collegiate sanctioning organization for Sandie, with the hope of applying to the NCAA for inclusion, and they understand the sorts of athletic activities of which the latter organization is likely to approve.

(7) They are the Scottish Sandie league, and, while they would love to schedule some games against American teams both in A-town and in Glasgow, only certain types of rules of play would be consistent with the way the game is played in Scotland.

(8) They are a group of local business people with a financial interest in the boost that international Sandie games in A-town would give to the tourism industry.

(9) They are the three gentlemen who actually invented Sandieball in Glasgow, and they have concerns about a bunch of Yanks calling some wildly different game "Sandie" without their permission (something that they complain has recently happened in Wales).

(10) They are the group of state legislators who managed, after four years of dealing with lobbyists, to get boxing outlawed in their jurisdiction, and would prefer to have Sandie start off as a safe, sensible sport than to have to go through the same sort of struggle with another pastime.

(11) They're from all over the world, and they really love watching only one particular sort of Sandie. All the other styles seem like rubbish to them.

These all describe "interests" and, with the possible exception of the last one, they all seem to be "objective" in some sense. Brighouse and Fleurbaey (2010) call such interests "stakes" and claim that their levels may be at least roughly quantified/estimated. It is not only the case that in their view (which, of course, is incompatible with the equality position taken here) votes should be proportional to stake level, but it is also true that their theory provides a handle on the boundary problem of who should be allowed to vote at all. It is boundary-destroying! Voting is called for when stakes are at or above some (unspecified) minimal amount, period. Brighouse and Fleurbaey take their position to be justifiable not only by considerations of utility, but by strictly procedural considerations involving respect for persons and their autonomy. The idea is that the "closer" an issue gets to an individual, the higher the stakes are for that person, and, thus, the more significant her vote on it should be. When the effects are de minimis, the right to vote on the matter may be allowed to disappear entirely. To the extent that effects circle outward from any activity, more and more people have a right to vote, though perhaps with lighter and lighter weights assigned to their preferences. Geographical boundaries are relevant only to the extent that they affect stakes.[2]

Let us look at the list of alleged Sandie interests a bit more closely in this light. The members of groups (1)–(3) surely have what Fleurbaey and Brighouse would call legitimate interests in the upcoming vote, but perhaps it can be objected that their claims may be ignored because, as voting members of relevant jurisdictions—the town, the state, or the country—they already have sufficient opportunity to put their desires into effect. For example, townspeople can be expected to have the opportunity to vote on field usage, either directly or through their local representatives, so perhaps they need not *also* be given a voice at Athletes meetings. And when it comes to (4)–(11), one might insist that the interests are insufficient or that there are other means to address them than allowing them to vote with the Athletes.[3] According to this way of thinking, Brighouse and Fleurbaey may be right about what is needed to get a vote, but either the criteria aren't met or there are other avenues that should be examined if we are to be certain that no person's interest will be multiply counted. How do we handle these issues?

Focusing on (1), it is true that, given some structures of local government, many of those living in A-town will have some manner of overturning certain votes taken on Sandie rules by the Athletes. But we can conceive of townspeople who will not have such opportunities, and in any case, we can imagine residents to think that their "proximity" to the matter entitles them to participate in *both* elections. On the other hand, it could be argued that the right of the Athletes to an exclusive vote on this matter and (thus) to exclude others from participation is fundamental. A democratic conception of what makes lives better entails that what is prudentially valuable for any group can be determined only by the proper aggregation of the largely unconstrained wishes of group members. And that in turn seems to require freedom of association. And perhaps *that* right suggests that if a bunch of people want to get together, form an athletic club, and vote on this or that matter—giving nobody else a vote, they may not be prevented from doing so.

Of course, if one were to take that position, it would seem to follow that the Athletes could not have the authority to *implement* the desires of their members. For surely that association can no more use the town field just as they like based on one of their own elections than they could enforce a rule they may have unanimously voted for allowing them to throw rocks at redheads without retribution. In other words, if democracy requires unfettered associating, voting, and expression—including the exclusion of others from participating—the effects of any votes on nonmembers will generally be flaccid. If elections of that type were not so constrained with respect to their implementation, contradictory edicts would occur as soon as another group is formed. To prevent that eventuality, it might be suggested that "stakes" could be used, not to determine who gets to vote, but to delimit the extent of the authority of any pronouncements. We may, however, want our votes to affect precisely some cohort that has the greatest "stake" in preventing an edict from affecting them!

What if we take a more limited view of the political rights of groups, and deny them the right to exclude participants? Could we then countenance a Proportionality principle more like the one proposed by Brighouse and Fleurbaey? It seems not, for the problem of the effects of multiple votes on the same issue in different forums would reemerge, again forcing the Proportionality defender into a position that involves implementation authority rather than the right to vote.

There are additional theoretical and practical reasons for dismissing Proportionality completely. To its credit, it dispenses with interpersonal intensity and capability measures, but vote weighting for reasons of *stake* comes with its own set of problems. For example, stakes may be increased or lessened by one's own activities—say, by monetary investment or changing a business location. Indeed, a Proportionality standard would allow certain voters—especially rich ones—to change their circumstances in ways that could increase their vote weights. In a word, Proportionality provides a clear path for those who want to buy elections. That seems like a very bad feature.

The impracticality of a Proportionality standard should be obvious, even if we ignore the problem of multiple voting opportunities. As the Sandie example shows, nearly anyone in the world could have a legitimate claim to vote in any election taking place anywhere. And the weight of each person's vote would need to be calculated based on some stake assessment. We would never have any way of knowing what portion of all the people eligible to vote was given the opportunity to do so, since every election—even one undertaken by a club in little A-town—would evidently need to be worldwide, extending through every time zone. As a result of such impracticalities, the notion seems useless.

POLITICAL RIGHTS BEYOND SANDIE

The Athletes are a tiny, private group, but I believe that what can be learned from this example about the fundamental importance of equalizing vote and voter treatment is universally applicable. According to the theory advocated in this book, only such rights as are needed to guarantee democracy may be taken to be absolutely fundamental (and thus, perhaps, "inalienable"). All other claimed entitlements are derivative of the axiom that the people must be allowed to govern themselves. But this is where we hit our boundary snag. Even if one agrees with the populist that it is all and only political rights that are fundamental and thus require equal and impartial distribution to all members of every relevant group, one will need to know which groups are the relevant ones. How is "a people" to be delineated?

The populist's elevation of democratic over "natural" rights can be seen as placing her closer to the "radical" endpoint on a liberal-radical continuum in which the liberals are more supportive of the Lockean claims for life, liberty, and property and the radicals are more concerned about democratic determinations of societal practices. David Miller (2009, 205) argues that such placement will have consequences for the position one takes on the problem of "who gets to vote." He writes, correctly, I think, that what he calls R-democrats (where the "R" stands for "radical") are likely to hold that:

> [D]emocracy is valued intrinsically and the idea of collective self-determination
> stands at the heart of democratic theory. Democracy is a system in which people
> come together to decide matters of common concern on the basis of equality,
> and the aim is to reach decisions that everyone can identify with, that is, can see
> as in some sense their decision. (Miller 2009, 207)

But the conclusions he draws from thus regarding an R-democrat's likely attitude toward boundaries seem to me confused. In fact, they even provide a good explanation of how "populism" came to become a dirty word. Miller (2009, 207) claims that while we can expect "L-democrats" (i.e., liberal ones) to be "subject mainly to an inclusionary push," R-democrats (radical ones) "will be subject to an exclusionary pull." This, he thinks, is because the latter theorists will likely take there to be "too little solidarity among the members on account of physical distance or cultural diversity." I take no position on where those closer to the L-democrat end of the continuum are likely to be found on boundaries, but Miller's assessment of R-democrat propensities seems entirely upside-down to me. I would argue that the distilled populist's devotion to voter equality along with her required agnosticism regarding most democratic *outcomes* (as opposed to procedures) will push her either toward unlimited inclusiveness (since all voters are taken to be equal), or to indifference/pragmatism on the boundaries front (since treatment of *votes* as equal may be all that matters to populists of her stripe). The exclusionary push that Miller attributes here seems clearly nativist and has no analytical connection with either L- *or* R-leanings.[4]

The populism endorsed in this book is a particular sort of procedural, aggregative democracy. As Sarah Song (2012, 44) summarizes positions of this type, they make all and only those rights that are "integral to the democratic process . . . such as the right to vote, freedom of political speech, freedom of assembly, and freedom of the press" constitutive of the very term "democracy."[5] On the other hand, populist approaches, when properly distilled, do not allow any inference to shared histories, shared cultures, and/or shared values—the items that comprise what Song calls "solidarity."

While Song finds solidarity to be a necessary condition of both fruitful deliberative interactions and the "pursuit of economic equality," I take it to be indicated *only if supported by the people in the group.* And what demarcates "the group" cannot itself be a function of "solidarity."[6] On the other hand, a matter that the distilled populist can agree with Song about regards the unacceptability of the views of Carl Schmitt (AKA "Hitler's favorite jurist") and Joseph Schumpeter.[7] According to those theorists, a group may use whatever criteria it likes to determine who shall be its voting members and who should be considered its "enemies." Both men insist that what they consider the obvious reasonability of denying the suffrage to young children, mental defectives, and convicted criminals shows not only that groups must be allowed to determine who get to be voting members, but that democracies have always made such determinations. In their view, it is thus self-contradictory to sneer at the use of race or ethnicity to include or exclude people from a polity.

I will turn to the issues of age, competence, and virtue momentarily, but want to consider first the possibility of using geographic lines to determine democratic inclusion/exclusion. Can such criteria be legitimately used even in instances in which the boundaries seem to have been explicitly placed to function in a manner antithetical to fair democratic procedures? Certainly, Song is not alone in arguing that the use of geography should be prohibited whenever it is availed for apparently discriminatory purposes.

I agree that the goal of discrimination against a race or ethnicity can never be allowed to provide an appropriate rationale for unequal treatment with respect to voting, access to relevant information, political expression, or any other bona fide political activity. In other words, if there were no borders, support of political equality would seem to require a prima facie position according to which everybody in the world ought to be allowed an equal vote on every matter. But that would be neither a reasonable nor desirable arrangement. And this is so whether or not considerations of "solidarity" or "enemyhood" have played (or even continue to play) significant roles in the placement of jurisdictional boundaries. Remember, our contentions are limited to what is necessary for democracy, a practice with procedures that require defense against unfair discrimination: they do not include prescriptions for clearing up all obstacles to what someone may consider a "good society." Democracy requires access and fairness, but does not guarantee a society that exemplifies decency, kindness, or "distributive justice." Thus, nothing prevents an excellent democracy from existing within a country whose citizens betray nativist prejudices (or countless other attitudes or activities we may find appalling) so long as such prejudices do not produce *political* inequalities, including, for example, lack of equal protection under the law. And, as we shall see, where there is procedural fairness, there will be both strict prohibitions on discriminatory treatment and a sort of flywheel mechanism that may limit electoral exclusion via boundaries of any kind.

There are two lenses that have traditionally been used to look at the boundary problem: *legalistic* and *moralistic*. The first method sets forth decisions by courts of competent jurisdiction on questions of alien suffrage, naturalization, and the like, and attempts to find some sort of coherent thread in them. The second method tries to tease out the features of a "just" approach to the "Who gets to vote on membership?" question by using "conceptual analysis" and/or the consulting of one's "moral intuitions" on these subjects. As I have not cited any cases, it might be thought that I am pushing for a *moralistic* solution that has not been offered hitherto. I am not. This may be easier to see if my own approach is contrasted with a clearly moralistic one.

A good example of the moralistic method of handling the boundary problem can be found in Michael Walzer (2010). Walzer there considers in what ways political membership seems more or less like neighborhoods, clubs, or families.[8] As he sees it, neighborhoods are at root geographic areas that people move in and out of freely; clubs are non-geographic collections of individuals which may be joined only by those who exemplify whatever criteria current members insist upon; and families are those to whom we have some moral obligations, whether we like them or not. By extracting various pieces from columns A, B, and C, Walzer fashions a loose theory that provides what he believes should allow for or require a right of entry to a polity. This methodology makes sense to him because, as he puts it (2010, 43), "Membership as a social good is constituted by our understanding: its value is fixed by our work and conversation; and then we are in charge (who else could be in charge?) of its distribution." There is thus, in his view, some *correct* theory of membership according to which rules of entry are sometimes a strict matter of what the current members want, but, for example, when those seeking entry or asylum are in grave danger, must instead be understood to be a function of some higher principle(s). He addresses issues involving alienage and naturalization in the same way. In a word, he trusts his intuitions on these matters and believes that if we consult our own, we'll agree with him.

That is as good an example of non-naturalized democratic theory-making as one is likely to find. Walzer is ambivalent, though. For example, he says (2010, 40) when discussing clubs, that "distribution of membership in . . . any ongoing society is a matter of political decision" rather than "some act of nature or of God." He also points out (2010, 51) the apparently supreme relevance of finding the answers to such questions as: "What kind of community do the citizens want to create? With what other men and women do they want to share and exchange social goods?" But he says that families are not like clubs because of "moral connections," and claims that it is only neighborhoods that can be construed as nothing more than "areas." Since, in his view, polities are in some respects more like families or neighborhoods than they are like clubs, we cannot simply take a poll to decide who may enter. And, of course, determining who could take the poll would require answering the boundary paradox in any case.

GETTING TO INHABITANCY

Let us see if our naturalizing gambit can assist us in getting to some answers about boundaries without appeal to moral intuitions. First of all, distilled populism requires us to take a position of modesty: no individual is expected to know—indeed, none *can* know—what is good for everybody in some group without a mechanism for aggregation of individual choices. What can be calculated to be (prudentially, not morally) best for the group is always a function of what everybody does (and will) choose, as well as of estimates of successes and failures given those choices. Understanding that the only way to find out what is good for any group is to aggregate individual choices leads us to the consideration of appropriate methods for doing this. What must be guaranteed by the choosers for the democratic mechanisms to work? We find that such guarantees involve the protection of such political rights as free speech, association, and non-discrimination. These must extend to everyone in any group for its general will to be properly assessed. Votes within the group cannot tell us what the boundaries of that group is, but fair voting *does* require specific kinds of treatment of every member *within* any specified borders.

We saw that some who have a "legitimate interest" in the A-town rules for Sandie may live on a different continent, so it seems that if democratic borders are to be a function of "stake" they cannot be derived from geographical closeness. But it is important to recognize that there are numerous rationales for territorial boundaries that have nothing to do with democratic principles at all. Consider, for example, military defensibility, access to fresh water, or desire to avoid expenses involved with multiple languages. It is thus unsurprising that many political boundaries are a function of natural geographic barriers like rivers or mountain ranges. Such barriers may have been conducive to "solidarity," but for democratic theory, those effects are nugatory. What is much more important is that the provision of democracy requires the possibility of administration in addition to the equal treatment of voters.

Deciding on geography as an essential characteristic simply follows from the conception of government as something that has, if not a monopoly on force, at least the most power of any internal institution to enforce rules within some geographical area.[9] For if democratic rights must be guaranteed, there must be places where they can be ensured. The world is currently such that it is impossible for political rights to be protected where there is no identifiable geographic region in which a government can enforce them. While some polities have considerable power outside their own borders, at least at present, they cannot have predictable authority except within some defined geographical ambit.

Put another way, our take on this matter makes the territorial boundaries of each polity in one sense irrelevant from the point of view of democratic theory. We know that on each side of any boundary, every choice must be accorded the same (fair) treatment. But this is not helpful because majority views will vary based on how groups are divided. One group may be socialist, another individualist, a third Georgist. Indeed, the members of one group may even stringently desire a sort of homogeneity that is clearly racist. As construed here, however, democratic theory can be used to combat racist views only by insisting that, *within the voting group*, treatment must be equal. That is, if we do not take a moralistic position, democratic theory can tell us only that whatever the state's boundaries happen to be, they may be defended in all and only such manners as the people inside them wish them defended. But however that is, each voter and vote within the polity must be provided fair and equal treatment. We may add to this that, if the jurisdiction is to be expanded or contracted, that also may be done only if and as the people want it, always making the full panoply of political freedoms available to all of its current or future residents. These would, of course, include the right to freely lobby for open or closed borders, or for lax or stringent immigration restraints. Whatever moral value such attitudes are claimed to have, they are orthogonal to democratic principles—so long as they do not infect domestic democratic practices. So, for example, if the citizens of country A are determined to accept only such members as are of particular races or ethnic backgrounds, a proper understanding of democratic theory will allow them to be inhospitable to outsiders and to keep an extremely close watch on their borders. But, if unwanted individuals nevertheless make it inside and establish residence, even for a relatively short period of time, the desires of those individuals on this issue (as well as all other public matters) must also be equally counted. Failure to do so would endanger self-government by creating the potential for incorrect assessments of "what the people want" simply because "the people" must include *all persons in the group*.

Walzer's claim that a state "owes something to its inhabitants simply, without reference to their collective or national identity" is, thus, accurate, but I think he is wrong to believe that the rights of entry or exit are among the items owed to members of democratic groups. Those "rights" exist whenever, and only whenever, a majority of the people in the groups in question want to make the borders of their polity open in each direction. Again, those to whom such a position seems cruel are free to exercise their political rights to the utmost to press for a different attitude and so ensure that their own states don't act that way, and that no one may be punished for lobbying. Democratic principles require that everyone is able to get involved in such ways—and, as we shall see, in much fairer and more effective ways than are now available in the United States. But naturalized democracy via CHOICE is unsympathetic to the view that, for example, there is a "natural right" to leave any territory and find a home elsewhere. There may, of course, be such a *civil* right, but that will arise where and only where the people in some jurisdiction legislate it into existence.[10] Distilled populism cannot declare barriers to entry or exit simply "unjust" as a matter of "natural law," even in cases in which there is little doubt that they are cruel. For nothing about a correct concept of democracy prevents a democratic polity from being cruel. In fact, it is hard to see how an authentically democratic polity might not be cruel if its population is. There are, however, strict limits to the types of cruelty in which a legitimate democracy may engage. For example, violations of equal protection to all those under its jurisdiction must never be allowed.

But if habitation is to be taken as the key to settling boundary disputes, it must be explained further. What is the exact criterion? Residence for a day? A month? Five years? Residence plus ownership of property? Residence with the declared intention of seeking naturalization? These questions will be taken up in chapter 6. First, however, I want to try to show that settling on some sort of residence criterion need not suggest that residence is being suggested as a good proxy for every type of "stake" or "interest."

Suppose we do a lot of business in some state where we do not live (call it "Old Hampshire"), have close relatives there, and visit it regularly. Suppose too that there is a prevalent desire, not only within Old Hampshire but outside of it, for retaining a particular way of life *inside* Old Hampshire. When one considers that this desired manner of living could have significant effects both on those who live in the state and on those who may want to enter it, one may wonder why giving outsiders a voice in these matters cannot be appropriate. Let us assume that the population of Old Hampshire is divided roughly equally into supporters of two opposing parties, the Public-School Advocates (PSA) and the No-Tax Libertarians (NTL). Suppose the PSA party is currently in power and they have proposed a bill that would forever bar entry into the state by any advocates of libertarianism. If people all over the world are allowed to vote on this, we can expect PSA regulars in the state to contact teachers' unions everywhere with the hope of getting members around the world to vote for "at least one safe harbor for educators, somewhere in the world." Similarly, NTL advocates will lobby anti-taxers worldwide to fight *for* "freedom of movement (and conscience)" and against discriminatory treatment against "the wise among us." Whichever side wins this election will clearly determine many aspects of living conditions for Old Hampshire residents for the foreseeable future. These will involve not only availability of public education but also levels of taxation, the characteristics of who is likely to become a future government official, and so on. Surely, a large contingent of active anti-taxers in Australia should not be able to determine these central aspects of the living conditions in far off Old Hampshire, or regulate who may immigrate into that state. We may not like the idea of a majority of voters passing a PSA measure that would prevent the entry of any forthright libertarians into their state, and no doubt Walzer would be joined by those to his right in considering any such jurisdiction "unjust." But such a measure seems to me clearly consistent with democratic principles, so long as the plebiscite takes the temperature of the correct group on the matter. That group seems clearly to be all and only those who actually live in Old Hampshire—not because of a correct demarcation of interests, but because in our world, capacity to govern is closely tied to geography.

These considerations may help us distinguish between what matters for political rights and what matters for citizenship/naturalization. When the NTL is in power, it might be true to say that that the people of Old Hampshire feel the need to hear a vow of eternal antagonism toward socialism and other methods of wealth redistribution before they will consider granting citizenship to any applicant. Perhaps they also want to make sure that all of their citizens are willing to carry arms, fight, and die for the right of every Old Hampshirite to smoke cigarettes in every room of every building and airplane—not only in Old Hampshire but in the entire world. If Old Hampshire wants to make all of those attitudes conditions for *citizenship* (not for voting rights), it must be free to do so—but only so long as it is really clear both that that is what the majority of residents there want and that full political rights there do not require citizenship. In that way only will the determination that the Old Hampshirites really do want those things be safely based upon appropriate democratic procedures.

Settling on some sort of residency as the key criterion for political rights leads us back to questions regarding what residency *is*. Supposing that it is granted that being an inhabitant is the appropriate criterion for determining who is to receive voting and other political rights, what is it that constitutes *inhabitancy*? I turn to that matter in the next chapter.

NOTES

1. Of course, the U.S. senate is—and was intended to be—violative of this principle.

2. The authors note, in addition (2010, 142–146), that insofar as we can quantify stakes and use them for voting, we will have no need to fear Condorcet/Arrow cycles, because we will be able to assign cardinal numbers to every possible position on the societal preference scale simply by summing and subtracting stake votes. This virtue is also claimed by supporters of certain types of Score Voting, which can be seen as one way to flesh out a simple variant of Proportionality. I say something about Score Voting in chapter 7.

3. For example, in the case of (9), there might be legal remedies for claimed harms.

4. I think Rogers Smith's (1988) take on exclusionary attitudes, discussed in chapter 1, is more insightful. See also Huntington (1981).

5. While populist theories, with their relative quiet regarding both such traditional alleged rights as life and property and—at least at the outset—any particular procedural niceties regarding deliberation, may seem quite minimalist when compared with those of "deliberative democrats" like Joshua Cohen, Amy Gutmann, and Song herself, they need not ignore the importance of equal opportunity to access certain types of information, government positions, and expressive outlets including mass media. Those kinds of opportunities seem to involve both sufficient resources to obtain crucial (accurate) information and a guarantee of nondiscriminatory treatment. All these matters will be discussed in later chapters.

6. Neither can such outcomes as "economic equality" of the sort sought by Song and many other theorists be considered indispensable to the determination of what the people want—so long as voter access to information, ballots, media, and offices all meet minimum thresholds. I will argue in chapter 9 that authentic democracy may require equal access to airwaves of a kind that I think can be achieved through such avenues as a media "fairness doctrine."

7. See Schmitt (1932) and Schumpeter (1942).

8. Interestingly, while Walzer (2010, 43) does not mention Schmitt by name, he gives an etymological explanation for Schmitt's most famous view—that nonmembers must be conceived of as enemies.

9. For a defense of this conception, see Dahl and Shapiro (2015) and Cudworth (2007).

10. For an excellent discussion of the origin and nature of civil rights and duties, see W. D. Lamont (1946). I will have more to say about rights of various types in a later chapter.

Chapter 6

Who May Vote II

Residence, Age, Criminality, and Competence

Among the many delightful nuggets to be found in the accounts of U.S. history by early twentieth-century progressives are the Beards' tales of the evolution of requirements for voting and holding office imposed by the various colonies—and later, the various states. To give a few examples:

> In New Hampshire, the governor had to be worth five hundred pounds, one-half in land; in Massachusetts, one thousand pounds, all freehold; in Maryland, five thousand pounds, one thousand of which was freehold; in North Carolina, one thousand pounds freehold; and in South Carolina, ten thousand pounds freehold. A state senator in Massachusetts had to be the owner of a freehold worth three hundred pounds or personal property worth six hundred pounds; in New Jersey, one thousand pounds' worth of property; in North Carolina, three hundred acres of land; in South Carolina, two thousand pounds freehold. For members of the lower house of the legislature lower qualifications were required. In most of the states the suffrage or office holding or both were further restricted by religious provisions. (Charles and Mary Beard 1921, 239)

The debates regarding what quantities of freehold, wealth, income, tax payments, and so on are sufficient to demonstrate a connection with a community that is stable enough for one to be allowed to vote or hold public office could often be a wonderful mix of subtlety, ferocity, and personal interests. According to Charles Beard (1913, 164–167), proposals to include those sorts of voting restrictions in the U.S. Constitution were defeated for economic reasons. Madison argued that small property requirements would likely be insufficient to keep out those farmers who were pushing paper money schemes, but imposing large landed property minimums might exclude mercantile and manufacturing interests. Charles Pinckney proposed that those having unsettled debts be barred from becoming Congressmen, but Governeur Morris realized that might keep any number of members of that very constitutional convention out of office, and so beat back all such proposals. In the end, for reasons having little to do with democratic principles but quite a lot to do with the personal interests of the conventioneers, no property qualifications either for voting or for holding office made it into the final draft.

It was different in the state constitutions, where, in addition to the instances of discrimination against slaves and women that *were* memorialized in the Federal Constitution, one could find a plethora of property-related requirements until quite recently. Richard Morris warned his fellow Virginians, "What better test of character could there be than property ownership? . . . Unless property is protected, it will be invaded [for] [i]f those without property can vote to take it away from those who have it, surely they will."[1] Ezekiel Bacon asked similar questions in New York.[2] It was also wondered how, if someone does not pay taxes of any kind, it can be fair for that person to vote on tax laws. What disincentive would he or she have for supporting the highest taxes possible?

In spite of the evident attraction of these sorts of arguments for elite groups, obstacles to voting were slowly but steadily defeated in the United States, in large part because of the steadfast work of labor advocates and supporters of the rights of women and blacks. Property qualifications and religious tests were gone by the mid-nineteenth century, gender disqualification by the 1920s, and the last racial and ethnic bars by 1952. In 1964, states were prohibited from denying the vote to those who owed Federal taxes, and in 1971, the voting age was lowered to eighteen nationally. As Cogan (1997, 496–497) explains, at some point America seems to have given up considerations of accidental properties of prospective voters, and instead "pursued the logic of the look within as far as it would take them." That sentiment was reflected in Justice Warren's 1964 declaration that it is the individual persons themselves, not any accidental properties they happen to have, that matters when considering democracy:

> Legislators represent people, not trees or acres. Legislators are elected by voters, not farms or cities or economic interests. As long as ours is a representative form of government, and our legislatures are those instruments of government elected directly by and directly representative of the people, the right to elect legislators in a free and unimpaired fashion is a bedrock of our political system.[3]

Naturally, this evolution has not cleared up all difficulties in the matter of who gets to vote. The relevance of a certain relational (or "outside") characteristic—*residency*, as well as that of several apparently "internal" factors—*age, competence,* and *virtue*—remains controversial.

WHAT CONSTITUTES RESIDENCE?

Currently, the right to vote in the United States is a function of *citizenship* rather than residency—permanent or otherwise. As I write this (February 2019) the United States is embroiled in fierce disputes regarding immigration that have already resulted in one lengthy government shutdown and may cause more. A significant percentage of the country would like to erect an enormous wall, with Mexico on one side of it, and California, Arizona, New Mexico, and Texas on the other. Others scoff at this idea, either because they believe it would be too expensive or ineffective, or because they would like our borders to be more open (or both). What is significant about this dispute for our purposes is that it illustrates that immigration into the United States— with or without a wall—is not, at present, intended to be easy. About twenty thousand employees of Immigration and Customs Enforcement are currently quite busy both trying to keep various non-citizens out and taking action to send back those who have sneaked in.

For it is not only hard to get in: those who are here legally often find it extremely difficult to *stay in* for more than a brief visit. Lawful permanent residents must obtain green cards, the application process for which is anything but trivial.[4] These cards can take years to obtain, and the wait depends on the place determined by Homeland Security to be the applicant's "country of origin."[5] Since the total number of immigrants to the United States is limited, it may simply be impossible to obtain a green card, even when a qualifying relative or employer sponsors the applicant. If there is the slightest indication that someone would not make a wonderful neighbor, his or her chance of obtaining a green card is quite remote. The barriers do not just involve paperwork. In his careful discussion of this issue, Rosberg (1977, 1130) points out that

> Resident aliens [must be] committed enough to the United States to serve in the armed forces, and they have been drafted into the army in the same way as citizens. A resident alien is admitted in the expectation that he will make the United States his home and remain here indefinitely.

Most current U.S. citizens were born on American soil because the constitution includes a guarantee of citizenship as a birthright. That may be considered a tremendous stroke of luck, since it is clear that a significant percentage of us would never be able to get green cards given the sort of scrutiny currently directed toward visitors with applications to stay here.

As mentioned earlier, however, the ability to vote currently requires not only "permanent residence" but *citizenship*. This may seem to be nothing but the exercise of additional prudence, since naturalization requires the holding of a green card for at least five years, along with (i) residence for the last three months in the same state, and (ii) success on a basic American history test. But it should not be forgotten that it is much easier for those with green cards to become citizens than it is to get a green card in the first place. And from the perspective of distilled populism this additional hurdle accomplishes nothing but the abrogation of a basic political right, possibly for a very significant period of time. Governmental activities cannot truly be democratic unless they reflect the voices of *all* those who are subject to them as a result of their residency. As Rosberg (1977) notes, there are a number of nonpolitical privileges such as the right to call upon the U.S. government for protection in certain circumstances that are available to citizens but not green card holders. Those need not concern us here. But the inhering of political rights—such as to vote and to hold public office—cannot be allowed to wait for the clearing of obstacles that many native-born citizens certainly could not clear. In sum, democratic principles do not allow political rights to be denied to green card holders with stable residences.

We have seen, though, that it can take many years for green card applicants to get even *those* approvals. Therefore, removing the distinction between *permanent resident alien* and *citizen* is insufficient to handle democratic concerns. There must be created a category of "Contingent Green Card Approvals": those that would occur if the availability of visas were irrelevant. Such contingent approval ought to be obtainable within a year or two given continuous residence in a single locale since application date. Meeting that burden should be sufficient for the obtaining of all political rights.[6] In a word, permanent residents must be allowed to vote and hold office, whether they are citizens or not.[7]

AGE OF COMPETENCY

Back in 1977, Rosberg (1977, 1150) wrote that "The exclusion of children from the franchise is itself a subject of much controversy," and cited *Oregon v. Mitchell*, 400 U.S. 112, 240 (1970) as evidence for his claim. But according to Sanford Levinson (2002, 1271) any such controversy must have disappeared entirely during the following twenty-five years, since he confidently asserts that "not even professors or students who take pleasure in offering provocative arguments suggest that . . . sixteen-year-olds should have the right to vote." Levinson goes on to assure his readers that "Whatever 'imperfections' may pervade the Constitution, no one has given that label to its presumptive permission to states to limit the suffrage to those older than eighteen years of age." Whether or not Levinson was correct in his assessment in 2002 (and I believe he was not), there is certainly public controversy to be found regarding age restrictions on voting today.[8]

Carl Schmitt and Joseph Schumpeter used "what everyone must know" about children to make what they took to be a telling point against egalitarians who objected to their view that any *polis* may limit its voting membership to a certain kind or class of individuals. Populists are subjected to arguments of this type even today:

> You say *everyone* is to be treated equally, that *all* must have equally weighted votes—whoever they may be and wherever they may come from—but you cannot actually believe this. After all, little children and the insane are people, aren't they?—yet you don't suggest they get the vote! You must at least realize that six-year-olds should not be given the vote in spite of their "personhood."

It can hardly be doubted that, up to some vague point, "maturity" does increase with age, and little could be clearer than that the average six-year-old doesn't know what a vote is, never mind much about the state of the world. But how can the populist consistently prohibit infants (or institutionalized psychopaths) from voting? If all the desires—whimsical, immature, ignorant, confused, malicious—must be weighed equally in calculations of the general will, what basis can there be for leaving *anybody* out? Let us look at this issue more closely.

The recent spate of school shootings in the United States has brought attention to the fact that, while high school students may appear on television and make speeches about the clear dangers that widespread gun ownership may present to them, they cannot vote on the matter. And it is worth noting that concerns regarding the limited rights of children have long been a popular subject in books, television, movies, and plays. To mention just two of the latter, Tony Awards have recently been won by both *Spring Awakening* (based on a play first produced in 1891) and *Dear Evan Hanson*. Each of these focuses on the complicated issues with which teenagers must deal, including those involving criminality. Rape, incest, child abuse, suicide, drugs—all are topics that come up and must be closely dissected by their dramatis personae. And in each work, feelings of powerlessness are often allowed expression only through the pathos-drenched silence of the performers.

But before we insist that since real-world adolescents face the same issues, they ought to get to vote on them, we must remember that we have already dismissed the idea of interest-based criteria for suffrage, beginning with our discussion of Sandie. And, in any case, rape, incest, child abuse, and drugs don't just affect adults and teens: they may victimize toddlers too. Surely the suggestion that six-year-olds or even infants be granted suffrage can be taken as a reductio of the whole matter of reducing the minimum voting age.[9] How can we resolve this? If neither knowledge nor virtue is to matter and we don't base suffrage on the possibility of being affected by the passage of laws, regulations, or orders by those who will be elected, what *can* be plausible bases for enfranchisement?[10]

One clue comes from the history of the juvenile justice system. Until about 200 years ago, U.S. children under the age of seven were believed to be incapable of forming criminal intent, and were thus considered to be exempt from punishment. In Britain, the Common Law allowed for a "Defense of Infancy" based on what was known as *doli incapax*—an age-based presumption of inability to know right from wrong. For many years the presumption of *doli incapax* was irrebuttable for those under eight, but rebuttable for those between eight and fourteen.[11] This approach to the issue is psychologically or cognitively based, rather than focused on knowledge, independence, tax liability, virtue, or interest-reach. A thorough examination of this matter may be found in Vivian Hamilton (2011). She notes, in accordance with my own views, that few people at any age are likely to be terribly knowledgeable about many of the "issues" that are relevant during elections, and adds, in accordance with the well-known conclusions of Anthony Downs (1957), that the cost of acquiring that kind of information nearly always swamps the expected benefit one could gain by voting with it.[12] While the quite specific second prong of CHOICE sets a high bar for a "correct vote," a competent vote does not require "full information" or even any general level of information at all.

So, what *should* voters be able to do? According to Hamilton (2011, 53), "a minimally competent voting decision involves the appropriate application and coordination of various reasoning processes to make a choice that could be justified by a good reason."[13] This is because, in her view (2011, 52–62), the ability to cast a non-random vote requires minimal competence in all of the following:

- The ability to learn and retrieve information.
- The ability to form mental representations of information.
- At least some ability to reason inductively, deductively, and analogically.
- The ability to apply and coordinate reasoned inferences to some goal, like the solving of a problem or the making of a decision.

Once there is agreement on these, settling on a minimum voting age is simply a matter of consulting the literature on the stages of psychological development. That is precisely what Hamilton does, with patience and care. I will not rehearse her generous summary of the research here, but simply report the absolutely decisive conclusion that, (i) prior to the mid-teens (i.e., sixteen or thereabouts) there is, on average, arguably insufficient maturity to meet

Hamilton's criteria; and (ii) after the mid-teens, there is, on average, no development in those areas significant enough to be declared relevant.

This result will not be surprising to anyone who has adult children. That something dramatic happens during the high school years is quite obvious. Athletes begin to have ninety miles-per-hour fastballs, close in on Olympic records, even get notifications of interest from professional teams. Musicians, visual artists, and actors begin to give performances or create pieces that could be staged without embarrassment anywhere in the world. Writers begin to compose publishable works of poetry and prose. Mathematicians suddenly make progress on matters that have stumped the world since the beginning of time. Chess and video game players become masters. Actors start to show multiple levels of depth and nuance of expression. Comedians become funny in original ways. Of course, some kids develop earlier, and some are late bloomers. But those of us who have gone to plays, concerts, games, art showings, and so on at our children's high schools will know that an incredible change takes place among the rank and file there. Clearly, if what the people in some polity want is a strict function of what (all) its people competently and autonomously choose, sixteen-year-olds must be allowed to express their desires and aversions in the same manner as older members of society.

Will the votes of sixteen-year-olds be independent, or will they just ape the votes of their parents or teachers? It really doesn't matter: nobody's vote is entirely independent of those around them. What about the danger of teens simply being instructed to cast their votes in a particular manner by those who feed and house them? The secret ballot is a wonderful protection against coercion of that type. Will they not care enough to vote, based on the belief—correct or incorrect—that most of the issues won't affect them? That is entirely up to them. Electoral indifference also provides useful information about the state of the populace. (And if they are made to go to the polls against their will, they can always write in Rihanna, Payton Manning, Zippy the Pinhead, or one of the Mutant Ninja Turtles: no harm will have been done.)

COGNITIVE IMPAIRMENTS, MALEVOLENCE, AND CRIMINALITY

According to a 2007 compendium on the subject,[14] most states have statutory or constitutional provisions prohibiting those with significant cognitive impairments from voting, although "the assessment of voting capacity, if necessary, must be made in a judicial proceeding that affords challenged voters their due process rights" (Hurme and Appelbaum 2007, 932). The decision in a 2001 case in the state of Maine sets the minimum standard as "the mental capacity to make their own decision by being able to understand the nature and effect of the voting act itself"[15] which, incidentally, seems to me a nice, compact way of expressing the rather complex list of cognitive requirements set forth in the previous section.

Hamilton (2011, 43) claims that there is an argument to be found for distinguishing between setting the basis for an age standard and setting one for alleged cognitive disabilities:

> The purpose of the standard used to determine [the competence of allegedly impaired persons] is simply to assess whether the nature of voters' cognitive impairments are such that they have clearly lost that competence. The purpose of a standard used to determine the electoral competence of young people, on the other hand, is to assess whether they have reached the stage of development by which they will have attained—as an initial matter—the array of cognitive capacities required for competent voting.

However, I find no argument to support this claim in her paper, and it seems unlikely that competence testing is universally thought to be relevant only for those who have *lost* some previously attained cognitive skills. I don't think this matters much, though, since I find no compelling reason to test *anybody* once they have reached an age at which the vast majority of individuals are competent. Once we depart from the eighteenth-century picture, according to which voting eligibility ought to imply a good chance that the voter in question will get to some *correct* answer (i.e., the answer in accordance with both eternal value-truths and solid empirical assessments of current facts and probabilities), there need be little concern that a handful of votes in any election may have been made, not only with little information, but with complete confusion regarding what voting is. While I have no objection to incompetent residents being barred from elections, the process seems to me a waste of resources and subject to abuse. Unless it is clear that campaigns are routinely scouring asylums and nursing homes with the intent of somehow forcing or inducing the inhabitants to vote for certain candidates, individual assessments of competence seem to me nugatory. If several dozen individuals scribble in the names of their pets, it will do no more damage to a large aggregation than those few teenagers who may write in the name of their favorite rapper.

The matters of criminality and maliciousness may be dealt with together. Like the setting of a minimum age, but unlike the cognitive impairment issue, the effect of rules regarding "felon suffrage" is far from trivial. According to Whitt (2017), every state except two (Vermont and Maine) disallow voting by imprisoned felons and thirty-five bar voting for some period even after time has been served. These policies have disenfranchised a very substantial number of individuals—especially in certain areas.[16] A number of apparently plausible reasons for this massive disenfranchisement may come to mind.

As these people have been convicted of crimes serious enough to result in imprisonment, perhaps they are too evil to be trusted with the vote. Or perhaps it is just one more penalty that has been tacked on to those involving freedoms of movement and occupation. Clearly, the view that evil intentions ought to bar one from the vote is another artifact of the eighteenth-century idea that votes are a manner of "getting to what is objectively best." According to that picture, just as one might fail to be a "good voter" by being stupid or ignorant, one might also fail by having a malicious bent. But if voting is understood simply as a way to tell what people want, neither intelligence nor beneficence is vital. There must be a minimum level of cognitive competence, but there ought to be no bars related either to information or benevolence quotients. According to distilled populism, the point of government is neither a just society nor a happy citizenry. For the former, one likely needs angelic wisdom and virtue, and for the latter, soma might work better than voting rights. As a mere champion of democracy, what the populist is interested in is preserving human autonomy.

Sigler (2014, 1737) has suggested that it is sensible to remove the privilege of voting from felons simply because they have "violated the trust of [their] fellow citizens by flouting the laws collectively established for our mutual benefit." She calls any such violation "a breach of our civic trust." Whitt (2017, 293) replies to that justification by claiming that, to retain its legitimacy, democratic regimes must operate on an "all-subjected principle" according to which (quoting Dahl) "The demos should include all adults subject to the binding collective decisions of the association . . . except transients and persons proved to be mentally defective." Whitt attempts to distinguish this principle from the sort of "everybody with a *stake*" proposal that I have criticized in chapter 5 in connection with Sandieball. In Whitt's view, the latter, which he calls the "all-affected principle," is insufficient since it does not, as he believes it should, limit required enfranchisement to those whose "behavior or status [is] governed by law on a regular and ongoing basis, with the coercive power of the state standing behind the law" (2017, 293).

I agree with Whitt on that point. Indeed, it should be clear from my remarks in chapter 5 that Whitt and I are in agreement on the defects of the "all-affected principle," for, as indicated there, I think, too, that it makes more sense to use geographical bases for enfranchisement. But it's not entirely clear what Whitt thinks this should entail for those who are incarcerated. We agree, I think, that if one lives in Florida for some period and is reasonably expected to continue to do so, one should be allowed to vote in Florida elections. I believe, however, that someone incarcerated in a Federal Penitentiary in Tampa, Florida, is only confusingly dubbed a "resident of Florida," since nearly all the rules she is under will be federally issued. Thus, based upon either a residence or an interest standard, this inmate might reasonably be excluded from such questions as property tax overrides and school committee elections in Tallahassee. An incarceree in that facility is certainly a resident of the United States, but she may just as well still reside in the Louisiana facility from which she was transferred, when we consider any right she might have to vote in a Florida or Tampa election.

What light does our inhabitancy perspective shine on Sigler's objection to felon suffrage? Are voting rights alienable based on certain types of conduct? I myself do not see how political rights can be alienable if the governors of the population inside the region in question are to be able to say that they are doing what their people want. For only when sincere attempts are made to give the people what they want can public actions be considered legitimate. There is a sense of "legitimacy" according to which democratic practices should not themselves be thought to be either legitimate or illegitimate—since it is only authentically democratic procedures that can *make* public policies legitimate. That is, democracy either exists or it does not, and various procedures are democratic or they are not. On the other hand, statutes and governmental activities may be called legitimate to the extent that they reflect appropriately democratic procedures. Thus, we may legitimately have fines or incarceration as penalties for certain activities. That legitimacy is a function of whether the people or their representatives (or courts) actually want these activities to be considered criminal and have properly enacted and equitably implemented penalties to enforce that desire. If the laws or governmental actions taken pursuant to them have resulted from undemocratic or discriminatory means, those governmental actions are in this sense illegitimate. It follows from this that we cannot appropriately make disenfranchisement a kind of criminal penalty: it is incoherent over the long term to claim that the people want that penalty when enforcement of it might make it impossible to find out what it really *is* that the people want. The same objection may be made when the disenfranchisement is termed a "removal of a privilege" (and attributed to "flouting") rather than being designated a penalty for committing a crime. Either way, a contradiction emerges, one showing that it can never be appropriate to alienate a political right.

Let me now summarize the conclusions of this chapter. First, all those (let us call them) "enduring" residents in any jurisdiction who have reached the age of sixteen should be allowed to vote in elections held for the purpose of determining the governance of that jurisdiction. Second, while there are certainly people who are over sixteen and cognitively incompetent to cast anything but a random vote, that is not a compelling reason for a widespread search-and-prohibition scheme. Finally, incarcerated felons should be considered to be residents of the jurisdictions controlling the facilities in which they are held. Neither freedom from confinement, discharge of a (just) penalty, wisdom, nor benevolence should be taken to be a prerequisite to enfranchisement.

NOTES

1. Virginia Convention of 1829, Statement of Richard Morris.
2. See New York Convention of 1821 (statement of Ezekiel Bacon). An excellent summary of these sentiments may be found in Jacob Katz Cogan (1997) from which these examples were taken.
3. *Reynolds v. Sims*, 377 U.S. 533 (1964)
4. U.S. Citizenship and Immigration Services (USCIS) provides the following information (https://www.usa.gov/green-cards):

> Someone usually must file an immigrant petition for you (often referred to as sponsoring or petitioning for you). In some cases, you may be eligible to file for yourself.

After USCIS approves the immigrant petition, and there is a visa available in your category, you file either a Green Card application with USCIS or a visa application with the U.S. Department of State.

You go to a biometrics appointment to provide fingerprints, photos, and a signature.

You are interviewed.

You receive a decision on your application.

And the application itself (https://www.uscis.gov/i-485) is formidable: fifteen pages, densely filled with questions regarding travel and employment history and plans, criminal justice experiences, current and future familial relationships, information about any organizations, societies, clubs or military entities you've ever belonged to, and your expenditures on nearly everything you've ever purchased.

5. According to USCIS data, it can actually take up to twenty years for applicants from certain countries!
6. Such contingent status would, of course, be revocable for cause.
7. Walzer (2010, 55–61) makes a case for contemporary "guest workers" from other countries, whom he takes to be like the metics of ancient Athens in being owed political rights even if they have no intention of ever becoming citizens where they are employed. He notes that metics "were occasionally enfranchised" and "played a part in the restoration of democracy in 403 B.C." This treatment seems reasonable to me as well, although I again think some minimum requirement of residency duration is sensible. My own view is that one year of residence prior to the political activity and a reasonable expectation of remaining for one year subsequent to it ought to be considered sufficient.
8. See, e.g., Whitt (2017), Beckmann (2017), and the many articles cited in those works. Note also that there are now several organized national pressure groups, including the National Youth Rights Association.
9. See, however, Weaver (2018), in which Professor David Runciman of Cambridge University is reported to argue that the voting age should be lowered to six. Runciman apparently bases this minimum on the unlikelihood of being able to read at earlier ages.

10. I don't here give any weight to consequentialist arguments about, e.g., increased expected turnout or allegedly better substantive outcomes. For a discussion of some of the empirical evidence on those matters, see Chan and Clayton (2006).

11. Not only the presumption but the last vestiges of the defense itself was abolished in 1996, largely for reasons of discrimination against "good families" and perverse disincentives to moral instruction. See Department, Law Lords. *House of Lords - R v JTB (Appellant) (on appeal from the Court of Appeal [Criminal Division]).*

12. Notwithstanding my substantial agreements with Hamilton, I don't concur with her view that, in spite of widespread ignorance, it makes sense to expect some "miracle of aggregation" to produce "collective decisions that reflect well-informed and coherent beliefs, because random or uninformed views cancel each other out" (Hamilton 2011, 46). I think it is a mistake to either expect or desire that votes reflect well-informed beliefs in the first place. I also don't agree with her—or the writers she cites on the matter—that voting ought mainly to be thought of as a "speech-act that has primarily expressive or symbolic (rather than instrumental) value" (Hamilton 2011, 47), largely because I am not entirely sure what Hamilton means by that remark. But I hope it is clear that, for my own part, I take voting to be non-epistemic in that it discloses—or at least ought to disclose—no more than what the people choose—whether or not that choice is viewed by this or that expert as "correct." But it should not be inferred from this that votes have no cognitive content at all. For a good discussion of the problems with customary epistemic theories of voting, see Saffon and Urbinati (2013).

13. I think this would be less susceptible to criticism if it were amended to read "make a choice that could be justified by *what might plausibly be taken to be* a good reason." I hope Hamilton would take that as a friendly amendment.

14. See Hurme and Appelbaum (2007).

15. *Doe v. Rowe, 156 F.Supp.2d 35* (D. Me. 2001)

16. Whitt (2017, 283) says (although he provides no citation for it) that "an estimated 5.3 million Americans of voting age are disenfranchised on the basis of present or past felony convictions; most of them are no longer serving time in jail or prison. This is more than 2 percent of the voting-age population."

Chapter 7

Votes and Their Aggregation I

Majority Rule and Majoritarianism

I have signaled my support for majoritarianism in this book, but, although I have provided numerous hints, I have not paused to discuss precisely what I mean by the term. Let me begin that discussion by quoting a couple of classic defenses of the idea, one from the seventeenth-century British philosopher Thomas Hobbes, and the other from the early-twentieth-century Austrian jurist Hans Kelsen.

> [I]f the Representative consist of many men, the voyce of the greater number, must be considered as the voyce of them all. For if the lesser number pronounce (for example) in the Affirmative, and the greater in the Negative, there will be Negatives more than enough to destroy the affirmatives; and thereby the excesse of Negatives, standing uncontradicted, are the only voyce the Representative hath. (Hobbes 1651).

Kelsen (1949) fleshes out the same basic notion—and with detail that accords nicely with the main sentiments of this book—as follows:

> The greatest possible degree of individual liberty . . . is guaranteed by the principle that a change of the social order requires the consent of the simple majority of those subject thereto. According to this principle . . . the number of those approving thereof will always be larger than the number of those who—entirely or in part—disapprove, but remain bound by the order. . . . The idea . . . is that the social order shall be in concordance with as many subjects as possible, and in discordance with as few as possible. Since political freedom means agreement between the individual will and the collective will . . . it is the principle of simple majority which secures the highest degree of political freedom that is possible within society. If an order could not be changed by the will of a

simple majority of the subjects but only by [unanimous consent] or by the will of a qualified majority (for instance, by a two-thirds or a three-fourths majority vote), then one single individual, or a minority of individuals, could prevent a change of the order. And then the order could be in discordance with a number of subjects which would be greater than the number of those with whose will it is in concordance . . .

The view that . . . freedom in society is proportionate to the number of free individuals implies that all individuals are of equal political value and that everybody has the same claim to freedom, [i.e., that] the collective will be in concordance with his individual will. Only if it is irrelevant whether the one or the other is free in this sense (because the one is politically equal to the other), is the postulate justified that as many as possible shall be free. . . . Thus, the principle of majority, and hence the idea of democracy, is a synthesis of the ideas of freedom and equality. (Kelsen 1949, 286–287)

Both quotations suggest that a majority principle implies that each person's desire, vote, or CHOICE must be given equal weight. That position allows one to *count* votes where other ideas of aggregation allow (or even require) weighting them based on some estimate of intensity, knowledge, virtue, justice, or whatever. But even what might seem to be a simple matter of counting can be fraught with difficulties. Condorcet, Arrow, and others have shown that if we want to know which candidate or proposal is "liked best" among some batch of candidates or proposals, both plurality and majority answers given simply by counting votes may reflect various sorts of irrationality. Even if no individual voter is irrational, a majority (or perhaps different majorities) within a single group can like A more than B, prefer B to C, and nevertheless like C more than A.[1] If "majority rule" means only that "the majority" (or plurality) always gets to have the candidate or proposal they "like best," having each voter simply indicate a favorite seems incapable of producing an unambiguous winner. It therefore seems vital that the selection procedures used by egalitarians like Kelsen and Hobbes somehow be devised so as not to countenance that sort of ostensible irrationality.

WANTING, PRAYING, AND VOTING

Obviously, different sorts of items must be "combined" differently. Bricks are not like water in this regard, and beliefs may not be like votes. Let us consider desires: what they are and what they do. Suppose you are severely disabled, confined to your bed, and you suddenly have a craving for an orange. You call out to anyone who might hear you and, although you've always been agnostic, you even take a minute to "send up your prayer" to any deity that might hear you. One philosopher might take your wish to be a pointless waste of whatever "mental or biological energy" it consumes. Another might think that your craving *might* be useful, but only to the extent that it gets you to holler, since that might induce someone to get you an orange. A third, more religious fellow might take the petitionary prayer to be helpful in the way that petitioning a king or other sovereign can "bear fruit," based on the theory that there is (or at least could be) a benevolent deity that might hear your prayer and arrange the world in some way that allows for your wish to be granted. A fourth analyst may take a similar tack, but try to "science it up" a bit after the manner of Spinoza. She could say, "I have heard of biological studies according to which, if a large number of some type of cells in one's body are short of vitamin C, this deficit can somehow result in a craving for a lemon or an orange. We may not know how or why, but various cells in our bodies 'desire' something (in the only meager, primitive way that cells can), and *voila!* we reach into our fridge for an orange and our wish is 'granted.'" This "new age" thinker might say that if that can happen strictly through scientific (if mysterious) means on the biological level, perhaps individual persons may be considered like cells in some larger, discontinuous organism composed of people. "In this way," she ecstatically concludes, "if enough people need or want something badly enough, the world may—without any external overlord, mind you!—arrange itself in a manner that causes this wish to be granted."

This new age pantheistic theory may reflect as needy a psychology as the more traditionally religious one, and some skeptics would say that the sentiment in question—whatever theory is relied on—was nicely explained by Freud in *The Future of an Illusion* and *Moses and Monotheism*. What matters for our purposes is that a proper understanding of democratic theory may allow us to understand voting as a matter of effectively combining wants while eschewing both the magic (religious or "scientific") and the need for an all-powerful father-sovereign. In a democracy, a plebiscite is intended to aggregate the perspectives of the voters. It does so publicly[2] and in such a setting that its results demand action (at least to the extent possible). Where there is self-governance, the people's power is not limited either to writing supplicatory letters to their king or to wishing upon a star. And while the piling up of additional beliefs may be thought by some to increase warrant, the piling up of individual desires increases aggregate force.

Precisely what is wanted by a group may not be known before a vote is taken and is partly a function of the type of election that will occur. But those facts should not suggest that voting is epistemic (i.e., essentially connected with knowledge or warrant). For some item X to be epistemic, it is not enough that (i) Xs can only be produced by sentient entities and (ii) when counted, Xs provide information about the entities that produced them. (i) and

(ii) both seem true of wants, but that does not make wanting epistemic. Even the existence of some arguably cognitive element is not enough. We may, for example, gain useful information about a group by aggregating its annual hamburger consumption or the number of umbrellas it has thrown away, but neither of those aggregates, which both satisfy (i) and (ii) (and arguably themselves require the existence of cognitive activity at some time or other) can correctly be called epistemic items. These distinctions matter when we attempt to figure out how votes should be aggregated.[3]

In a recent work, Christian List (2014) has distinguished three sorts of collective attitudes toward any proposition that can be found among groups of individuals: he calls them "aggregate," "common," and "corporate." While both common and corporate attitudes seem to require unanimity among the members (and corporate attitudes need the group to itself be a sort of intentional entity, like Star Trek's Borg), voting, unlike some sorts of deliberative procedures, produces an *aggregate attitude* toward some proposition. Such attitudes, according to List's illuminating description, are *supervenient* on (entirely determined by) the individual attitudes of the group members toward that proposition. He explains (2014, 1607) that,

> It should be clear that the supervenience relation holds only relative to a given aggregation rule. Once we have settled on the majority rule, for example, the aggregate attitude on p straightforwardly supervenes on individual attitudes on p. By contrast, it would be a mistake to think that there is a fact about what a group's aggregate attitude on p is, independently of the aggregation rule. The political scientist William Riker famously emphasized this dependence of aggregate attitudes on the aggregation rule when he argued that there is no such thing as the "will of the people," independently of the voting procedure used to generate it.

This is an important point, but one must also remember that the "will of the people" should not be thought to mean whatever any political theorist wants it to mean. Some sorts of aggregation rules accord much more closely with our pre-analytic understanding of the phrase than others do. That is, we may correctly say of certain rules that they do a poor job of capturing the will of the people instead of saying that there is no such thing as a relevant aggregate attitude in some instances simply because different aggregation rules can be concocted. A principal ingredient of political theorizing seems to me to be precisely to find good aggregation rules. In other words, not every conceivable voting procedure can plausibly be said to generate something that ought to be called "the will of the people."

But we must not think that that some particular rule is more *just*, whether or not we think we can know what that is by intuition or careful cogitation. Our CHOICE rule makes no pretension to the delineation of results that are consistent with any conception of justice: the latter presumably involves certain kinds of ethical propositions, and CHOICE is no more than a standard for *prudential* values—indicating, for example, whether action X is likely to make life better for some person or group than action Y is. It does not claim that X is more ethically appropriate than Y, so it cannot take a position on whether it will tend to produce a more *just* result than Y would. It may well be that good aggregative procedures will sometimes produce unjust results (assuming there *are* principles of justice). But assessments of those alleged characteristics should not be considered relevant to the quality of aggregation rules as that matter is to be understood here. I may hate the results of some perfect election or consider some meticulously elected representative cruel or incompetent. That's democracy.

While aggregative collections all share the supervenience characteristic indicated earlier, List (2014, 1606) points out that their aggregation may have either of two importantly different goals:

> The purpose could be descriptive: to give a maximally accurate or representative description of individual attitudes, as in an opinion poll or election. Or it could be revelatory: to extract as much information as possible from individual attitudes, as in a prediction market or in a scientific community, where we seek to "harvest" the wisdom of the crowd.

As will become clear, we shall want to utilize two quite different sorts of aggregative rules to suit two, perhaps analogous, purposes. One is to be used to discover who (or what) would be the best choice to satisfy a large number of individuals with conflicting interests. The other is intended to help determine what candidates would best represent various subsidiary groups of individuals where the members of each of those groups are in general agreement with each other on the matters they consider most important. The first (A-type) is a tool intended for district-wide elections; the second (B-type) is a method for achieving minority or proportional representation for various groups in a diverse populace.

WHAT IS MAJORITY RULE?

The metaphor of conglomeration of individual conative entities or cells (Spinoza compared an idea to a "worm in the blood") used by our imagined new age spiritualist may remind some of John Locke's corporeal argument for majority rule in his *Second Treatise*:

> When any number of men have so consented to make one community or government, they are thereby presently incorporated, and make one body

politic, wherein the majority have a right to act and conclude the rest. For, when any number of men have, by the consent of every individual, made a community, they have thereby made that community one body, with a power to act as one body, which is only by the will and determination of the majority. For that which acts any community, being only the consent of the individuals of it, and it being one body, must move one way, it is necessary the body should move that way whither the greater force carries it, which is the consent of the majority, or else it is impossible it should act or continue one body, one community, which the consent of every individual that united into it agreed that it should; and so everyone is bound by that consent to be concluded by the majority. (Locke 1680, Ch. VIII, 95–96)

It is important to note several things here, however. First, there is nothing about *consent* in the cell story. It is intended only to suggest the existence of what might be called "combinatory levels" of conation. There is no requirement for the parts to have "consented" before the combination can take place. Transferring the cell picture to societal groups thus requires nothing like a "social contract," either historical or hypothetical. Second, the power angle that is so important to Locke in this passage doesn't really make sense in the context of the corporeal combinations hypothesized in the "lives of cells" story, where a sufficient conglomeration of wants might be enough to produce the fetching of the orange, regardless of the indifference or even antagonism of others in the group. Third, while the new age conception of "scientific prayer" may seem to explain the "right" of the corporate entity's actions, it fails to give much reason for any of the dissatisfied members to go along with the result. It may be that the dissenting portion is too weak to prevent it, but that is not enough to underwrite their *support*—or even acquiescence. Indeed, Locke seems simply to have described a corporeal variant of "might makes right." Finally, while Locke may have wanted to use his metaphor to support an uncomplicated summing of consenting individuals, it seems obvious that the body will move in the direction that the *stronger* or more "interested" parts carry it—even if there are fewer of them. Equality of desires is no part of the construction of this metaphor, and it cannot emerge from it: equal votes is something that must be stipulated to. While the Lockean/Spinozistic versions of corporeal mythology may not countenance it, my own view clearly involves an endorsement of what has been sniffed at as "head counting."[4]

Let us pause for a moment to consider the third point here, the "might makes right" issue. It is important, since the question of why we should obey majorities is often seen as the core question of democratic theory. Consent/contract theories have long been a popular answer. And, of course, landing upon such a theory would seem to shed considerable light on the boundary problems discussed in previous chapters: from the answer to *why* there should be obedience, we may be able to glean *who* it is that must obey. But consent has its shortcomings as a basis for democratic authority.

A. D. Lindsay (1929, 62–63) nicely summarized his own doubt that consent could be the key here as follows:

> [G]overnment and the organized force of government in the support of law are possible because most people give government their loyal and unforced support and because most people mostly wish to obey the law. But the acts of government and laws have to apply to everybody all the time. Most people usually wish to obey the law. Everybody has to obey it always. An organized force is at the disposal of government behind the law because most people usually want to obey the law. It is necessary to fill up the margin between most people and everybody, between usually and always. . . . If most people did not have confidence in government, there would be no government. . . . All this is a long way of saying that no government, however democratic, can be founded on consent, in the sense of particularized consent.

As we look for "fair" democratic procedures, let us keep in mind that what they need to do is "fill up the margin between most people and everybody." They must be rules which are such that, when we don't get what we want, we may still feel as though we have had our fair say, that we really couldn't have done better otherwise. Perhaps, if we wanted no change in the status quo and the result of an election calls for a change, we may feel that, if we were on our own, we might be better off. But if the election "incorporates" our own view in a way that seems fair to us, we might not have any reason to think either that we are not an integral part of this group or that the group is not doing precisely what its members (including us) want.

As general wills are only confusingly called "epistemic," our electoral procedures should not be expected to comport with Condorcet's Jury Theorem, wherein widespread agreement on some matter is thought to take us toward its increased probability of being "correct." In our view, a polled majority does not suggest any outcome that may be claimed to be most likely to be true, to have the highest utility, or even to have the highest probability of obtaining the highest utility. We learn from the vote only what will be a "success" according to an ex ante take on the matter, but that is the best that *any* procedure could provide. In looking for good voting rules, then, our goal must be limited to finding mechanisms that will tell us what—or who—the people want. There is no call for it to help us get to what is *right* or *true* or *good* or *probably correct* or *utility-maximizing*, or *just*. And as we have seen, good aggregations should never have been expected to reflect majority *favorites* in the first place.

Well, what sort of aggregation procedure(s) do mesh well with CHOICE's concepts of success and net prudential value? Let me now try to offer a precise answer to that question. In his seminal work on social choice, Kenneth Arrow (1951) pointed out that coherent preference orderings must, inter alia, be both transitive and complete.[5] These requirements have been echoed by a number of other social choice theorists.[6] Condorcet had long before shown how the aggregation of perfectly transitive individual rankings could not be trusted to produce unambiguous social rankings. But with his Impossibility Theorem, Arrow demonstrated that this was no accidental result, but an unavoidable feature of the construction of any social choice function that he believed was worthy of a claim to rationality. Of course, Arrow has had his critics among political theorists too. Some of these commentators[7] have maintained that one can make too much of majority cycles and that Arrow's worries about them are overblown. But what if we step back farther and consider instead whether the entire program has been misguided from the start? Let us begin with transitivity. Whatever one thinks about the likelihood of voting cycles or their dangers for democracy, it has become increasingly clear that even individual rankings (not only those made by rats but also those made by college students) often fail to be transitive.[8] Grether and Plott (1979, 623) have summed up the situation with respect to transitivity as follows:

> A body of data and theory has been developing within psychology which should be of interest to economists. Taken at face value the data are simply inconsistent with preference theory. . . . The inconsistency . . . suggests that no optimization principles of any sort lie behind even the simplest of human choices and that the uniformities in human choice behavior which lie behind market behavior may result from principles which are of a completely different sort from those generally accepted.

One line of response by preferentists (e.g., Hausman 2011, 36–47) to problematic rankings on either the personal or social levels has been simply to define their terms in such a manner that nothing can be a preference unless it satisfies the transitivity and completeness axioms.[9] The idea is that for preferences to be useful in studies of price optimization or voting, they must be rational, so it is best to label any (now merely ostensible) "preferences" that do not satisfy all required axioms, irrational and simply ignore them. Obviously, social scientists are free to use terms as they please. I would caution, however, that the results of such restriction are likely to be that at prices and votes so calculated, products won't *quite* clear markets and election results wouldn't necessarily reflect what people actually want. It seems, then, that—whether because of Arrovian problems stemming from aggregation or from the psychological eccentricities of individual human beings—economists and voting theorists may no more safely depend on individual preference rankings to obtain social desiderata than they have ever been able to rely on interpersonal utility comparisons.[10]

Fortunately, unlike Buridan's ass, both people and groups can and do make unambiguous choices between items considered to be roughly equivalent, even if the choosers are not always sure why they've picked one rather than another from among the alternatives open to them. According to CHOICE, only such "revealed successes"—publicly expressed, uncoerced choices from among actually available alternatives—may be safely aggregated in the search for non-paternalistic indicia of what social groups "want."

Social choice functions that utilize only unambiguous choices between two alternatives have been claimed to be immune to preference problems as well as majority cycles as far back as the early 1950s. In fact, both Arrow and Kenneth May included such requirements in their checklists of necessary and sufficient conditions that can be used to help observers determine whether any proposed voting system will dependably capture "the will of the people." May (1952, 682) claimed that we can trust a "simple majority decision" to render a group decision regarding two alternatives to be faithful to the preferences of the individuals in the group, because such decision methodology may be constructed in a way that guarantees "decisive, egalitarian, neutral, and positively responsive" outcomes. Such a voting method will be fair and accurate because it treats each voter and each alternative impartially, produces an unambiguous winner, and never produces results that change in a direction differing from the direction of changes in individual preferences (i.e., it exemplifies "monotonicity"). And according to May's Theorem, only two-alternative plebiscites that select as winners those receiving the majority of votes[11] meet these criteria in every conceivable case.

It might seem, then, that the concerns of Condorcet, Arrow, and their followers ought to have been allayed since the publication of May's Theorem. That has not been the case. There have been two main lines of objection to limiting the democratic influence of citizens to simple majority voting over two alternatives. First, it is claimed that the restriction of information collected by such balloting to which of two candidates (or ballot questions) has amassed the most votes has provided an insufficient sense of what voters want. At least as far back as the eighteenth century, it has been noted that in the sort of procedures that are eligible for May's imprimatur, "voters cannot give a sufficiently complete account of their opinions of the candidates" (Borda 1784). More recently, Goodin and List (2006, 941), citing Dummett (1997), point out that "collecting only a single vote from each voter is not ideal [since] the number of voters who think each candidate the worst is no less important than the number of voters who think each candidate the best. A balloting procedure that collects only voters' revealed 'top picks' takes no account of that." Second, there is a danger that the method for reducing the number of alternatives to two will be inappropriate. Riker (1982, 60) has warned,

> [T]here is no fair way to ensure that there will be exactly two alternatives. Usually, the political world offers many options, which, for simple majority decision, must be reduced to two. But usually also the way the reduction occurs determines which two will be decided between. There are many methods to reduce the many to two; but . . . none of these methods is particularly fair. . . . [A]ll methods can be rigged.

For these reasons and others, it has seemed to many observers that a robust democracy requires more than can be delivered by conformance with May's Theorem.

Riker himself was content with low-information elections. Rather than take problems with simple majority voting to be evidence that a more information-rich methodology ought to be found, he concluded that such problems actually demonstrate that desires for a particular sort of democracy ought to be abandoned. His solution was to distinguish between two basic types of democratic rule. There is *populism*, according to which "what the people, as a corporate entity, want ought to be social policy" (1982, 238). And there is *liberalism*, according to which "voting [solely] permits the rejection of candidates or officials who have offended so many voters that they cannot win an election" (1982, 242). In his view, if it really is the case (as he believed) that there can be no versions of populism that are both coherent and fair, we ought to make do with liberalism—a Madisonian position according to which the ability to "throw the bums out" is all anyone really ought to desire.[12]

Fortunately, for those who actually *like* the idea of self-government there are alternatives to Riker's proposals. As I have suggested, one way out of this conundrum is to acknowledge that no fewer than two sorts of voting procedures are needed. And we might also suggest that it has been insistence on no more than one mechanism that has produced pseudo-democratic systems that are either impossibly thin or non-majoritarian. Michael Dummett (1997, 2) made much the same point when he explained that two different sorts of things are decided pursuant to a British election. First,

> who is to represent each individual constituency in Parliament; and what the overall composition of Parliament by political party is to be. . . . [T]he composition of Parliament decides which party shall form the Government. . . . [H]owever, it is also important whether those elected for the constituencies truly represent the constituencies that elected them. . . . [T]hey speak in Parliament as the elected representatives of their constituencies. . . . They must represent the interests of the locality that returned them to Parliament.

It is my view that any good representative government must capture both of these aspects. Each of the two procedures must, of course, be egalitarian in two ways. First, they must, to use the old Benthamite language, "count each vote as one and none as more than one." That is, they cannot countenance weightings of most kinds[13] based either upon ordinal rankings of voter preferences or on any third-party assessments of the alleged differing value of this or that vote or voter. Second, they must require that the governmental authority granted to electoral winners accurately reflects the ratio between the number of eligible voters and the number of votes received by that winner. (I shall return to this second requirement in the next chapter.) So, let us now look for good electoral procedures. The remainder of this chapter will be devoted to the "A-type" (overall or majoritarian) element, leaving the minority representation provisions to be taken up in chapter 8.

APPROVAL VOTING

Suppose eight people (A, B, C, D, E, F, G, and H) are having a party and are trying to decide what soda to bring. (For simplicity, I here require a single winner by adding the assumption that, for whatever reason—maybe it would be a major hassle or much more expensive for there to be more than one choice of beverage at the party—only one sort of soda may be bought.) Now, let there be four possible choices: cola, lemon-lime (L-L), orange, and root beer (RB). There is no unanimity among the planners and, being the good (small-d) democrats they are, they think that the majority ought to have its way and plan a vote to decide the matter. One of the eight is made secretary and, as we shall see, keeps careful track of the votes cast. Figure 7.1

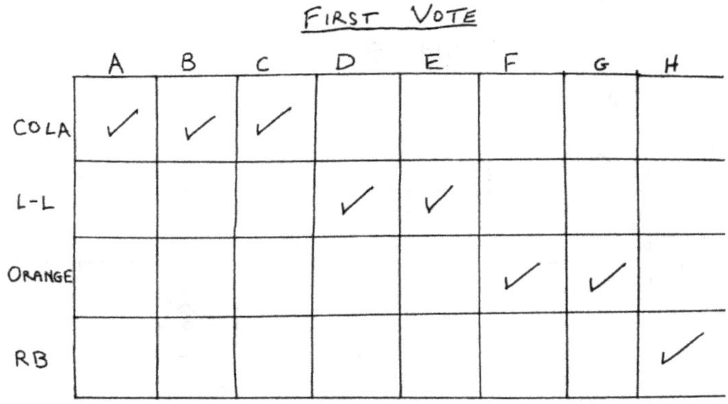

Figure 7.1 First Electoral Tally.

is the result when they are asked to give their favorite soda of the four (here designated with check marks).

While cola receives a plurality of the vote, no flavor gets a majority. One member of the group therefore suggests a run-off election among the first and tied-for-second contenders only, leaving off RB all together since it did so poorly. Figure 7.2 shows the results of this run-off election with "A" indicating an abstention.

Obviously, this second vote does not help. There has been no movement at all because voter H absolutely loathes all the flavors except RB and refuses to pick any of them as even passable choices for the party. The revelers aren't completely stuck though, because there are other possible voting schemes. I will suppose that they are skeptical of ranked choice voting (RCV),[14] not because they have heard criticisms of it involving vote splitting, non-monotonicity, or insincerity,[15] but because they worry that it may not get partygoers what they actually want. They take this to be a possibility because someone might prefer one flavor to another even if she really dislikes both of them. So, perhaps unlike other democracy investigators, our group's dismissal of ordinal methods does not involve concerns that the unavailability of intersubjective measuring sticks might allow for a huge divide between one person's first and second choices and hardly any at all between another person's two top picks. Instead, they just doubt whether a collection of preference orderings can ensure that they will meet their goal of landing on a beverage that the partygoers actually want to drink, something that will be a "successful choice" for the participants generally. This concern can be taken to be a recognition that a sort of cardinality is required here, something that, at the very least, allows the assignment of a "yes" or a "no" to each flavor, where a "yes" means "this is better than nothing" and a "no" means "this is useless or worse." Such assessments can correctly be said to mean the same thing to everyone. These reliably correlate interpersonally in a way that ordinal preferences do not.

RUN-OFF VOTE

	A	B	C	D	E	F	G	H
COLA	✓	✓	✓					(A)
L-L				✓	✓			(A)
ORANGE						✓	✓	(A)

(A)=ABSTAIN

Figure 7.2   Run-off Results.

Two members of the group have suggestions. One has been swayed by literature she has received from a group advocating AV,[16] and the other is a sports and cinema fan and understands that rankings of teams and movies usually use some form of Score Voting (SV), where each voter gets to assign a number of points (or stars) to each candidate, and the points are summed to find a winner or produce a ranking. This two-member subcommittee decides to allow points to be assigned, but only if the system excludes everything that seems to them impossible to compare. That is, they agree to keep out any allotments of point differentials that might suggest "a little better than" to one voter but mean "much, much better than" to another. In their search for additional trustworthy information, they come up with the following (arguably cardinal) scale:

BOTH ENJOYABLE AND THE BEST OF THOSE LISTED   [4 PTS]
GOOD ENOUGH (WOULD DRINK IT IF AVAILABLE)   [3 PTS]
PASSABLE (NEVER HAD IT BUT WOULD TRY IT IN A
    PINCH)   [2 PTS]
NOT OK (NEVER HAD IT AND WON'T TRY EVEN
    IF THIRSTY)   [1 PT]
REALLY DISLIKE IT   [0 PTS]

The AV supporter insists on an additional condition. She agrees with the use of this scale only if the assignments of 4, 3, or 2 points are also counted as "approvals," and assignments of 1 or 0 are considered disapprovals. This is settled upon as well, and the third vote is duly taken. The secretary represents the approvals here with a check mark, and circles the two sums representing the highest number of points and the most approvals (see figure 7.3).

The results are disturbing. While the plurality victor was cola, the SV winner is orange and the AV winner is L-L!

Perhaps it will seem that this embarrassment of winners is the result of the weirdness of there being so many "never tried it" votes with respect to what seem like common carbonated drinks. But it is important to realize that an attitude of "I really don't know much about her (or it)" toward a political candidate or proposal is not unusual at all. Look at the secretary's registers again, but this time, think of them as the results of a political election for a representative, each of whom is put up by a different party. (Perhaps replace "cola" with "corporatist"; "L-L" with "liberal"; "orange" with "outsider," and "RB" with "republican.") We can also think of the individual partygoers above as voting blocs. This may make it clearer that there can be a large number of decisions in which the assignment of the sort of SV points allowed by our partygoers would largely be a function of the varying amounts of risk that voters are willing to take. Some people will be OK with this or that

SCORE/APPROVAL VOTE

	A	B	C	D	E	F	G	H	TOT.	APPS.
COLA	4✓	4✓	4✓	2✓	2✓	1	0	0	17	5
L-L	2✓	2✓	2✓	4✓	4✓	2✓	2✓	0	18	⑦
ORANGE	3✓	2✓	0	3✓	3✓	4✓	4✓	0	⑲	6
RB	3✓	0	0	0	1	3✓	2✓	4✓	13	4

✓ = APPROVAL

Figure 7.3   SV/AV Tally.

relatively unknown candidate or proposal; others will not be willing to take their chances.

Brams and Fishburn (2007), perhaps the most complete and ardent work written in support of AV, do not say very much about what "approval" means. They merely note in passing that it is "voting for" something/someone or "finding it acceptable." It is important to recognize that in some cases we may find none of the candidates "acceptable" even though one or two seem to us a bit better than the others. In such cases, do we "approve" of any of them or not? Should we understand approval to mean *Is OK with? Thinks is pretty good? Supports? Hopes will win?* Something else? Couldn't each of these understandings of "approve" produce different results in an election?[17] This is a matter, discussed in previous chapters with reference to CHOICE, that I believe to be central to the question of what matters when one votes. And it is my view that the soda story is quite helpful here. We have taken the first three on this list to be approvals:

BOTH ENJOYABLE AND THE BEST OF THOSE LISTED	[4 PTS]
GOOD ENOUGH (WOULD DRINK IT IF AVAILABLE)	[3 PTS]
PASSABLE (NEVER HAD IT BUT WOULD TRY IT IN A PINCH)	[2 PTS]
NOT OK (NEVER HAD IT AND WON'T TRY EVEN IF THIRSTY)	[1 PT]
REALLY DISLIKE IT	[0 PTS]

This is because, ex ante, we do not think our lives will be better off if anything satisfying either of the bottom two lines is picked. We might say that those two bottom lines seem to us to be *Equal to Or Worse than Getting Nothing at All.* In this view, those only are the unsuccessful choices, and all others may be called successful—even though we may not particularly look forward to the obtaining of those we deem only "PASSABLE" and would admit that we may discover that we hate them. That is how affirmative votes (or *approvals*) should be understood throughout this book. It is a conception tightly connected with the concept of *success.* Notably, it does not involve favorites or preferential orderings, and so, perhaps, could not be used to construct an indifference curve. A choice should be deemed "successful" at time t if and only if its result is expected by the chooser to provide something that, at t, seems like it would be better than nothing at all. Of course, this is consistent with the unpleasant fact that when we make poor choices, our lives may get worse in spite of that "success."

So, who (or what) should the authentic majoritarian take to be the winner in this election? The corporatist (or cola), because he (it) is the favorite of the largest number of voters? The outsider (orange), who/which got the highest score? Or the liberal (L-L), who/which most voters found to be at least minimally palatable? In my view the third answer is the best: it is the number of approving voters that the best democratic practice should take to matter most. Why? Just as we ought not to be stuck at parties with nothing we can stand to drink, we ought not to be stuck with ruler/representative A when more people among us can stomach candidate B. This is the position that I believe produces the nearest thing to a consensus victor and, is thus more likely to knock out the sort of outliers who are most discordant with anything that might be considered a general will. So, it is my view that if it is to be used to determine what the people do or do not want, aggregation should be taken to be the counting of approvals, where each person's approval is given the same weight as everyone else's, regardless of how enthusiastic or tepid it is.

Surely this tack will be more conducive to stable regimes than ones according to which candidates whom a majority of the populace absolutely do not want may get to take office. Obviously, I cannot insist that nobody could mean anything else by "consensus" or that "egalitarian democracy" simply must require AV. But I believe that mine is at least a reasonable approach that not only does well against known competitors but captures much of the commonsense understanding of "consensus."

AV has some obviously desirable characteristics besides being uniquely competent to reflect the principles that motivate CHOICE. First, while it can countenance more than two candidates in a single-winner election, it is not susceptible to transitivity cycles, since it allows us only the choices of approval and non-approval. Thus, in a situation with seven candidates, whether we approve one, three, or six of them, there is never a danger of intransitivity. Second, it is consensus-building/revealing by its very nature.

Indeed, in legislatures and committees, substituting simultaneous approval votes on alterations of proposals (placed beside both the original proposal and "no bill at all") for the current practice of successive votes on amendments would vastly democratize procedures by eliminating the absurdly inappropriate power now held by agenda-setting moderators (Riker and Weingast 1988). Finally, it is easy to understand.[18]

Criticisms of AV[19] have focused on a claimed likelihood of producing unsatisfactory results if voters bullet their favorite candidates in violation of the system's explicit instruction that *all* approved candidates be voted for. Perhaps it would help in the effort to resist the lure of preferentism to put specific instructions on ballots indicating that what is wanted are bare approvals only: indications of which candidates are "passable."[20] Thus, perhaps:

Vote for every candidate you think would be minimally OK; that is, you would give a grade of PASS to them if they were considered strictly on a PASS/FAIL basis.

Insisting that such instructions will always be resisted in favor of doing whatever one can to elect one's favorite[21] is an empirical assertion of psychology, and those making it should understand that if they are right, the irrationality of social choices is inescapable, and reaching consensus will always be mere luck. This is because, as Arrow has shown, use of ordinal scales provides no possible means of coherently determining what would make a populace relatively content with governmental actions.[22] Fringe candidates that most voters find abhorrent could always be selected. In the next chapter I will suggest a way one might overcome preferentist defeatism of this sort by buttressing minority voices in government.

It is interesting to consider Lindsay's appraisal of theories according to which deliberative *consent* is a solution to the main problem of democracy in light of AV. Lindsay was a strong proponent of small group, Protestant-style deliberation as the best model for democratic practices. But he saw the limits of unanimity-building when he indicated that the margin between most and all must be filled. Why? Consider a church group of fifty people who cannot agree on whether to tear down their building and put up a new one, fix up the current one, or do nothing at all. Suppose the split is thirty-five for repair, ten for tear-down, and five for nothing whatever. They debate and debate but make no progress. What happens? Do the five ("do nothing at all") folk win if unanimity is never reached, or do we excommunicate them as "others" as Schmitt would have advised, and achieve unanimity that way? One devout Calvinist to whom I put this question, responded that, "Usually the dissenters get tired and concede or move on. Often folks just smile and ignore them like you do with a crazy old uncle."

But, of course, there are two ways to "ignore" this group of five. One is to pretend they are not there, the other is to halt the proceedings until these dissenters retire or die off, which would, in this case, be allowing the proposal with the fewest supporters to win the day. Lindsay saw the hopelessness of the "perfect accord" approach in such situations and so might have supported AV, according to which the church would have been repaired—the moderate position. The "do-nothing" group would not have gotten their way, but, assuming adequate and fair deliberation took place, they would have had their appropriate say both prior to and within the election. It would not be *might* that made the result *right*, but the group's fairly assessed and aggregated desires, since nothing else (that the vote might have missed) is "really right." As I will discuss further below, I don't believe that AV is *quite* enough to guarantee the entire filling of Lindsay's margin between *most* and *all* within large, necessarily non-deliberative groups like U.S. voters in large electoral districts, but I do think it is a crucial first step.

AV AND MAJORITARIANISM

Is AV majoritarian? It might be asserted that no AV system can properly be characterized as majoritarian because AV does not comport with what is commonly known as "the majority criterion." That is the simple requirement that if there exists a majority that ranks a single candidate higher than all others, that highest-rated (i.e., *favorite*) candidate must win. To be clear, I argue for a view that shares with simple majoritarianism the tenet that political actions and offices must be taken and distributed on the basis of the number of voters who want or don't want something (as well as on the other matter involving ratios that I'm putting off for now), giving no weight to how *much* they may want them (or which is their favorite). But the failure of AV to maintain the majority criterion may still be pressed. The candidate with most approvals always wins, but that person may not always be the "favorite candidate," at least according to some construals of that expression.

It is worth noting in this context that majoritarianism hasn't always been framed in terms involving "favorites." We saw that Hans Kelsen (1949) held that "the right track to understanding the majority principle" is to focus on its insistence that "as many people as possible shall be free, that is, as few people as possible should find their wills in opposition to the general will of the social order." His Hobbesian approach of "counting heads" on either side of an issue does not require the picking of favorites. In any case, if one insists that "majoritarianism" be defined simply by satisfaction of the "majority criterion," perhaps I can express my fellow feeling with that slant by calling my view "neo-majoritarianism." That could distinguish it from a "simple majoritarianism" that relies solely on the majority criterion.[23]

Whether or not AV should be considered a majoritarian system is not as important as whether it is competent to provide an adequate response to Schumpeter's (1942, Pt. IV) objection that combinations of inchoate thoughts, impulses, and so on ought not to be counted as "rational unities." I believe they can, so long as votes are not mischaracterized as batches of beliefs. And when supplemented by a second procedure (to be discussed in the next chapter), one that provides additional information about who various subgroups most want to represent their views, election results may correctly be taken to specify the general will of a populace.

DOES AV SOLVE "THE INTENSITY PROBLEM" OF MAJORITY RULE?

I have sung the praises of AV in this chapter, but even if one were to accept its claim to the merits set forth, there has been no mention of how it addresses "the problem of intensity"—and, as we have discussed, that has been one of the main objections to majoritarianism. I believe, however, that AV can reflect voter intensity without either relying on intersubjective comparisons or dispensing with vote equality. To see how this can be we must start by more carefully demarcating the sorts of attitudes discussed earlier in distinguishing the soda drinkers so that some may be called "intense" without that implying anything about ordinal valuations.

Let us take as a proxy for intense support for something, that the voter approves of, no other available item, and designate such support with "F+" (for "fervently supports"). While this may seem a bit different from being passionate or nearly indifferent (after all, why couldn't such a person not like any of the candidates very much?) the fact that one would "bullet" a candidate even without any "insincerity" or strictly strategic motives might indicate that they have more than mild interest in the bulleted person being elected, since all of the others are considered by that voter as being beyond the pale. Second, let us take "F−" to be a fervent disapproval of some candidate, and define that to mean that F− is present if and only if no other candidate is disapproved by the voter in question. Continuing, we may indicate mild or moderate support ("M+") by defining it as approval for some candidate that is accompanied by concurrent approval of at least one other candidate, and designate mild or moderate opposition ("M−") as non-approval of some candidate that is concurrent with non-approval of one or more other candidates.

We have so far defined fervor and moderation for individual voters, but we can do something to characterize groups as well. Let us say for any group

G, that G is M+ with respect to some candidate if and only if at least half of the members of G are M+ with respect to that candidate, and make the same sort of move for a group attitude of M−. But let us define fervor within groups more narrowly and insist that a group is F+ or F− with respect to a candidate only if *all* its members are F+ or F− (respectively) with respect to that candidate. I should not be thought to be claiming that one can take an F+ or F− position only if one has intense preferences. Similarly, one with vehement likes or dislikes may fail to utilize these methods.

Let us now look at some examples. Obviously, in a two-person race, the results of a plurality, AV (or RCV) election would be identical. After all, there is little point in voting to approve both candidates, and all systems allow for the blanking of all candidates (or nonattendance).[24] So, for example, we can imagine in the 2020 Presidential election a race between Donald Trump and Elizabeth Warren, and hypothesize further that Warren is supported by 40 percent of the populace and Trump by 38 percent. If we ignore Electoral College provisions and only consider the popular vote, the result will be the same whether we conduct the election on a plurality or AV basis: Warren wins. But things change once a third candidate, say, John Kasich (who we will here, for illustrative purposes, suppose to be ideologically exactly halfway between the other two) is added to the mix. Let us imagine the preference breakdown here to be that 40 percent of those who will vote favor Warren, 38 percent prefer Trump, and 22 percent like Kasich best. In a plurality election, Warren again wins, and intensity of support is completely irrelevant. What happens with AV? First let's suppose the supporters in all the groups are half-hearted (M+) with respect to their favored candidate as follows:

- Half of Trump's supporters also approve of Kasich, another 2 percent only approve of major party candidates and so approve of Trump and Warren only.
- A little more than a third of Kasich's supporters—8 percent of the total vote—also approve of Trump, a second segment, 7 percent, approve of Warren instead, with the remaining 7 percent approving of Kasich alone.
- Half of Warren supporters also approve of Kasich, and an additional 2 percent of them, again fearful of the consequences of having a president from an unfamiliar party, approve of Trump and Warren only.

With these facts, Kasich would win easily, with his original 22 percent + 20 percent from Warren supporters + 19 percent from Trump supporters = 61 percent of voters approving his candidacy. That would beat Trump's 48 percent and Warren's 49 percent. This very different result may seem surprising, but it is consistent with what one would expect the results to be in elections between Kasich and each of the others in a jurisdiction where a majority is required to win and run-off elections are implemented.

Let us now suppose the voters are more gung-ho in various ways. If the Trump supporters are F+ for him (i.e., approve of no one else), and the other groups continue to have the same M+ attitudes toward their favorites as above, the result would be

- Trump 38 percent + 8 percent (from Kasich's group) + 2 percent (from Warren's group) = 48 percent
- Kasich 22 percent + 20 percent (from Warren's group only) = 42 percent
- Warren 40 percent + 7 percent (from Kasich's group only) = 47 percent

In this scenario, Trump narrowly ekes out a victory over Warren in a race that, with less equanimity among democrats, could just as easily have gone to their standard-bearer.

Now suppose both the Trump and Kasich supporters fervently oppose (are F− with respect to) Warren, and the Warren supporters are F+ with respect to their favorite. In this case the results would be

- Trump 38 percent +22 percent = 60 percent
- Kasich 22 percent + 38 percent = 60 percent
- Warren 40 percent + 0 = 40 percent

Here, Trump and Kasich tie (or, more realistically, the results are too close to call).

Obviously, the possibilities are endless, so I'll just give two more. First, in a campaign flooded with negative ads by each of the two major party candidates against the other one, suppose Trump supporters are F− to Warren and would all approve of any alternative, Warren supporters are F− to Trump and would approve of Kasich to avoid him, and Kasich supporters (disgusted with the whole scene) are F+ to their hero. We get

- Trump 38 percent + 0 = 38 percent
- Kasich 22 percent +38 percent + 40 percent = 100 percent
- Warren 40 percent + 0 = 40 percent

This, obviously, is an absolute landslide for the (positive-advertising) centrist.[25]

Finally, let us imagine that the Kasich supporters aren't really enthusiastic, but just uncertain what to think about the other candidates, and again split their second-choice approvals. Let us also suppose that the Trump campaign goes negative on Warren, which results in an F− attitude toward her, but the Warren campaign does not follow suit, and simply runs puff pieces on their hero, leaving the other candidates alone; that is, they are F+ for Warren. Here, we might get something like this:

- Trump 38 percent + 8 percent = 46 percent
- Kasich 22 percent + 38 percent = 50 percent
- Warren 40 percent + 7 percent = 47 percent

A narrow win for Kasich.

Again, there are limitless other scenarios that may be imagined and many other definitions that could be used to capture fervency. The point is that, given AV, intensity of a kind *does* matter and can produce different outcomes, even with no assumptions of interpersonal qualitative measures, ordinal preference lists, or "insincere, strategic" activities involving the violation of instructions.

As indicated earlier, I do not believe that the virtues I have discussed here in connection with AV are sufficient to show that the sole use of such an electoral system can truly be said to specify what "the people want." I would not even use it, for example, to narrow a field to a handful of finalists. In short, my answer to the "Does AV solve the intensity problem?" is "Not entirely." I believe two criteria must be satisfied for an aggregation to show/determine what a group wants. It must be something that indicates the direction forward, by providing a general consensus on the matter of what is to be done: I do believe AV meets that criterion. But the result must also capture the (more particular) zeitgeist of the populace in question. And because the virtues of AV depend in part upon a loss of information (Who or what does each voter think would have been ideal? Who should the candidates be that will be considered for approval?) it cannot alone provide an ample picture of the general will. I will argue that a completely satisfactory system requires AV to be supplemented not only with an additional type of aggregation (and the appropriate combination of the two aggregative schemes) but also with guarantees that include easy ballot access, limitations on election buying, effective deliberative and bargaining requirements for the representatives chosen, and real means of enforcing implementation of political rights, including possible removal of disappointing leaders.

Some of these requirements were nicely put by Hans Kelsen (1949, 287):

> The principle of majority in a democracy is observed only if all citizens are permitted to participate in the creation of the legal order, although its contents are determined by the will of the majority. It is not democratic, because against the principle of majority, to exclude any minority from the creation of the legal order, even if the exclusion should be decided upon by a majority. . . . The

system of proportional representation is the greatest possible approximation to the ideal of self-determination within a representative democracy, and hence the most democratic electoral system.

NOTES

1. Overlapping majorities with such "revolving" preferences within a group are often called voting "cycles" and are thought by some to make the process of aggregating societal choices incoherent. See, e.g., Arrow (1951) and Riker (1982). Majority rank orderings have also been demonstrated to change as a function of the order in which choices are offered to electors.

2. In the sense of honestly and effectually. Ballots can and should be *secret*, but they are not just silent prayers sent heavenward. They must be correctly tallied and acted upon.

3. Coleman and Ferejohn (1986, 13–16) are fuzzy on this matter. They make a cogent argument that voting is epistemic in the (quite limited) sense that we cannot infer the object of any population's desires from the results of an election without first specifying the sort of aggregation procedure that will be used. And they take from this that only the "right procedure" can ensure a "correct" result. But evidence that doing X is the appropriate expression of a group's general will is not evidence that X is correct (i.e., that such group "ought to" do X), unless one accepts the premise that group actions "ought to" follow the promptings of their general wills. Coleman and Ferejohn are silent on that proposition, which I take as axiomatic.

4. See, e.g., Dworkin (2013).

5. Transitivity requires of any preference ranking that, for all alternatives x, y, and z, if x is preferred to y and y preferred to z, then x must be preferred to z. Completeness requires of any alternatives x and y and ranking relation R that either xRy or yRx or (where R includes indifference) both. That is, one must be put higher than the other or have the same rank: no other possibility is allowed.

6. Harsanyi (1985, 43), for example, has written that the preference model used by economists can explain an agent's priorities, "provided that these preferences satisfy some suitable consistency requirements (namely, transitivity and completeness)."

7. See, e.g., Tullock (1967) and Mackie (2003).

8. "Experiments have shown that when rats are sufficiently hungry they will prefer food to sex, sex to avoidance of pain, and avoidance of pain to food" (May 1954, 7). The completeness of individual rankings has also taken a beating. That a person's absence of preference between two apparently competing alternatives cannot always be interpreted as indifference between them has been demonstrated by failures of those doing the preference ordering to move toward one of these alternatives based on "small improvements" being made to it, such as giving an extra dollar to those who pick it. See Peterson (2009, 170)

9. This is sometimes called "laundering" preferences. See Reiss (2013, 216–219). This gambit may remind the reader of attempts to "idealize desires" or "render judgments coherent" discussed in previous chapters.

10. While it has been suggested by, e.g., Graaff (1957, 33–35) and Nozick (1977, 373–375), that real preferences may be revealed not only by actual choices but by the answers to questions involving subjunctive conditionals, it seems obvious that questionnaire responses may be as incoherent as preference orderings.

11. Or the plurality of them. What matters here is that there be only two alternatives.

12. Both Riker's critique of populism and his support for liberalism have been subjected to extensive criticism as well. As indicated earlier, some of his critics, like Mackie (2003), have focused on what has been decried as over-concern regarding both (i) the actual incidences of majority cycles (or other alleged incoherencies) and what might follow on them on the rare occasions when they *do* occur, and (ii) purported evils stemming from strategic voting (or other types of alleged "rigging"). Others, like Coleman and Ferejohn (1986) and Radcliff (1993), have pointed out that Riker's proposals for citizen "vetoes" of sitting officials are vulnerable to some of the same objections that Riker leveled against populism

13. As will be discussed later, weighting of votes is allowed to preserve or ensure the equality of voter treatment when, for example, districts have significantly different population sizes.

14. Under RCV, voters rank as many of the choices as they would like. If no candidates receive enough first-choice votes to win, the candidate receiving the least first-choice votes is eliminated, and the vote counters see what the second choices were of the voters who most liked this eliminated candidate. Those second preferences are then distributed as if they were first-choice votes. This process is continued until some candidate(s) have/has enough votes to win. RCV is thus a way to conduct iterative instant run-offs, dropping the bottom candidate each time. Without specifying more complete preference orderings of our party planners, it is impossible to determine which type of soda would come out on top pursuant to RCV.

15. See Brams and Fishburn (2005).

16. The voting rule for AV is quite simple: vote for all and only those candidates you minimally approve of by making a mark next to the name of such candidates. These votes/marks will be summed. The candidate getting the most votes wins.

17. I have benefited from discussions with Kevin Zollman on this matter.

18. It will likely be observed that everyone who writes about voting rules seems to have her own particular favorite. Sometimes such promotion stems from the calculation of likely outcomes given various estimates of voting strategies among the electorate. But theorists also attempt to demonstrate that their pet mechanisms provide the most accurate aggregations of individual preferences over a set of more than two options. But AV is not intended for that purpose at all: it maps (much easier to sum) approval profiles rather than preference profiles. In the next chapter we will look at another mechanism that eschews ordinality, but does so for a different purpose. Both procedures reflect my view that general wills are not ordinal rankings.

19. See, e.g., Nagel (2007).

20. Notwithstanding current television ads insisting that "Just OK is not OK," most people will agree that a grade of pass is better than having to retake a class. What is actually "Just OK" or acceptable/approvable need not be *best*, anybody's favorite, or even terribly good.

21. Caleb Huntington has speculated in conversation that this predilection might be related to the utility gain, for primitive hunters, in choosing only one antelope in the herd to focus upon and chase, even though any number of others would do just as well.

22. With respect to compiling ordinal lists, I agree with Riker and Weingast (1988, 382) that "tinkering with the mechanism" is pointless. There simply is no coherent way to sum individual rankings to determine what a group wants. In my view, to find the general will, one must scrap preferentism completely.

23. Indeed, even if one were to loosen the definition of "majoritarian," as Risse (2004) does, by requiring only that majoritarians focus on whether it is a majority or a minority that wins, one might reasonably wonder if counting approvals under AV ought to count as satisfying such a focus.

24. It is, I suppose, possible to imagine a regime that, over-anxious to determine the general will with exactitude, not only makes voting compulsory but also insists that even where there are only two candidates, every voter must indicate all and only those of whom they approve. That would, very occasionally, produce a different (presumably more moderate) winner than would have been produced by the current method. But such a scheme is quixotic as well as costly and unpleasant, since it would almost never alter the result.

25. As can be seen, by its very nature, AV encourages third-party candidacies. In this scenario, a candidate who is the favorite of only 22 percent of the electorate nevertheless wins quite easily. Those sorts of results are bound to be extremely encouraging to marginal candidates.

Chapter 8

Votes and Their Aggregation II

Minority Representation and How It
Must Be Combined with Majority Rule

As discussed in the previous chapters, some approaches to aggregative puzzles have left democracy in a feeble state, allowing some semblance of majority control, but providing no voice at all to minority viewpoints. A government should be a place for the presentation of alternative positions—and where the changing of minds is possible. In a democracy, the majority must rule, but a representative body must do more than "rule." As James Hyland has put it,

> The illusion that, in the nature of the case, political disagreement is a winner-takes-all game is created by the fact that when decisions are made via a majoritarian system the decision-making procedure itself transforms the disagreement into the limiting case of zero-sum conflict in which the most preferred option of the majority is implemented, with maximum pay-off to the majority and zero pay-off to the minority. There are normally any number of alternative possible outcomes that would distribute the pay-offs more evenly. . . . [T]here is no justification whatsoever for the claim that simple majoritarianism is the only system consistent with political equality. (Hyland 1995)

Many in the United States think that, at least on the national level, our federal structure is the best way to cure the problem that they find in the concentration of population in urban areas. How better to ensure that farmers in Iowa and miners in West Virginia will have a chance to counteract the power of city dwellers on the two coasts than give each state two senators and utilize our Electoral College? And it cannot be denied that the federal structure of the United States has done much to ensure that minorities have a voice.

But even if we ignore that this structure has often provided voices with volumes well above what their numbers justify, what the defender of geographical curbs on majority power misses is that such a solution requires that like-minded people always live near each other. If agrarians, socialists, libertarians, gun collectors, or railway aficionados are scattered evenly throughout the country, they may have insufficient numbers in any particular place to get a say in anything anywhere, even if there are quite a lot of them in the country. Why think that either nativist city haters or gun-averse socialists will always pick the same areas or states to live in? And why should they be required to live near each other in order to have a voice? Couldn't it be that the majority of libertarians don't want to live near people who think just like they do? Unfortunately, no richer method than geographical districting has received widespread support among those who believe that the theorems of Arrow and May cannot be ignored without violating some principle either of fairness or of coherence. In this chapter I will argue that the SNTV),[1] a hitherto widely derided method for producing minority representation, is uniquely competent to provide populist democracies with minority representation. It is a system, moreover, that can do its work without any danger of engendering Condorcet voting cycles. I will defend SNTV against claims that its defects have impaired numerous elections in Japan, Korea, and elsewhere, and argue that the problems that have been reported were a predictable result of a fundamental misunderstanding of the nature of representation under SNTV and a resulting mis-implementation of the procedure. I will also attempt to provide a way in which a reformed SNTV can be coherently combined with representation via AV. Even that would not be sufficient, however. To do all that democracy requires, additional political rights must be guaranteed. For example, ballot access must be nearly frictionless and available to all, geographical subdistricts must be abolished to the greatest extent possible, unequal campaign access to media must be mitigated to some extent, and deliberations of those who are elected must be appropriate and fair. Discussion of some of these will be postponed to later chapters.

I spoke in chapter 7 about objections to AV stemming from the empirical claim that voters in AV elections will be unable to suppress the impulse to bullet their favorites even when they actually approve of multiple candidates. No doubt, such acts could cause disliked candidates to win elections. I suggested beefing up instructions as a way to curtail that practice. That should help, but a more important means to overcoming any tactical impulses to violate the AV ethos may be to provide additional elections that use a voting method that is specifically intended to give voters a chance to indicate what is *most important* to them. With SNTV elections available, I think we could expect a more sincere search for rough consensus via AV.

SNTV AS B-TYPE REPRESENTATION

Once a group has decided on a representative form of government, we can expect the individual voters there to desire stand-ins that they believe will accurately represent their desires within governmental bodies—people they respect who will provide a *voice* with which they nearly always agree. It is not the job of any B-type representative to try to assess or implement what the majority wants. This is a very important difference from that which A-type representatives must do. When a constituency picks its favorite representative through SNTV, each person will have voted precisely for someone to be *her* voice in government. In such B-type elections, no voters or candidates need be concerned with the interests of anyone else, except to the extent that such concern might help get their own policies agreed to by the majority. It is not only that this sort of representation does not *require* consideration of the interests of those not in the represented group: it is inconsistent with it. Others must receive their representation by picking their own favorites, getting their own voices. Thus, if we add B-type representation into the electoral mix—we can make up for some of the information loss stemming from AV elections of single representatives. SNTV tells us what the first, second, and lower preferences are of the entire electorate.[2]

Clearly this type of representation, which cares nothing for "compromise candidates" who may be acceptable to everyone throughout a large area, will not do for presidents, governors, mayors, or other executives who are intended to be the only person with the job in question. But in B-type elections there is no need to seek candidates to whom no one will vociferously object. This is the main way in which B-type representation fundamentally differs from majoritarian (A-type) representation, which seeks the general consensus.

It may seem that the choice of a B-type representative from among more than two candidates might violate the conditions for fair, rational elections set forth by May, but that is only because the term "alternatives" is ambiguous. When, under a system like SNTV, we choose one winner from among, say, ten candidates, and there is no relevance whatever to the ranking of also-rans, there is an important sense in which it is true that there are but two "alternatives" (yes and no). That is why such a procedure satisfies all of the Arrow/May criteria. It is thus not quite right to assert that picking between two candidates is the only method that can yield a rational social choice function.[3] It should be clear, however, that for a system like SNTV not to devolve into a search for least bad compromises, the purpose of this electoral mechanism must be understood by the voters. In addition, there must be no hard-to-clear barriers to nominate candidates. If it is not easy for like-minded citizens to get their favorites on ballots, the information lost when each may make only one choice will indeed be destructive to the determination of the general will.[4]

Another important consideration regarding B-type representation is that if majority rule is to be enforced not only on the level of the voting citizenry, but also when their representatives vote on government policies, the authority afforded each official elected via a B-type balloting must reflect the total number of votes which he or she has received from electors. That is, the power of each such representative must be equal to the proportion of the total electorate that finds him or her best. Failure to weight representational authority resulting from B-type elections in this manner leaves not only a voting mechanism that is not an example of majoritarianism, it is mismatched with majority rule.[5] Once a government is composed, when we harmonize all the hitherto independent notes, we must keep in mind that the composition that ultimately emerges will be incorrectly balanced if small constituencies are given all the melody lines.

The literature regarding weighted voting of representatives—both among democracy theorists and in SCOTUS decisions—has sometimes involved formulae intended to procure a fair result for all the voters in the district.[6] As Still (1981) points out, equal shares may be carefully allotted based on overall and district-only head counts, but, for example, if district A is more populous than district B and both are winner-take-all, the voters in district B may have no real say in polity-wide activities. To illustrate this, Still considers an election for the mayor of a city with 100,000 voters (each of whom has one vote). Suppose the voters are divided into two precincts, one containing 60,000 voters and having six electoral votes, and the other containing 40,000 voters and having four electoral votes. The electoral votes are here appropriately weighted, but if all of the electoral votes for each district are awarded to the candidate carrying the district, the winner will always be the candidate favored by the larger district, and all the voters in the smaller district might as well stay home. The Banzhaf and Shapley-Shubik indices[7] were developed to prevent this sort of result, by ensuring that each vote is weighted in a manner that will provide each member of the populace an equal probability of turning the election. I do not press for probability weighting here, but, where possible, I would prohibit winner-take-all provisions in any elections (for non-executive officials) to avoid this deleterious effect. One thing that should be absolutely clear from these considerations is that the present use of the Electoral College to select U.S. presidents[8] is completely antithetical to democracy and should be eliminated.[9]

Those who are fond of the retention of the EC will undoubtedly complain that presidential candidates would visit only urban areas under such rules, ignoring more sparsely populated rural and agricultural areas entirely. But as Justice Warren has opined, in a democracy, representatives are of people, not acres or types of employment.[10] Of course, elimination of the EC would do nothing to provide minority representation: in fact, it may seem antithetical to that goal, since the ostensible point of that method of election was to prevent the majority from having all the say. The EC's defect as a provider of subgroup representation is that no system relying solely on geography, as it does, can ensure the proportionate expression of minority voices.

Returning to SNTV, it should be noted that even where the representation of interests via B-style mechanisms has been utilized, there has been precious little literature on apportioning the authority of representatives on the basis of the number of Yea votes candidates have received, rather than on the total of potential voters. In the case of SNTV, it will only be where the voting powers of elected officials are appropriately weighted, that we can be assured that the minority representation afforded will not be violative of majoritarian principles. It is, no doubt, tricky to get the proper implementation of SNTV exactly right, but the reward is great. If it is accomplished, the fairness and coherence standards required by Arrow and May can be met without the danger either of extremely limited voter information (and majority tyranny) on the one hand, or minority rule on the other. Whatever additional features may or may not be desired to ensure the fostering of naturalized democracy, SNTV provides precisely the characteristics necessary for the sort of B-type representation that must be part of any robust populism.

A CLUSTER OF CRITICISMS OF SNTV

I expect that my characterization of the virtues of SNTV will have been met by close observers of international electoral processes with raised eyebrows (at best). After all, attacks on SNTV, a system that has been used for various purposes and at various times in Japan, Hong Kong, Taiwan, South Korea, Afghanistan, Jordan, Indonesia, Puerto Rico, and Libya, have been both plentiful and loud. In fact, the system has been blamed for everything from electoral corruption to civil war (Hamid 2016). Furthermore, a number of jurisdictions where SNTV was being used subsequently discontinued it precisely because of these alleged failings. The complainants have made both empirical and theoretical indictments. Shadi Hamid (2016) has called it "one of the world's most counterproductive electoral systems" and in a survey (Bowler, Farrell, et al. 2005) of election specialists at the Political Studies Association, the American Political Science Association, and the International Political Science Association, it was ranked dead last of the nine systems that were compared on such matters as accountability of government and the representation of minorities. Surely, then, it must take extreme audacity—if not utter incomprehension—to suggest its reinstatement anywhere!

SNTV's poor performance around the world is generally said to be the result of two basic defects of the system: an unavoidable tendency to foster intraparty competition, and a fairly high likelihood of giving governmental authority to individuals whose views do not actually have the support of the majority of the citizenry. That these problems are not merely academic has been amply demonstrated in a series of studies,[11] one of which provides no fewer than ten ways—ranging from malapportionment and manipulation to party factionalism and corruption potential—in which use of SNTV is said to have been detrimental to democracy in Japan (Grofman 1999).[12] Surely it must seem, then, that the jury is out: SNTV has had more than a fair chance in Japan alone, having been given widespread use in that country's lower house between the years of 1948 and 1993, when the law authorizing its use was finally (some would say "mercifully") repealed. Before responding to these objections, I want to remind readers that I do not myself think that SNTV can be used as the sole electoral system—even on a strictly legislative level that eschews single-member districts. It is designed to give voices in government to significant minorities. But that is not all that democratic devices must do. B-type representation is insufficient to provide for appropriate self-government and can be expected to be harmful if used as the exclusive mechanism for determining representation.

VOTE DISTRIBUTION IN THE JAPANESE HOUSE OF REPRESENTATIVES ELECTION 1980

I nevertheless think that many of the criticisms of SNTV have been misplaced. We can begin by taking a moment to look at some of the real-world illustrations of under- and overrepresentation that have been laid at the doorstep of SNTV. Table 8.1 using data from A. Lijphart, Pintor, et al. (2003, 160), contains information compiled from elections for seats in the lower Japanese House in 1980 and allegedly provides stark examples both of misallocation of votes to or from various parties and of over- and under-nomination of candidates by those parties.

Tables 8.1 and 8.2 are examples taken to be proof of the dangers of split-votes, wasted votes, under-nomination by large parties, and over-nomination by small parties—all thought to flow irresistibly from the structure of

Table 8.1   A. Alleged Under-Nomination: Tokyo, Eighth District, Three Seats

Takashi Fukaya (Lib. Dem.)	76,254	elected
Kunio Hatoyama (Lib. Dem.)	70,866	elected
Mitsuhiro Kaneko (Communist)	46,208	elected
Yoshirni Nakagawa (Komeito)	45,029	
Yuji Sato (Socialist)	16,476	
Total votes	254,833	

Table 8.2   B. Alleged Unequal Vote Distribution: Niigata, Fourth District, Three Seats

Katsuhiko Shirakawa (Lib. Dem.)	67,549	elected
Osamu Takatori (Lib. Dem.)	65,434	elected
Kihei Kijima (Socialist)	57,261	elected
Toru Tsukuda (Lib. Dem.)	53,886	
Tomosaburo Sudo (Communist)	7,089	
Total votes	251,219	

SNTV.[13] However, when we take a closer look at what these results would have entailed if winning candidates had been given the weighted authority they deserved based on their vote counts, a quite different picture emerges. The results in district A are supposed to suggest that if there had been a different system in place and the Liberal Democrats (Lib. Dem.) had put up three candidates instead of two so that the roughly 147,000 Lib. Dem. votes could be split three ways approximately evenly, that party would have won all three of the seats. I note first that such a revision would have provided no minority representation at all and, in addition, relies on the assumption that voters ought to be indifferent with respect to all candidates from the same party. But, ignoring these debatable virtues of "superior" systems, it may seem that the Communist Party candidate ought not to be claimed to deserve as much as one-third of the governmental authority. After all, that candidate received about 24 percent of the votes cast for the three elected representatives and only about 18 percent of total votes cast in the district.

But consider: this misallocation of power would not have been present if the winning candidates had had their authority to act in government weighted by the percentage of the number of votes received by each candidate from eligible voters in the district. I do not know the precise percentage of those eligible to vote who actually did turn out in any of the three cases depicted in table 8.3, but if we suppose it to have been 55 percent,[14] then about 32 percent of the total possible district authority ought to have been accorded to the two winners of the Lib. Dem. Party combined, while the Communist Party winner should have received about 10 percent of the district's total influence in the

Table 8.3   C. Alleged Over-Nomination: Oita, First District, Four Seats

Isamu Murakami (Lib. Dem.)	104,522	elected
Chubun Hatano (Lib. Dem.)	86,255	elected
Eijiro Hata (Lib. Dem.)	72,093	elected
Keinosuke Kinoshita (Dem. Socialist)	70,206	elected
Tomiichi Murayama (Socialist)	69,466	
Kirnitake Hongo (Socialist)	65,081	
Koichi Hamada (Communist)	11,450	
Total votes	479,073	

lower House. While this would have been only slightly less than one-third the authority granted to the Lib. Dem. Party winners, such a result seems to me precisely fair, partly because the power of all three would have been reduced in virtue not only of the poor district-wide turnout, but also because candidates from other parties were also supported, even if not elected. It can also be seen that under such a rule it would not have been better for the Lib. Dems. to have put more candidates forward: on the contrary, doing that would quite likely have hurt them.

Turning to district B, we are told that this case, one in which the Lib. Dem. Party nearly got all three seats but lost one of them to the Socialist Party, is an example of "Unequal Vote Distribution." And, surely, the voters of the Lib. Dem. Party again seem to have been short-changed by SNTV, something that would not have occurred if the voting had been either on the at-large system or via party lists. But (again waiving the obvious objection that there is no reason to believe that every candidate put up by a party is or ought to be seen to be absolutely equivalent to every other candidate put forward by that party), I maintain that scenario B actually provides a clear example of how over-nomination can result from the failure to weight the authority of winning candidates based on total votes received. Restriction of the number of Lib. Dem. nominees would have been quite appropriate under a corrected system: it would merely be an expected artifact of divvying up authority as it should be divided, that is, by the percentage of votes received rather than by the percentage of seats won. The Lib. Dems. put up three candidates because they believed they had a legitimate chance of taking all three seats. However, if the number of representatives to be elected was not confused with the amount of governmental power to be won, that party would likely have put up only two candidates, and the authority of each of their winners would have been enhanced by the votes not wasted on Toru Tskuda, who was not among the top three vote-getters. So again, what seems like a defect of SNTV is really a product of its incorrect implementation.

A review of district C produces a similar diagnosis. There, the Socialist Party was clearly harmed by putting up two candidates rather than one. Each of those aspirants came quite close to capturing a seat in this four-member district, but each narrowly failed. One can only surmise that if it had been clear that the party's role in government would not have been impaired by having one of their members receive all or most of the votes that were actually cast for both of the socialist aspirants, they would have put up one candidate only and the socialist citizens of Oita would have received an appropriate level of representation in the Japanese House—rather than none at all.[15]

Thus, in each of the three examples, it has been a misconstrual of the nature of B-type representation, not SNTV, that has produced unfortunate results for the voters of Japan. The original confusion of what such mechanisms are intended to (and do) provide caused the mechanism to be misapplied at the outset, and its continued misapplication naturally resulted in party activities that were designed to take advantage of the system as actually, though inappropriately, used.

SNTV is easy to understand, and its results are easy to aggregate. It obviously affords minority representation, and if implemented appropriately, will capture the most important and intense voices of the people. While numerous experts have plumped for Hare, Coombs, Condorcet, or Borda (or, like Riker, have pushed for nearly nothing at all), I believe that no other system for minority representation has all the virtues of SNTV—so long as its implementation is corrected as noted earlier. Single-member and at-large systems can provide only geographically concocted minority representation (or none at all), while proportional representation systems other than SNTV generally assume measurable utilities or reliably coherent individual rankings, and may even fail to provide a non-arbitrary manner in which choices may be aggregated.[16] These other systems may also be considerably more difficult for unsophisticated electorates to comprehend. Under SNTV, if 35 percent of the citizenry believes in a certain economic theory or identifies closely with some minority cultural or racial group, and that belief or identification is what is most important to all the members of that group, they ought to have 35 percent of the governmental authority: not enough to generally win the day, perhaps, but enough to be a strong minority voice in debates and in the drafting of laws. I don't believe that any other proportional electoral scheme can provide the entire basket of advantages that SNTV offers.

To repeat, I do not claim that critics of SNTV have been mistaken, either with respect to alleged theoretical defects of the system or to the consequences of actual elections where SNTV has been in operation. Indeed, it seems to me utterly unsurprising that the system as implemented would have the flaws that have been enumerated by Grofman, Cox et al. After all, why would any party *not* reduce (or increase) the number of candidates it puts up for election if failing to do so would be likely to diminish its ability to make public policy? Wouldn't such behavior be extremely foolish? And if SNTV has also been disparaged for its contribution to inefficient governments that are far from fulfilling the clear wishes of the populace, one should ask in response how a system that is interpreted in a manner that allows not only for minority representation but also for minority *control* could be expected to do the bidding of the general will? To my knowledge, SNTV has nowhere been implemented in a fashion that recognizes that, because the mechanism involves B-type representation only, the weight of the authority distributed to winning candidates must be varied according to the ratio of the number of votes each candidate or question receives to the total population of the citizenry that is eligible to vote for those candidates.[17]

It should be obvious how elimination of this defect in allocation of power would be expected to alter the electoral strategies not only of parties, but of regional, ethnic, class, religious, and other interests. After correction, the position of no group could be harmed by one of its candidates receiving "too many votes." The practice of running fewer candidates when such a move would more likely produce winners would no doubt continue—perhaps even increase—but in no way is such a strategy "manipulative" or otherwise inappropriate. Voters simply pick their (single) favorites, and those who win seats receive authority commensurate with their vote totals. The M+1 rule, according to which exactly one more candidate than the number of seats available is likely to be put forward,[18] might well remain in play, but it is hard to see what harm that creates for democratic principles. So long as the allocation of power is always made to be a strict function of the number of votes received rather than of the number of seats held, B-type representation will be fair.

WHY B-TYPE REPRESENTATION CANNOT BE THE EXCLUSIVE VOTING MECHANISM

In spite of the highly favorable picture I have painted of SNTV earlier, however, I should repeat that B-type representation is insufficient to be the exclusive electoral system in any jurisdiction.[19] One consideration that shows that Dummett is correct on that issue is that B-type systems can result in a (possibly quite large) segment of the population having no representation at all. That is, even if we correct the application of SNTV as set forth earlier, there would remain the serious defect that those who did not vote for any of the winning candidates would have no representation whatever. This is because B-type representation cannot legitimately afford the sort of squishy "representation" that, under the current single-member system in the United States, winning legislators claim to provide to *all* who live in their districts. To give real voice to those who elect SNTV representatives, the electoral winners are bound to do as they believe those who actually voted for them would want: that is their prime directive. As those voters only are their constituency, these representatives should not be expected to consider the interests of anybody else in their deliberations, their bargaining, or their final votes—except insofar as such consideration helps them get their proposals enacted. But, of course, no genuine representative democracy can leave any of "the people" entirely without representation. Thus, A-type representation must always be part of the mix. But exactly how is this combination supposed to work?

Imagine there is to be an election for four Congresspersons in some state. Suppose that ten candidates get enough signatures to make it onto the ballot, but the leading contestants are:

L   Liberal
C   Conservative
R   Radical "Leftist"
N   Nativist "Rightwinger"
M   Moderate
S   Silly Party

It might be suggested that the top three vote-getters in the SNTV election get seats—and receive the aliquot authority as explained earlier—and that one seat be reserved for a representative for all those who didn't vote for any of the top three. So, for example, suppose the results were:

L was the favorite candidate of 20 percent of the SNTV voters
C was the favorite candidate of 15 percent of the SNTV voters
M was the favorite candidate of 10 percent of the SNTV voters

That result requires the allocation of only 45 percent of the total government authority to be divvied up by this district. How should we treat the majority— the remaining 55 percent of that total political authority? And how shall we guarantee their representation? This issue was considered by the progressives William U'Ren and Herbert Croly early in the twentieth century. Their solution[20] was to assign the seat and the appropriate authority (in this case 55%) to whichever candidate finished second in the most recent gubernatorial election in that state. Presumably, if that person were not interested in the job, his or her party would be entitled to select a substitute.

While clever, the U'Ren/Croly solution does not work. To give just one problem with it, in this imagined jurisdiction, the second-place finisher in the last gubernatorial election is quite likely to have been a member of the Liberal, Conservative, or Moderate parties, and those parties have already won congressional seats in the SNTV election just held, so giving that party the remaining 55 percent of authority in addition seems inappropriate. Another possible suggestion might be to allow the seven candidates who did not get seats to pick someone to be the 55 percent winner. But it is not clear how that determination would be made—and there is no reason why any person or party that received far fewer votes than any of the three winners— the quite congenial Silly Party candidate, for example—should end up with more governmental authority alone than the three actual SNTV winners receive in total! A third suggestion might be to have voters indicate on their ballots, in addition to noting their favorites, all the candidates they approve of. In that way we could look at the ballots of just those voters who did not get their favorite elected and use AV to find a representative for them. The problem with this suggestion is that the AV winner is quite likely to be one of the three candidates who have already won seats, and it seems inappropriate to reduce the number of total seats to three—even if we increase the authority of one of three elected members by 55 percent. Furthermore, the selected candidate would likely then cease to be a very good B-type representative of the group that liked him or her best.

I believe that what makes most sense here would be to separate the A-type and B-type candidates and elections—one via AV, the other via SNTV, but to hold the elections simultaneously. For the reasons set forth earlier, no candidate could appear on both the SNTV and AV ballots, and it would not be clear in advance whether the top vote-getter in the SNTV election or in the AV election would end up with the most power in the relevant legislature, since the AV winner would always receive an authority allotment equal to 100 minus the sum of the percentages received by the SNTV winners. When thinking about which election to run in, the prospective candidates with small but loyal followings of strong supporters would be expected to look more closely at the SNTV seats, while those with views more likely to be palatable to a (perhaps less fervent) majority would be more likely to opt for the single AV-elected seat. As indicated, no candidate could know the percentage of voting strength ultimately to be received by becoming either the AV winner or one of the SNTV winners. I would suggest, however, that the AV seat come with the perquisite of a longer term, higher salary, and more staff, since that representative will have the additional burdens of attempting to represent everyone and the added constituent service that comes with that obligation.

What *is* clear is that, for all the reasons explained in this chapter and the last, if such a bipartite system were implemented on the U.S. congressional level, there would be much less reason for anyone to complain that the structure of the voting system is inconsistent with them getting a voice in government that is entirely reflective of their wants in both quality and loudness. If correctly administered, these procedures would guarantee (to the extent that any electoral system can) not only that the will of the majority of voters would carry the day in government, but that minority voices would be heard in proportion to the size of their followings.[21] Use of SNTV as an alternative to geographical districts would ensure that true voter concerns are substituted for current inferences of like interests based on residence proximities and would eliminate all danger of gerrymanders. Indeed, there seems to be no good reason for giving geographical identification pride of place when, as Mill said, other issues (say, views regarding free trade or subsidies for the arts) might well be more important to voters than where they happen to live.[22] Furthermore, SNTV wisely avoids issues surrounding the question of which minority groups "deserve" representation, since it allows each voter to indicate precisely which identification—issue, race, gender, region, religion, class, and so on—is most important to her when she picks someone to be her voice in government.[23]

I have already discussed the significance for democracy of ensuring correct apportionment and preventing both quantitative and qualitative vote dilution. Use of SNTV could help achieve those goals, including a decreased need for district map-making. The importance of eliminating gerrymanders cannot be overstated. In the words of Polsby and Popper (1991, 305) "Gerrymandering introduces a chronic, self-perpetuating skew into the business of popular representation. . . . Those in control of the districting process can gerrymander the opposition into electoral irrelevance." Indeed, Martin Shapiro (1985, 239) has called the practice "a pathology of democracy." Many suggestions have been put forward to take districting out of the hands of politicians and, via "optimal compactness" (Polsby and Popper 1991), "simulated annealing" (Browdy 1990), or "split-line algorithms" (Smith 2005), put the matter into the care of (hopefully impartial) computer programmers. But all these solutions are themselves controversial, and to the extent that large multi-member districts can replace smaller single-member districts, such solutions are rendered unnecessary. Pressing for SNTV is in large part an advocacy for such replacements. For reasons discussed earlier, I am not confident that small districts can be done away with entirely at this time. But any reduction in them that can provide appropriate minority representation is to that extent alone beneficial.

THE APPROPRIATE NUMBER OF SEATS

I have said that SNTV can provide appropriate representation for significantly sized minority groups. But what is a significant size? Regrettably, neither SNTV nor AV is superior to other electoral systems in providing advice or direction with respect to optimal overall-seat numbers. For the answer to that, we must defer to the empirical matters of cost and deliberative efficiency. Will having too many representatives result in a "confusion of the multitude" or in more influence peddling? Condorcet reasoned that, on the one hand, "A National Assembly that was too small would be weak in moments of crisis, because, on those occasions when courage is needed, each must fear compromising himself personally." On the other hand, he warned that an assembly that was too large "could become detached from the general will, and cease to be effectively representative" (Williams 2004, 215). Madison had similar concerns:

> No political problem is less susceptible of a precise solution, than that which relates to the number most convenient for a representative legislature; nor is there any point on which the policy of the several states is more at variance. . . . Sixty or Seventy men may be more properly trusted with a given degree of power than six or seven, but it does not follow that six or seven hundred would be a proportionally better depositary. . . . [T]he number ought at most to be kept within a certain limit, in order to avoid the confusion and intemperance of a multitude. (*Federalist #55*)

Others have been more confident—or perhaps just less modest—than Madison or Condorcet. Weighing all the various constraints, Auriel and Gary-Bobo (2012) concluded (based on their "square root theory") that the United States, with its roughly 325 million inhabitants ought to have about 800 representatives.[24] I suppose another approach—though one that does not consider cost or efficiency—might be to require a confidence level X at which we want to be sure we are getting a view on some person or referendum "correct" (in the sense of appropriately reflecting the views of the voters) within some specified margin of error Y. For example, where X is set at 90 percent and Y is set at 3 percent we would need about 750 representatives for a population of 325 million. Again, one might consider the question from the angle of minority threshold: When is a group so small that it can be considered an outlier and the electoral system may ignore it? During the U.S. Prohibition era, Rice (1928) argued that, barring a good case being made to the contrary, political opinions ought to be assumed to have a normal frequency distribution. Someone might use this estimate to deem positions not garnering the support of at least .0015 of the populace (what remains outside of three standard deviations from the mean: that is, the views of 487,500 voters in an electorate of 325 million) to be outliers—too small to need representation. Such an estimate would require about 667 representatives in the U.S. House.

Waldron (1995) notes that deliberativists have generally sought to reduce, rather than increase the number of participants in decision-making bodies, and he quotes Descartes, Mill, Rousseau, Blackstone, and Bagehot on the near-impossibility of getting anything coherent out of a large, diverse group. For his part, David Altman (2014, 13) suggests that a group of twenty-one individuals is optimal for a deliberative body. The search for perfectly sized legislatures and committees is fascinating,[25] but, as should be obvious, good answers will not be derivable from either the structure of the voting systems we have settled on or from any obvious precepts of democracy. Rather, they are practical matters that should rely on empirical research regarding deliberative efficacy in reaching various goals, as well as cost considerations. I will discuss this in more detail in later chapters.

But there are some provisions about which I believe we should now feel relatively comfortable. We have said that the majority should rule and that (significant) minorities should have their say. If we are also resolved to weigh the authority of representatives, it is no hard trick to apportion power fairly among all subsidiary jurisdictions in a federal system, no matter how many representatives each such jurisdiction is allotted. That is, if we were to leave the number of U.S. House members about where it is, we could set a minimum number of seats for any state at three or four, thus guaranteeing minority voices everywhere, have a maximum number of fifteen or twenty for the most populous states, and always be sure that apportionment is fair by weighting the authority of all representatives in a manner that guarantees that characteristic.[26] As indicated earlier, all but one of the representatives from each state should be elected via SNTV with the final representative elected via AV—and perhaps given a longer term (though be subject to recall). When the votes of members need not have identical weights, we can guarantee that the votes of the people always will.

HOW OUR COMBINATION OF AV AND SNTV PROVIDES A SORT OF DEMOCRATIC LEGITIMACY

As already touched upon, the traditional problem of political authority found in democracy textbooks involves the question of why the government ought to be obeyed when we disagree with it. One reason this has been difficult to answer is that it conflates two questions:

(A) Why is this or that coercive action by government allowable? and
(B) Why should anybody who disagrees with this or that governmental edict go along with it?

As noted earlier, A. D. Lindsay made a lovely consequentialist start to an answer to (A) back in 1929 when he pointed out that while most people usually wish to obey the law, the acts of government and its laws must apply to everybody all the time. Why? If there were no coercive force behind an unpleasant obligation created by some law,

> most of us would occasionally break it and in these matters example is contagious. We, most of us, for example, pay our taxes with comparative cheerfulness and from a sense of duty; but if we knew that taxpaying were left to a citizen's sense of duty and that we had to pay higher taxes than were our share because other

citizens with less sense of duty than ourselves refused to pay . . . we should all,
to say the least of it, find our sense of duty considerably strained. (1929, 62)

Lindsay here suggests that governmental coercion is justified when we are
cheerful about complying and do so with a "sense of duty." Perhaps these
sentiments reflect the idea that when truly democratic means are utilized, a
fairly enacted law can be expected to reflect what the people want. In any
case, Lindsay says we can provide a sort of utilitarian justification for the
government's implementation when those feelings are in place. But even if
this is a satisfactory answer to (A), it does not actually imply any answer to
(B), since the latter question involves the troublesome word "should."

Douglas Rae (1975) characterized one anarchist's (Robert Paul Wolff's)
refusal to be shoved into obedience by any amount of factual information as
follows:

(1) Citizens should do as they think best.
(2) This is possible if they must obey only those laws and policies to which
     they have each given their consent.

In (1), we not only have "should" but "best." Putting an ethical spin on those
words, the anarchist may conclude from (1) and (2) that exactly *nothing*
can "fill up the margin between most people and everybody": there must
be unanimity. And the view that even complete agreement can get us to
what is "best" requires both a utilitarian conception of ethics and a Paretian
conception of how one can reach an optimal number of utiles.

But this conclusion requires a moralistic construal of "should" and "best."
Those taking a prudential view of these terms are free to say that, just as an
autonomous individual *will* do what she wants—and *should* do what produces the most prudential value—a group will and should do likewise.[27] I
hope it is clear that the anarchist's (1) plays on these ambiguities of "should"
and "best." If there are moral truths, perhaps what both people and groups
should do is precisely what they *don't want* to do, even what they *think is
worst*. Now, the anarchist may allow here that the "best" anyone can do is
follow what *seems* to them to be *best*. But what reason is there to believe
that imprecation if "best" is understood as a moral term? Why should some
individual's intuition regarding what is appropriate always take precedence
over, for example, the aggregated moral intuitions of a group consisting a
thousand individuals? The point is, if one insists on a moralistic understanding of "should" in (1), no guarantee of correctness results from an individual
following his or her own impulses. What of the claim that each of us should
do what we want on a non-moralistic understanding of "should"? If we strip
the moral aspect from "should" in (1), is it then compelling? In my own view,

the question of what both individuals and groups should (prudentially) do is answered by CHOICE. We should do what produces the most successes over the long term.

Well, given the response to (1) provided by CHOICE, what of (2)? Can it plausibly be claimed that individuals should defer to the polis as a whole when they disagree? Wouldn't that consent-eschewing move require one to concur with Rousseau that when an "opinion that is contrary to my own prevails, this proves neither more nor less than that I was mistaken"? My view here is that we can be expected to accept such a quasi-corporeal model, when and only when we agree that the procedures used by the government to make and implement laws are close to perfect. That is, we ought (prudentially) to defer to the "whole body" when (i) we believe that no alternative set of feasable procedures is demonstrably more reflective of what the people (including me) want: this means that no one has suffered from unfair discrimination and everyone has therefore gotten precisely the "say" to which "equal treatment" and appropriate aggregation entitles them; (ii) we believe that our representatives will, in accordance with their charges at all levels of government, make legitimate attempts to faithfully carry out the acts of the (deliberative) bodies representing us; and (iii) we believe that there are fair mechanisms in place for the authentically democratic reversal of policy decisions and the recall of electoral victors. This will be enough, at least for those with little interest in living as isolated hermits. The rest of us can be expected to try to find a group with rules that require the appropriate treatment of the wants of all their members. If it seems that my own government fails in this, I *should* (prudentially) try to change it or look elsewhere for a more congenial group. But if it seems that my own government is proceeding in accordance with the above-listed criteria, I have no good reason not to comply with its commands and will have the reasonable expectation that reasonable others will do so as well.[28] That I would have liked the government to do something different in some instance neither will nor should move me toward rebellion, because I have the warranted belief that no worthy democracy could have acted differently given the same general will. Again, I may try to find another more congenial group, but in the meantime, I will have no reasonable basis for not obeying. That, at any rate, is the non-consent-based answer to the age-old question regarding the basis of political legitimacy that is available to those accepting the CHOICE standard.

NOTES

1. Under SNTV, each voter is entitled to one vote only in multi-winner elections in his or her jurisdiction. That is, no second, third, or lower preferences are to be

recorded, and votes are not "transferred" from one candidate to another as they are pursuant to Ranked Choice Voting. SNTV simply requires that if in some electoral area five candidates are to take office, those five candidates receiving the most votes from among the voters' (single) choices win seats. The case of ties will be discussed later.

2. Support for B-type voting (via Hare's transferable ballot plan) was endorsed by Mill (1861, 142–143) in the following terms:

> [I]t secures a representation, in proportion to numbers, of . . . every minority in the whole nation consisting of a sufficiently large number to be . . . entitled to a representative. . . . [N]o elector would . . . be nominally represented by someone whom he had not chosen. Every member of the House would be the representative of a unanimous constituency. . . . Under this relation the tie between the elector and the representative would be of a strength and a value of which at present we have no experience. Every one of the electors would be personally identified with his representative, and the representative with his constituents. Every elector who voted for him would have done so either because he is the person, in the whole list of candidates for Parliament, who best expresses the voter's own opinions, or because he is one of those whose abilities and character the voter most respects, and whom he most willingly trusts to think for him. The member would represent persons, not the mere bricks and mortar of the town.

3. Those wanting a formal demonstration of this can find it in Goodin and List (2006).

4. It can be seen that this sort of election can be for representatives (or finalists) only: it cannot work for votes for executives, or those on initiative petitions that would apply to everyone in some area, or even for such matters as choosing one or more employees from among a larger number of job seekers. In those cases, we would indeed face concerns regarding the loss of information needed to make good compromise choices. It is also important to recognize that for resolution of ties in B-type votes among the nth and nth + 1 candidates in an n-member jurisdiction, any revotes could only involve those who had not already voted for winning candidates. Those who voted for winners should not be allowed to vote twice and, by being part of a second "constituency," get an additional representative.

5. See Croly (1914, 284–302).

6. See, e.g., Banzhaf (1967–1968), Toplak (2008), Anon (1969), and *Reynolds v. Sims*, 377 U.S. 533 (1964).

7. These are both discussed in Anon (1969).

8. SCOTUS has recently heard—remotely because of Covid-19 considerations—oral argument on two cases (*Colorado Department of State v. Baca* and *Chiafalo v. Washington*) that nicely demonstrate that failure of proportionality is not the only defect of the EC. There is the additional danger that an elector may not be required by a state to vote as the electorate there does. Even a prohibition of the acceptance of a bribe to vote in a manner contrary to the majority has been claimed to be beyond a state's power!

9. I have already made several (perhaps startlingly) specific recommendations regarding how governments exemplifying distilled populism ought to be structured and will, as we proceed, more frequently engage in this perhaps pointless activity

of suggesting overhauls of the U.S. Constitution that would make it acceptably populistic. I am well aware of the quixotic aspect of most of these recommendations, but I think it is illustrative to spell out the real-world implications of what might otherwise be seen as entirely academic philosophizing. Remedial proposals help provide a sense of the range of changes that would have to be made to achieve a truly democratic state—whether or not there is much hope of those changes ever being accomplished. Furthermore, proposals that may have little or no chance of adoption on the U.S. national level will sometimes "have legs" at the state or municipal level, or seem promising to foreign groups looking for ways to make their own governmental procedures more democratic. At least I harbor that hope.

10. Or cows. See Pecanha (2020).

11. See, e.g., Cox (1996), Reed (2003a), and Grofman (1999).

12. Cox (1996) claims that in Japan and Taiwan SNTV has had the dubious distinction of being both sub-proportional and super-proportional, i.e., it has awarded both too few and too many seats to dominant parties.

13. It is perhaps worth pointing out the obvious here, however: no electoral system has been entirely immune from such criticisms. Grofman (1999, 401) notes, "It is remarkable to what extent the complaints by reformers about SNTV, namely, that it fosters localism and parochialism, entrenches incumbents, and gives rise to very expensive campaigns and the potential for corruption, are mirrored by the complaints of reformers about STV [the single transferable ballot] and SMD [single member district] systems."

14. Japanese turnout generally runs about the same as that of the United States (Desilver 2017). Calculating weights by putting the number of eligible voters in the denominator rather than either the number of votes cast or the number of votes cast for winning candidates seems to me the method most consistent with democratic principles.

15. And it is not solely policy-making power that is at stake here. In regions where significant patronage accompanies electoral victory or where elective office is seen largely as an employment opportunity, it may be necessary to consider those benefits as part and parcel of governmental "authority." That is, more votes should also entail more of such trappings.

16. It is well known that under some systems of proportional representation, the same votes can produce different winners depending on the order in which ballots are counted.

17. If never correctly implemented, the essence of SNTV *has*, at least, been previously understood. Oregon's People's Party, through the agitation of W. S. U'Ren, got right its necessary connection to the weighting of governmental authority in the 1890s, and the issue was later picked up by Herbert Croly.

18. See Reed (2003b).

19. Interestingly, however, it may be more appropriate than AV, majority or plurality systems for determining a list of candidates to be subject to a final approval vote by the total electorate. In preliminary elections, like U.S. primaries, it is reasonable to expect voters still to be creating a list of favorites to represent them. The current party system distorts that purpose to a significant extent.

20. See Croly (1914, Ch. 14).

21. American readers may note that while voters in B-type systems will know who their representatives are, since geographical districts are not relevant, representatives will not know who their constituents are—only the "interest" they are representing. This has been seen by some to require political parties to take a more active role in constituent service or to reduce funding and staff for such services and increase it for A-type representatives. If there is concern about the effect such a change might have on citizens wanting assistance from their representative with respect to some nonlegislative governmental matter, it is important to remember that any problems of that sort arise in every PR list system as well, and there have been no reports of widespread deterioration in constituent services in such areas. Future prospective voters retain their value to future prospective candidates. A good discussion of these issues may be found in Lundberg (2007).

22. One has to be careful here, however. There may well be geographical constraints that simply cannot be ignored. Perhaps the day will come when electioneering will nowhere need to be a local matter, but it has not come yet. Grofman (1999, 381) notes that in Japan,

> [T]he Lib. Dem backbenchers who are not blessed with the opportunity to inherit an established campaign machine from a father or mentor will seek to build a reliable electoral base by enlisting the support of family, friends, and elites in the district. Most candidates seek out local politicians who can claim to "deliver" the votes of their own supportive constituencies as officers in the personal support organizations (*koenkai*).

Grofman found things much the same in Korea while SNTV was used there: political loyalty was "based mainly on personal ties such as alumni, clan, and other professional and recreational groups," and candidates were said to offer such favors as job opportunities, chances to attend ceremonial events, and even help in finding marriage partners.

23. According to Grofman (1999, 403) the use of SNTV in parts of Alabama where "same-race bloc voting is over 80 percent" ensured that blacks would always get at least one representative where they were not in the majority.

24. I note that their calculations are based on the assumption that each representative is to have one (presumably equal) vote, an assumption which is inconsistent with the B-type representation defended here.

25. A nice chart (derived from Pew) showing how much larger American congressional constituencies are than those represented by one legislator in other countries can be found in Matthews (2018).

26. We might similarly insist that a national SNTV preliminary to a final presidential election produce four or five candidates who will contest via an AV vote. The current primary system makes this impossible both by the coercive imposition of state and party affiliations as the only important considerations for all voters and by limiting parties to one general election candidate each. I note here that in a large-scale, single-vote election like that for a U.S. president or senator, there need be no worry about "a game of chicken" tainting election results. Nagel (2007) points to an 1800 decision in which the use of AV created what he calls a "Burr Dilemma." But

that series of votes among a tiny "electorate" involved "inside baseball" being played by a few men with personal interests and a lot of information about what every other voter was is likely to do.

27. No doubt, for either person or group to simply do what they want may be morally wrong if there are violable moral values, Again, I don't want to be thought to be categorically denying either that there are such obligations or that they should not be taken to prevail over "merely" prudential considerations. If morality does take precedence, both the autonomous individual and the autonomous group sometimes *should*—in the moral sense—do something other than what increases prudential value. I take no stand on those matters here. But ethics backers should be open about the fact that when there is a conflict between principles, they will be required to entirely ignore what makes people and societies better off—even over the long term.

28. As Nadia Urbinati (2010, 153) puts it, "Citizens who happen to be in the minority don't feel oppressed or excluded because even if they suspect beforehand that they will end up in the minority they know they have participated in the making of the law and the expression of the majority opinion."

Chapter 9

Political Representation I

Direct Participation, Delegation, or Controlled Trusteeship?

In chapter 7, I briefly discoursed upon the relations between wanting, praying, and voting. A suggestion was made there that contemporary democrats might be thought of as substituting voting for the sort of petitionary prayer one makes to a lord or sovereign. Having one's "prayer" be a part of the motive force of a demos seems less diffident, more *stout*, than any form of abject begging. For if a democracy is structured correctly, we can *know* that our "prayer" will have effect, that it will do its work.[1] But what, precisely, is the nature of the item that one "produces" when one votes? And in what does this activity of voting consist?

WILL OR JUDGMENT?

In her illuminating discussion of the history of these questions, Nadia Urbinati (2010) spends considerable time on the distinction between will and judgment. The importance of this matter to democratic theory may not be obvious at first, but Urbinati's careful analysis shows that views on that matter have had a major impact on discussions regarding the nature and limits of sovereignty and representation. If, as Rousseau believed, sovereign edicts should be considered acts of will, then it is what the sovereign *wants*, not anything that anybody *believes*, that is the law. And Rousseau gleans from that stance that the expertise of representatives must never elevate representation to sovereignty. The supposed superior wisdom of elected parliaments, even with the greater opportunities for deliberation and bargaining with which their members are provided, can hone judgments only: any alteration of the people's *will*, whether or not based on parliamentary wisdom or experience, would be an illegitimate usurpation of sovereign authority. So, from a view about the nature of wants,

155

Rousseau infers that if we must have representatives, they should be seen as no more than discretionless delegates who may not exercise independent judgment. For even the smallest alterations in the instructions given by the populace would involve a change in the general will in addition to a refinement in the people's judgment. Nadia Urbinati puts the Rousseauian position this way:

> Delegates are administrators, judges, experts, and wise leaders, but not political actors in the lawmaking sense Rousseau attributed to political action. This means that they cannot claim a share in decisions unless they simultaneously change their status and usurp the sovereign. A servant who decides in his master's place ceases to be a servant and becomes master of his own activity. (2010, 81)

Rousseau seems to me to have been somewhat less careful regarding the extent to which the (legitimately) sovereign pronouncements of the people are themselves entirely free of all judgment. For *Let there be war!*, *Taxes shall now be levied!*, and *Jones shall lead the deputation to Japan!* all seem infected with propositional content, whoever may issue them. As suggested in the discussion of voluntarism earlier, valuations may be predominantly *conative* and *affective*, but they are never purely so, because wants include what is wanted in some fashion.[2] We should therefore not think there can be no propositional content—no *judgment*—involved in the expression of a public preference just because *hate* and *love* are involved in sentiments like *We hate France* and *I love having Jones as a deputy*. And although affective attitudes need not be rational or well informed, it is generally sensible to combine valuations with factual information where that information is relevant and such combination is feasible. We have been warned by Rousseau that such combination may involve alteration, but before we can have a good sense of whether any modification of the judgmental aspect of a decree constitutes a usurpation, we need to know the nature of the decree. For example, if the populace proclaims, *Taxes shall be assessed at a rate that is high enough to educate all the children but low enough not to hurt the economy*, ministers would seem to have leeway to decide on a specific rate—something which may be seen as an alteration of the original judgment—without suspicion of usurpation. And if the people should say, *We want to be led by Jones in all matters*, there would seem to be an inappropriate arrogation of authority only at the point at which Jones tries to prevent his removal or at which "all matters" is construed in some way that is violative of democratic principles (say by including the right to call off future elections or prohibit voting by members of some class).

Concerns about the actions of ostensible representatives that seem to violate the "representation relationship" have only increased since Rousseau's time. Over 100 years ago, Herbert Croly warned that

A clear-sighted, self-confident and loyal democracy will keep in its own hands the active control of all the agents and instruments of its own fulfilment. The instinctive repugnance which the American democracy has always exhibited to the delegation of too much power to any one of the separate departments of government is explicable and justifiable. No plebiscite can bestow authenticity upon an ostensibly democratic political system which approximates in practice to the exercise of executive omnipotence. No intermittent appeals to the people for their approbation can wholly democratize a system which approximates in practice to the exercise of legislative omnipotence. (1914, 279)

And Hanna Pitkin has despaired that

Despite repeated efforts to democratize the representative system, the predominant result has been that representation has supplanted democracy instead of serving it. Our governors have become a self-perpetuating elite that rules—or rather, administers—passive or privatized masses of people. The representatives act not as agents of the people but simply instead of them. (2004, 339)

There is not always a bright line available between what we want and what our elected officials must not fail to do, of course. One way of dismissing all concerns about this fuzziness leading to usurpation would be simply to eliminate representative government entirely and make all governance direct. Since experimentation with direct democracy in ancient Athens, literature on the feasibility of government *by the people only* has grown quite large, and I will not rehearse those issues in detail here.[3] Instead, I want to leave for a moment the question of whether representation is sensible and simply insist that, up to the point of clear usurpation it is at least *allowable*.

THREE TYPES OF GOVERNMENTAL PRONOUNCEMENTS

As I indicated at the outset, there have been many different types of polities that have been called democracies. Since this study is normative rather than descriptive, it seeks to delimit those structures that may be called *real* or *worthy* democracies. Imposing such limitations involves judgments that have required me to rely on axioms or defining properties of democracy, and I have suggested that we assent to something like the following:

(A) Democratic polity must at least try to do what its citizens indicate that they want done. (There is no "higher authority" to which one may appeal for better or more legitimate instructions regarding what must be done.)

(B) Each citizen in a democracy must be treated equally when it comes to the determination of what its citizens want their government to do.

The combination of these sets forth both minimum requirements for (worthy) democratic procedures and limits beyond which choices may not go. While these axioms clearly require apportionments of both numbers of representatives and their individual authority so that equal treatment of voters and votes will be guaranteed, such matters as the length of terms, the size of legislatures, or the appropriate nature and duration of legislative deliberations must be based on best estimates of what will work best. In fact, assuming that Dahlian criticisms of direct democracy are based on empirical considerations, even whether representative bodies should exist at all ought to be regularly revisited. The idea that we must have elected legislatures or executives of some kind may seem so obvious to us that we will be extremely tempted to "constitutionalize" them—even to the point of making them absolutely impervious to amendment or removal. But treating them as foundational puts improper limits on what the people should be allowed to choose and change based on considerations of utility.

As difficult as it is in many cases to determine where the "deducible-from-axioms" group ends and the "reasonably-expected-to-be-beneficial" group begins, there is a further complication. It is that an important subset can be found within the latter group that consists of propositions that, while not absolutely essential to democracy (and so not deserving of complete immunity from modification or deletion), are nevertheless too deeply ingrained to alter or strike without the creation of huge upheavals. Many rules involving federalism, governmental structure, and geographical boundaries will be of this kind. For example, there would be nothing contrary to democratic principles for the borders of each U.S. state to be annually redrawn to ensure that each one contains the same number of residents. Or perhaps someone might want to propose that Congressional elections take place monthly or that the justices of the highest court in the land be selected for a two-year term as follows: *If it is an even-numbered year, by the president; if it is an odd-numbered year, by the Congress.* It is neither that it is inconceivable that there is a sensible argument for adoption of these proposals, nor that such suggestions are inherently violative of democratic principles. It is simply that, once the basic structure of government has been fixed for a significant period, it becomes clear that changes of such a radical nature would be destabilizing. Thus, it makes sense to put non-absolutely fundamental, but deeply entrenched structural provisions into a third bucket, one in which the provisions are not absolutely safe from alteration, but where such change can only be accomplished with difficulty.

The entire issue of constitutional change is perplexing, since it involves the paradox discussed earlier of how a demos can alter apparently essential democratic procedures. Constitutions must be changeable in a democracy. But democratic principles require that certain provisions, elemental if not quite foundational, should be amendable or removable only with great difficulty.[4] I think the best way to handle this is to have the two sorts of propositions that belong in any constitution—the foundational and the elemental—clearly delineated. The first group may only be lightly tinkered with—perhaps made clearer or easier to implement—but they may be neither substantially altered nor removed. I shall label such *foundational* principles with an "[F]" and attempt to distinguish them from what I take to be *elemental*, if not actually axiomatic, "[E]" propositions. Those involve the structural, if not absolutely essential, propositions that also belong in constitutions because they should only be altered or struck with significant difficulty. Ideally, well-drawn constitutions would contain only [F] and [E] items and would be perfectly perspicuous regarding which of these two groups every included proposition belongs to.

Unfortunately, constitutions generally contain much material that is neither [E] nor [F]. In addition, the U.S. Constitution requires supermajorities (of both branches of Congress and of states) to change anything at all in it. That is, unlike regular statutory changes, the U.S. Constitution makes it insufficient for the people to want some particular amendment made to it: a very small minority of people and/or a very small minority of states can prevent any change at all. For legitimate [E] propositions, this *almost* makes sense. Since structural changes can be tectonic, we don't want them to be made on a whim (and majorities can sometimes be quite whimsical). However, I don't think the solution the "Founding Fathers" landed upon is quite apt even for this subgroup of constitutional matters. Proof that a change to an [E] proposition is indicated should not be a function of supermajority bingo. A much more appropriate way to determine whether a desire is "entirely settled" among the people is to have it approved by a majority of the populace more than once, with sufficient time elapsing in between to ensure that a majority of another (presumably somewhat different) totality of individuals also indicates support. To amend their own constitutions, a number of states require the approval of consecutive legislatures and even subsequent referral of the matter to the voters for final approval. Such a process seems appropriate for [E] propositions on the Federal level as well. The electors of House and Senate representatives may be different from those who elected the president because of timing, so the incumbent executive (or consecutive executives) ought also to be required to assent to the change before referring the matter to the people for their additional approval. This is a lot of process admittedly, but it nowhere requires either a majority in excess of 50 percent plus one or separate state plebiscites. As Kelsen pointed out, democracies ought to be generally suspicious of supermajority requirements.

When thinking about foundational versus elemental propositions, it may be instructive to again consider what the electorate may sensibly vote on. One might answer this by simply saying *Everything*—or at least *Everything not inconsistent with one or another of the democratic axioms*. These answers are attractive since a free people cannot appropriately give up their sovereignty and remain free, any more than an autonomous individual can choose to enslave herself and remain autonomous. But it does not follow from the fact that one *may* vote on everything that is not democracy-destroying, that it would be prudent to set up a system that puts large, complicated matters before the entire electorate at every turn. If, for example, the voting public were to realize that it is really not up to the task of writing complex legislation, it might, contra-Rousseau, wish to delegate that authority to representatives who are more expert at such tasks. Making a structural decision of that kind (*The people shall be represented in the following way*—) seems not to exclusively involve [F] propositions, but does seem to require the inclusion of a number of [E] propositions into one's constitution. The fact that such structural provisions are elemental indicates that they should not be subject to quick or easy change, but we cannot infer that no polity could be a worthy democratic entity without having any specific group of them in its constitution. Neither the modification nor the deletion of any particular [E] proposition within/from a constitution necessarily constitutes the electorate's alienation of its sovereignty.

DIRECT PARTICIPATION OR REPRESENTATION?

To repeat, so long as no alienation of sovereignty is allowed to occur, both direct and representative governments seem to be consistent with our axioms. That means we must consider only what works better, what makes more practical sense. Perhaps strangely, the choice between the two has, in theory if not in practice, remained stubbornly controversial. It may seem obvious that only polities consisting of no more than five or ten thousand people could successfully be directly governed. But some have suggested that where the numbers or distances seem to provide a barrier to direct participation, the initiative petition and referendum provide a reasonable facsimile, especially in an internet era where computers are available to nearly everyone. Some of these direct democracy advocates have complained bitterly about representative government in the real world. Nadia Urbinati has nicely summarized a number of their arguments as follows:

> [R]epresentation has been associated with the weakening of self-government. For democrats in particular, it has held little appeal, first because it is seen

as justifying a vertical relation between the citizens and the state, and second because it is seen as promoting a passive citizenry. Even the attempt to make it more consistent with the democratic principle of equality, for instance by making it proportional, has been considered not only useless but also insincere. (2000, 759)

It is not only for reasons of feasibility that agitation for direct democracy has not carried the day. I have argued that fair voting is analogous to autonomous choosing on the individual level. As successful individual choices always involve the *getting* of something, successful voting (i.e., voting for a winner) should also. Thus, to the extent that our political theory reflects the principles advocated here, we should, where possible, restrict voting to cases in which something is actually obtained by successful voters. This does happen when we vote for candidates: winners will take office, at least where there is no fraud or other untoward behavior by the candidate, the government or any rebellious faction. But when we vote on issues, as we sometimes do on ballot questions and would always do in a direct democracy, matters of implementation will generally interpose themselves between the voting and the getting. A winning vote on, for example, the building of a bridge, may never result in a bridge. Maybe work is started but never finished, or perhaps there is insufficient money or know-how to even begin construction. Thus, while it may seem that direct democracy cuts out a middleman absent from the personal level, that appearance can be misleading. Initiative petitions share this defect. It may be then that we should try to reduce the number and sort of popular votes where groups that win are not guaranteed real success. It might, then, be most effectual to restrict official citizen participation to voting in elections for representatives, referendums, recalls and reversals.

There are numerous other arguments against the expansion of direct democracy. In the case of the initiative petition, it is obvious that if the people don't write the individual alternatives that will be voted on and cannot amend them, there must always be the danger of manipulation, misunderstanding, and minority control. And initiative petitions are not the only examples of citizen participation that have come under attack. Lynn Sanders has provided several reasons to be wary of making deliberative activity among the general populace generative of governmental authority. She writes,

Appeals to deliberation . . . have often been fraught with connotations of rationality, reserve, cautiousness, quietude, community, selflessness, and universalism, connotations which in fact probably undermine deliberation's democratic claims. . . . Some citizens are better than others at articulating their arguments in rational, reasonable terms. . . . [T]aking deliberation as a signal of democratic practice paradoxically works undemocratically, discrediting on seemingly democratic grounds the views of those who are less likely to present their arguments in ways that we recognize as characteristically deliberative. In our political culture, these citizens are likely to be those who are already underrepresented in formal political institutions and who are systematically materially disadvantaged, namely women; racial minorities, especially Blacks; and poorer people. (1997, 348–349)

Sanders is correct, I believe, that even if all the characteristics making for good deliberators are admirable, we cannot require them to be exemplified by every voter without abandoning our equality axiom.

And there is also a good utility argument according to which representative structures can be more advantageous to minorities than deliberative democratic activities among the electorate. Sherman Clark (1998) has noted that direct democracy can create obstacles for beneficial bargaining. He argues that minority initiatives are much more likely to prevail inside representative bodies, where logrolling and other forms of trading can more easily reflect intensity of support than can "head-counting" among the entire electorate. In Clark's view, even without the availability of proportional representation, minorities (especially wealthy ones) will do better with representative structures than they can among the general electorate. Clark's argument is concerning, however. The sort of deliberation and bargaining that can create excellent laws and their fair and efficient implementation seems quite different from the sort of bargaining that results in the making of odds by bookies or the setting of prices by retailers—and those are the models Clark seems to have in mind. Even if logrolling is in some ways analogous to markets in what it can provide for intense minority interests, it seems clear that it should not be the sole deliberative paradigm. A different sort of nuanced collaboration and bargaining is required for the most advantageous overall results. Combining Sanders's suspicions of the benefits of direct democracy for disadvantaged groups with worries about the effects of well-heeled interests upon bargaining within representative institutions leaves us where I think we belong: more supportive of some types of deliberative procedures than of others, and conscious of their varying utility in different contexts. In sum, we should consult the voluminous literature on the costs and benefits of different deliberative methods and not suppose that every environment is equally conducive to each technique.

That stance puts me somewhat at odds with Urbinati, who shares with me the sentiment that representative government is essential to modern democracy, but differs in her attitude toward the possibility and advisability of voter participation at some local level. She has voiced concern that an occasional election is insufficient to make a polity a real democracy because she takes more to be required of "wholly active citizens," I take the less utopian, but still sanguine view that, with respect to the populace at large, all we need do is ensure that the right sorts of things are voted on, that representatives are given sufficiently short terms, and that referendum, reversal, and recall are available with respect to certain sorts of laws, decisions, and personnel. I do not think that other sorts of "active participation" by the electorate are either required or particularly beneficial to democracy. In fact, the continued enthusiastic encouragement of heightened citizen participation might even be taken to be counterproductive if I am correct that the expected benefits of such activity mostly result from utopian fantasies.[5]

It might be suggested that my views are in concert with Rousseau's on this matter, since he too preferred isolated reasoning to community agitation and discussion (not to say badgering). But my doubts that deliberative activity can bear much fruit in the area of fostering democratic values (or in increasing prudential value generally) extends only to participation among the electorate at large. On this matter, I agree with Amy Gutmann that

> Accountability, not direct participation, is the key to deliberative democracy. Accountability is a form of active political engagement, but it does not require continual and direct involvement in politics; it is fully compatible with the division of labor between professional politicians and citizens that is characteristic of representative democracy. Whereas participatory democracy points toward a polity in which all actively participate in making decisions, deliberative democracy takes account of the burden of political action and the advantages of a division of labor. Deliberative democracy insists on ongoing accountability, not direct participation in politics. Those who act on our behalf must be accountable to us, and we must hold them to account. (1993, 143)

I will come back to the theme of appropriate places and types of deliberation shortly, but now I want to revisit the question of what sort of representatives we should have in the first place—and what sort of instructions they should be required to follow.

REPRESENTATIVES AS DELEGATES OR TRUSTEES?

I mentioned earlier that estimations of the utility effects of various democratic structures can be extremely difficult. It is fortunate, then, that this matter has long engaged keen observers. If asked to give the name of the most acute foreign observer of American government in the nineteenth century, most political theorists would unhesitatingly answer "Tocqueville," although a few might suggest Lord Bryce. One person whose name is unlikely to be mentioned in that context is the prolific Victorian novelist, Anthony Trollope. I believe, however, that his 1862 nonfiction opus, *North America*, is at least the match of the excellent studies by those more famous for their discourses on American government. Trollope was particularly suited for this investigation. He was traveling in the states just as the Civil War was about to begin and had the opportunity to discuss political issues with northerners and southerners in every station—from small farmers to high-ranking officials. He had long been a close observer of English government, writing many political novels, not only about Parliament, but also about the civil service (in which he had been employed for many years). He ran for Parliament himself in 1868, but was defeated.[6] Many of his novels are well known for their keen observations regarding representation, political bargaining, suffrage, sovereignty, home rule, discrimination, patronage, civil service tests, administrative efficiency, corruption, nepotism, rotten boroughs, and so on.

In *North America*, Trollope devoted lengthy chapters to the constitutional provisions of various state governments, the nature of representation, the reasonings employed by the "Founding Fathers" for various aspects of the U.S. system, the effects of slavery on the current crisis, and so on. We will focus here, however, only on a few of his comments regarding delegation and trusteeship. Remember that in the 1860s, U.S. senators were not yet directly elected by the voters, but were selected by the legislatures of the various states. Trollope expressed concern that some of these state legislatures held the reins of their appointees too tightly, and, at least on certain controversial subjects, the senators would be required to submit to voting instructions from their home states and would use the fact that they had received such instructions to justify themselves in voting contrary to their personal convictions. According to Trollope,

> Such a practice, even with the members of a House which has been directly returned by popular election, is . . . false to the intention of the system. It has clearly been intended that confidence should be put in the chosen candidate for the term of his duty, and that the electors are to be bound in the expression of their opinion by his sagacity and patriotism for that term. A member of a representative House so chosen, who votes at the bidding of his constituency in opposition to his convictions, is manifestly false to his charge, and may be presumed to be thus false in deference to his own personal interests, and with a view to his own future standing with his constituents. Pledges before election may be fair, because a pledge given is after all but the answer to a question asked. A voter may reasonably desire to know a candidate's opinion on any matter of political interest before he votes for or against him. [But] the representative when returned should be free from the necessity of further pledges. . . . Nevertheless, it is the fact that many Senators . . . do hold themselves absolved from the personal responsibility of their votes by such dictation. (1862, Vol. 2, Ch. 9)

A unique perspective, that! In Trollope's view, submitting to instructions from constituencies—an activity that has seemed to some theorists as precisely what is required by democratic principles—should be frowned upon as mere pandering, perhaps even constituting dereliction of democratic duty! Of course, it could be suggested that Trollope was just giving in to elitist leanings here, demeaning the common folk he'd met on his work for the postal service all over England and Ireland. But it should not be denied that the complexity of the issues that arise in the House of Commons and the U.S. House of Representatives as well as the study required to master them, seem to make legislatures more fitting places for barristers than for brewers. It should also be pointed out that a position favoring trusteeship is buttressed by the nature of SNTV elections. If we really believe that we have found a good B-type representative to advocate for our own positions in government, someone who not only shares our values but whom we believe to have the intelligence, creativity, and craft to get them implemented, why should we not simply get out of her way and let her do this job?

That that answer is too simple is suggested by the Croly and Pitkin quotations quoted earlier. Appropriate representation must always be a balancing act. If our representatives feel entirely safe from any effective disapprobation until the next election, they may well cease to see themselves as representatives at all, especially if they have no credible opponents. It is true, on the other hand, that we voters usually share a fairly strong sense that we are not in a position to provide detailed instructions on every matter. The issues are too many and too complex, which means that "instructions" (and initiatives) will either be poorly written, miss some of the main points, or actually be composed by some other "expert representative"—a party functionary, for example. A good assessment of our needs, authority, and limitations suggests that, while we ought to be proposing policies only via our choice of representatives, to be safe, we must reserve the right to recall at least some of those representatives as well as repeal those policies we disapprove of. A real threat of both referendum and recall are thus essential constituents of any system in which the people can truly be said to rule. The specific mechanisms and their application may be [E] elements, and so not entirely determinable by foundational principles. But, assuming a representative system, their general availability is crucial.

RECALL, NOT IMPEACH

While nineteen U.S. states have provisions for the recall of state officials, it is doubtful that the recall of any Federal official is allowed by the Constitution. Where the term of office is two years or less, this makes sense. Recall

elections are time-consuming and expensive—especially so for the individuals subject to them. Furthermore, a recall provision would, in a system
utilizing representation via SNTV, be at best highly impractical, and at worst
entirely incoherent. (E.g., how many votes for recall would be necessary
to remove a representative who is in office in virtue of being the favorite
candidate of 15 percent of the electorate?) But where there can be no recall,
terms must be short. Thus, no one elected via SNTV should have a term that
exceeds two years.

As described in the previous chapter, where there are SNTV representatives, there must also be representation by a majority system, preferably AV.
Here, however, a longer term makes sense and in fact may make such positions more desirable in spite of the uncertainty of the percentage of governmental authority that will accompany winning the seat. But a sensible term
of, say, four to six years must always come with the possibility of recall by
an unsatisfied electorate. And just as governors are subject to recall petitions
in many states, the president of the United States must be removable, other
than via impeachment. Trollope explains why:

> We know that he can be impeached by the Representatives and expelled from
> his office by the verdict of the Senate; but this in fact does not amount to
> much. Responsibility of this nature is doubtless very necessary, and prevents
> ebullitions of tyranny such as those in which a sultan or an emperor may
> indulge; but it is not that responsibility which especially recommends itself
> to the minds of free men. So much of responsibility they take as a matter of
> course, as they do the air which they breathe. It would be nothing to us to know
> that Lord Palmerston could be impeached for robbing the treasury, or Lord
> Russell punished for selling us to Austria. . . . We are anxious to know, not in
> what way they may be impeached and beheaded for great crimes, but by what
> method they may be kept constantly straight in small matters. . . . [T]hey must
> be . . . of one mind with the public. Let them be that; or if not they, then with
> as little delay as may be, some others in their place. That with us is the meaning
> of ministerial responsibility. To that responsibility all the cabinet is subject.
> But in the government of the United States there is no such responsibility. The
> President is placed at the head of the executive for four years, and while he
> there remains no man can question him. . . . There are no reins, constitutional
> or unconstitutional, by which he can be restrained. He can absolutely repudiate
> a majority of both Houses, and refuse the passage of any act of Congress even
> though supported by those majorities. He can retain the services of ministers
> distasteful to the whole country. He can place his own myrmidons at the head
> of the army and navy, or can himself take the command immediately on his
> own shoulders. All this he can do, and there is no one that can question him.
> (1862, Vol. 2, Ch. 10)

And, Trollope adds with disdain, "Seeing that Mr. Buchanan has escaped any punishment for maladministration, no President need fear the anger of the people." It is just such considerations as Trollope puts so well here that ought to make it obvious that in presidential systems too, a praiseworthy democracy requires the ability to recall all elected officials with terms greater than two years. State recall provisions vary, but I would recommend that a total of certified signatures equaling perhaps 25 percent of the number of voters in the last election for the office in question should be required to put the question on the ballot. A majority of those voting for recall in the subsequent election would prevail only if some minimum percentage of the electorate participates, perhaps 90 percent of the total number of those who voted in the election that put the individual in office. While such elections are indeed costly in many ways, democracy seems to me to require that recall of these officials be allowable at least once in any two-year period. Where any recall election is successful, a new election must be held as soon as possible.

JUDICIAL "INDEPENDENCE" AND "SEPARATION OF POWERS"

It is interesting to note to what almost incredible extent the eighteenth-century constitution-builders in America amplified Montesquieu's "separation of powers" trope into a principle that could be used to fuel the fear of any scent of "despotism."[7] I will be discussing this matter in relation to bicameralism and the executive veto shortly, but it is important at present to distinguish what any parliamentary system shows to be largely a red herring, from the separate, and I think defensible, tenet of judicial independence. This matter is important here because the precept of independence must be made to harmonize with democratic principles when considering the selection of judges and the prospect of the revisability of their decisions by the people. Obviously, judges—particularly those who will sit on the highest courts—must have a specific sort of expertise. While this may be true of legislators as well, judges are not correctly viewed as our representatives. Where legislators will be chosen largely because of the concord between the voters' views and what the candidates say they intend to do, judges—while also having political perspectives—clearly need to have legal expertise of a type that the electorate is unlikely to be in a position to assess. But even if, as I think, high judges must therefore be selected by the executive, the legislature, or both, there should be no imputation of "separation of powers" here. Such "independence" as is required must be consistent with a judiciary that will remain responsive to the general will. As Paine pointed out, the distinction of government into executive, legislative, and judicial branches is more a distinction of words than of things.

The sort of responsiveness needed, even among the judiciary, seems impossible where judges are elected for life terms. And as Croly (1914) warns, a too-powerful judiciary makes us a nation not of laws but of lawyer-sovereignty—a country ruled almost entirely by unaccountable attorneys.[8] Selection of judges by the executive and confirmation by the legislature thus seem to me appropriate, but only if appointments are for fixed (perhaps) twelve-year, though renewable, terms. Those judges wanting to remain on their benches at the end of their terms should be required to apply for continued service to the executive, who could either agree or dismiss them and make alternative choices, with such decisions again being subject to confirmation by the legislature.[9]

Judicial independence is, of course, more than a matter of selection and retention or dismissal of judges. There must be reasonable confidence, not only among members of the judiciary but also among contesting parties, that decisions will be made based on the merits of cases, rather than political considerations or estimates regarding whether some decision may be overturned by an executive or legislative edict—or even by the results of a plebiscite. But such judicial power must nevertheless not be itself used to entirely upend the will of the people. As Amy Gutmann (1993) points out, judicial review of legislative acts must go no farther than *delegation* of popular control, and not move on to the complete *alienation* of it.

There has been no end of disputes about this issue, not only in academic works, and in legislatures and courthouses around the country, but on battle-fields of the Civil War. There are today numerous subjects where one can find the demos on one side and the courts on another. Gun control is a good example. But thorny as they are, I believe these issues are resolvable if we correctly distinguish among types of cases. State legislatures and executives have long been jealous of what they take to be the rights of their constituents to live as they please, and they have been quite willing to set aside criminal and civil cases and focus their objections to judicial power on those specific matters wherein a Federal judge strikes down or preempts a state law or constitutional provision based on an interpretation of the (U.S.) Constitution or a Federal law.[10] The distinction the states have tried to make here is on the right track but insufficiently careful. Justice Marshall was right concerning *some* matters. There ought not to be "second-guessing" of the Federal government or its high court by a state, either on what I have called [F] or [E] matters, or on criminal or civil cases. There must be a final say regarding what is the foundation (or at least the current basic structural law) of any nation, and, since elections are not truth-tracking, voters should not be used to weigh evidence or retry cases. Neither, however, should the Federal courts be substituting their judgments for what the people in some state want—so long as there are no national laws on the matter. One obstacle to a correct parsing here is that there are so many pro-visions in the U.S. Constitution that are treated as [F] when they are actually [E], and so many others that ought not to be in the document at all. Remove the latter, and states would immediately have more leeway in areas where the nation's voters as a whole have not expressed their will. Thus, it seems to me that there are *some* court decisions that ought to be reversible by popu-lar vote—no matter how high the court. These must, however, be only such decisions as are both (i) contrary to some legislative or (state) constitutional provision, and (ii) not essentially tied up with any matter(s) correctly desig-nated as [E] or [F] in an applicable constitution. Of course, there would still be disputes about whether some case really *is* "tied up with" a foundational or elemental matter. For good or ill, those would have to be finally determined by the appropriate courts themselves, if only because it seems too messy to try to resolve them in any other way. In any event, even in cases where reversal is not allowed, the demos should have its (indirect) say about the judges them-selves when they come up for reappointment.

What should happen in these non-[E] or -[F] cases? Disgusted about the regular striking down by various courts of popular legislation involving such matters as child labor, workers' compensation, and sanitary conditions in tenements, Roosevelt wrote,

> It is the people, and not the judges, who are entitled to say what their constitution means, for the constitution is theirs, it belongs to them and not to their servants in office—any other theory is incompatible with the foundational principles of our government. If we, the people, choose to protect tenement-house dwellers in their homes, or women in sweat-shops and factories, or wage-earners in danger-ous and unhealthy trades, or if we, the people, choose to define and regulate the conditions of corporate activity, it is for us, and not for our servants, to decide on the course we deem wise to follow. We cannot take any other position without admitting that we are less fit for self-government than the people of England, of Canada, of France, who possess and exercise this very power. (Roosevelt 1912)

Roosevelt's solution was not to move to a parliamentary system, but to require that a certain subclass of judicial decisions be subject to overturn by votes for reversal. He wanted the courts to be independent, but believed that such independence was more at risk from corporate and legal special interest groups than it was from "popular tyranny." He gives some minimum delib-erative requirements for these actions (e.g., the plebiscite would have to wait at least two years from the election of the legislature that enacted the law that was struck down), but he isn't quite clear on how to interpret the results of these votes. He writes, "It is a matter of mere terminology whether this is called a method of 'construing' or 'applying' the constitution, or 'a quicker method of getting the constitution amended'" (1912). This is glib, I think: it is important for any democratic populace to be able to know what is in its constitution. Roosevelt was wrong to suggest that this doesn't matter, but the difficulty he points up with his remark is not easily handled. Both the constitutions and the statutes of all the various states involve specific methods for amendment, and they may not include language regarding "amendment via court decision" due to alleged unconstitutionality. Let me here provide my own tentative suggestion for the availability of reversal votes when a statute (not touching on any [F] or [E] matters) is deemed unconstitutional.

A successful vote to overturn a decision of any court regarding its opinion that a law involving the general welfare violates the provision of any constitution shall be construed as a remand to the court issuing the decision as well as to the legislature and executive created by the constitution deemed to prohibit the law in question. Such remand shall include instructions that either (i) the court revise its view of the conflict within some specified period of time; (ii) (a) the court advise the legislature regarding how to draft another bill producing substantially the same result but which in their unanimous opinion would pass constitutional muster and (b) the legislature and executive enact this statute within the same specified period; or (iii) the court provide constitutional amendments that would, in the unanimous opinion of the judges, handle the alleged conflict and request that such amendments be placed on the ballot forthwith. Said instructions must be clear that if, by the date specified within them, there is in effect neither a policy tantamount to that desired by the voters nor an amendment to the constitution on the ballot that would allow such policy in the opinion of that court, then each member of the court who voted that the legislation be struck down as unconstitutional be forthwith removed from his or her office for cause, unless either two-thirds of the legislature in question indicate by open vote that they are opposed both to enactment of any such legislation or constitutional amendment, or the executive of that government agrees that it is his or her own responsibility that no bill has been enacted and no constitutional amendment has been placed on the ballot.

It is quite likely that others can come up with a less convoluted procedure, but the reasons for at least some complexity should be clear.[11] The judges may have been quite right that the new law conflicts with one or more constitutional provisions; the legislature might pass new laws according to the judicial recommendations and have them vetoed, or the executive might receive nothing to sign that would address the matter. It therefore may be hard to find duplicity or, if it is found, it may be difficult to parse it. But what should not be lost in these weeds is the necessity, as Roosevelt, Croly, Beard, and a number of other progressives understood, that *some* method must always be available for the people to get what they want. In a democratic country, citizens cannot be left, as the American people are today, with so little recourse to change things, to have their way.

I have not spoken highly of the initiative petition, instead taking an attitude that may make my views seem undemocratic.[12] It is my view, however, that considerable expertise and diligent study are necessary to make good laws, and that those achievements are not generally dispersed throughout a broad populace. Furthermore, the initiative is, as already indicated, highly manipulable. But the referendum, which enables only the striking down of statutes or executive orders the electorate does not like, is markedly different, and, within strictly demarcated areas, must be available. Surely, on such matters as whether a country should go to war, the population at large must not be relegated to the position of ineffectual boosters or protesters. It is generally fairly easy for people to know that they don't want this or that thing that has been thrust upon them. I believe the mechanism for overturn of a law should be similar to that suggested earlier for the recall of an elected official: there should be minimum numbers set for both signatures and Yea votes. And the demand for substitute action by the legislature or executive (though not instructions regarding precisely what it must be, which would turn the event into an initiative) could be required. The point is that spontaneous actions by legislators and executives must be subject to repeal by referendum—as long as the issues do not involve matters that are fundamental to democratic principles.

Another look at the "There ought to be a new bridge" dispute discussed earlier, may help to clarify the specific roles and limitations of voters and representatives. The voters know better than anybody else can what they want and don't want. Their representatives are expected to be able to go some way in figuring out what to do with that information. But neither the voters nor their representatives may know whether such actions will be "good for the people." That matter calls for special sorts of scientific expertise, as it is a function of what various courses of action can be expected to produce in terms of future attractive options and successful choices. Neither the general populace *nor* their representatives ought to be expected to be extremely proficient in that area of prognostication. It is not always easy to disentangle the wants either from the ways or from the expected and actual values of the results: there will be overlaps, gaps, and disagreements.[13] But democracy should allow us to do the best we can. The availability of referendums ensures that neither representatives nor experts appointed by legislatures or executives can usurp the basic democratic right of the people to indicate what they *don't* want—and have what is unacceptable removed where possible.

As noted earlier, it is reasonable to be concerned that a "majority veto" by the electorate at large could cost minorities gains that they might make in legislatures through logrolling or strategic contributions, because, while intensities matter in deliberative bodies, they do not play where we simply count heads.[14] But while a distilled populism intentionally ensures an equitable voice to minorities, it should not be expected to provide strategies to achieve minority rule. The people at large must be convinced. Of course, it is not always possible to know that our representatives actually approve of some action or do so in light of their general agreement with us on the issues: it may be that they are lying or have been bought. Vigilance is crucial in the area of public corruption, and the opportunity and means to cure illegitimate encroachments must be in the voters' arsenal. In a word, the Progressives of Teddy Roosevelt's time were right about the gradual usurpation of the people's power, even if their proposals need tweaking. Confusions and conflations (as well as the intentional smokescreens sent up by traditional liberals and conservatives) have managed to deprive U.S. citizens of real democracy since the country's creation. Yes, equal protections must never be violated. Yes, the judiciary must be independent. No, we cannot allow tyranny—even by the people. But it is possible to have real democracy for all that.

NOTES

1. Replacing a transcendent lord with *ourselves* seems to me akin to something discussed by William James in his *Varieties of Religious Experience*. He there writes,

> Let me . . . propose, as an hypothesis, that whatever it may be on its farther side, the "more" with which in religious experience we feel ourselves connected is on its hither side the subconscious continuation of our conscious life. Starting thus with a recognized psychological fact as our basis, we seem to preserve a contact with "science" which the ordinary theologian lacks. (James 1917, 512–513)

2. See Hall (1961, Ch. 8). Compare also W. D. Lamont (1955, 239): "[A]pproval is primarily a conative attitude . . . when we speak of approval, we are referring to a total mental state or activity which is at once cognitive, affective and conative, but with the emphasis on the conative aspect."

3. Perhaps the best discussion I have seen on the subject can be found in the debate between "James" and "Jean-Jacques" in Dahl (1989, Ch. 16). Any lingering hope for widespread "citizen rule" is there obliterated by a combination of simple arithmetic and a couple of obvious truths about human nature and the finitude of life. As Dahl demonstrates, for even relatively small jurisdictions, participatory democracy itself requires certain forms of representation.

4. J. Allen Smith (1907) seems to have missed this point in his savage denunciation of the monarchical Hamiltonians among the Conventioneers in Philadelphia:

> All democratic constitutions are flexible and easy to amend. . . . Such a constitution cannot be regarded as a check upon the people themselves. It is a device for securing to them that

... without which popular government exists only in name. A government is democratic just in proportion as it responds to the will of the people; and since one way of defeating the will of the people is to make it difficult to alter the form of government, it necessarily follows that any constitution which is democratic in spirit must yield readily to changes in public opinion.

It follows, however, that a democratic constitution cannot allow such amendments as would make it difficult to (otherwise) amend. In a democracy, democratic principles must be sacrosanct.

5. It may be complained that there is considerable irony in one who proposes as many practically impossible governmental reforms as I do, calling anybody else's views utopian. But let me say in my defense that my proposals are far-fetched in a different sense than are the proposals I am criticizing here. My recommendations may be utterly unfeasible given our present circumstances, but they are, I believe, all consistent with human nature as we find it. I suggest what I think is required by distilled populism, but I make no claim that reaching that goal is either dependent upon or likely to contribute much to the making of a different sort of populace.

6. He stood as liberal, for the borough of Beverly.

7. An excellent discussion of this metamorphosis can be found in Gordon Wood (1969). It is fascinating to discover that at the time of the signing of the Articles of Confederation, many of the individual states were extremely democratic, providing limited terms for judges, broad impeachment processes, little in the way of executive vetoes of legislative actions. As J. Allen Smith (1907, Ch. 2) notes, "In this respect the early state constitutions anticipated much of the later development of the English government itself." Smith attributed this radicalism to the fact that the checks and balances in the English system and in the colonies first established in America "resulted from the composite character of the English Constitution—its mixture of monarchy, aristocracy, and democracy." When the democratic spirit grew in the new world, there (at first) seemed little reason to retain all the restraining mechanisms. And so the Articles, like the state constitutions, entirely omitted them.

8.

No reverence for the law can guarantee political and social liberty to a body of democrats who confide their collective destiny to written formulas as expounded by a ruling body of lawyers. In practice each of these systems develops into a method of class government. The men to whom the enormous power is delegated will use it, in part at least, to perpetuate the system which is so beneficial to themselves. (Croly 1914, 279)

See also the careful demonstration of the unavoidable defects of judicial lawmaking and the consequent importance of legislative codification in Austin (1869) (Lect. XXXIX).

9. Dismissals and appointments should be considered separate actions, since the legislature ought to be able to overturn a dismissal, perhaps by a 3/5 vote as if it were a veto. Since I have criticized the use of supermajorities earlier, I should note here that I have no problem with them when they are used exclusively to overturn contrary (simple majority) actions by another legislative branch or the acts of an executive elected by the same (or roughly the same) electorate.

10. See, e.g., Ransom (1912), Culp (1929), and Beard (1912). This issue was a stalking horse for Teddy Roosevelt during his Progressive period.

11. A simpler, if less radical approach, according to which legislatures may overturn certain types of judicial decisions has recently been suggested by Ganesh Sitaraman (2019).

12. As already indicated, that is the response that I'd expect to be taken by Nadia Urbinati, given what she says in *Democracy Disfigured* (Urbinati 2014). For a more favorable view of strictly "yes/no" plebiscitary arrangements, see Jeffrey Edward Green (2011). My own view, like Croly's, falls somewhere in between.

13. Urbinati (2014) is instructive on the nuances of what she calls the "diarchy" of decisions and opinions.

14. See, e.g., Clark (1998).

Chapter 10

Political Representation II

Deliberation, Camerality, Term Limits, and Judicial Review of Legislative Procedures

For at least fifty years, deliberation theorists have stressed what they take to be the irreplaceable benefits to the public weal that can result from certain types of discussion.[1] And in spite of my doubts with respect to what can be accomplished by the use of deliberative procedures among the electorate at large, I am convinced of its value within legislatures, courts, juries, and so on, and disagree with those who seem to think support for extensive deliberation is antithetical to majoritarianism. Jeremy Waldron, for example, tells the story of Ronald Dworkin's failure to answer when asked how those in a lifeboat are to decide between leaving to chance which passenger should be sacrificed or settling the matter by majority decision. Waldron (2010, 1051) takes Dworkin's reticence to be "as striking an instance as one could find of the cheerful view—common among 'deliberative' democrats—that colloquium-style deliberation (if only it goes on long enough) obviates the need for voting." I myself see no reason why consensus-building might not do just that in some cases, even if not in every imaginable lifeboat scenario. That we should not insist on Pareto optimality does not mean we should not look around for it and take it when it is available.

THE BENEFITS OF DELIBERATION— REAL AND IMAGINED

In the last chapter I noted that the usefulness of various forms of deliberation in reaching concord has been held by some to largely depend on the size of the groups utilizing them. Jon Elster (1998, 109) writes,

> The dynamics of large assemblies, small *bureaux*, and small specialized committees are likely to be very different. In a large assembly, it is not possible to

pursue an argument in a coherent and systematic fashion. The debates tend to be dominated by a small number of skilled and charismatic speakers, a Mirabeau or a Lamartine, who count on rhetoric rather than argument. . . . Although the speakers themselves need not be swayed by emotion, they hope to gain cause by playing on the emotions of the audience. In the *bureaux*, one is more likely to observe the substance and not only the form of deliberation. The small size reduces the scope for demagogy and allows all speakers to be heard. . . . In functionally specialized committees, the technical quality of whatever deliberation takes place, especially on factual matters, is likely to be higher than in the *bureaux*. Yet because the members are less likely to adopt an impartial attitude, there will be less deliberation and more bargaining.

Elster finds the middling size of the *bureaux* optimal for producing defensible compromises. That is fortunate for us, because, with respect to the general populace, we have agreed with Gutmann (1993) that it is the demand for accountability to the populace, not the latter's active participation, that is the key to self-governance.[2] But what are the goals that we expect deliberation to help us reach where we think it can be beneficial, and what are the ideal procedures thought to be for reaching those goals? For reasons already given, we will neither be able to conceive of deliberation as providing "truth-tracking" powers[3] nor will we be able to follow the Rawls-Dworkin axis when they insist that appropriate participants must be motivated by a conception of the public good. But we may nevertheless find common ground with at least *some* of the deliberativists' prescriptions. For example, as our conception of democracy essentially requires the equality of individuals, it makes sense to insist that members of deliberative groups be treated with equal respect. To give one example we could say that, whether or not they are allotted different amounts of political authority, each representative must be allotted an equal amount of time and (to the extent possible) attention. In the words of Joshua Cohen (1986, 73), participants must "recognize one another as having deliberative capacities . . . and for acting on the result of such public reasoning." We have seen that majoritarian principles may require providing differing weights to the votes of representatives. But the best deliberative practices nevertheless require a certain sort of equality among them. According to Cohen (1986, 74) "Everyone with the deliberative capacities has equal standing at each stage of the deliberative process. Each can put issues on the agenda, propose solutions, and offer reasons in support of or in criticism of proposals." In addition, the deliberations of representative bodies must be transparent[4] and reasonable allotments of time (both minima and maxima) must be provided to every voice. Both silencing and filibustering are destructive to democracy. Finally, deliberation should aim for a "rationally motivated *consensus*—to find reasons that are persuasive to all who are committed to acting on the results of a free and reasoned assessment of alternatives" (Cohen 1986, 75). Again, to the extent that discovery of a Pareto-optimal solution to a dispute is feasible, there is no reason why it should not be welcomed.

Ian Shapiro (2003, Ch. 2) has argued that lengthy exercises in deliberation (i) can be costly in money as well as time, (ii) can produce disagreements more virulent than they would otherwise be, (iii) are useless when conducted by individuals who are absolutely sure they are right, and (iv) may be especially problematic when parties are relatively ignorant of the details of their adversaries' positions. But to a large extent these problems stem from failing to distinguish citizen participation from deliberative activities undertaken by their representatives. In the latter context, (ii) and (iv) seem over-anxious: professional participants can be expected to know the views of their adversaries fairly well, and it is less probable that their positions will move farther apart in a committee-type session. (i) and (iii) are more realistic, but both the costs of patient discussion and the pointlessness of arguing with fanatics are simply unavoidable components of the human condition. Furthermore, as I will discuss later, any costs of prolonging legislative activity could be more than offset by another indicated change involving legislative structure. In any case, the benefits of beefing up legislative deliberation seem clearly to be worth even those costs Shapiro can point to that cannot be recouped.

In sum, a naturalized populism will likely find the expansion of deliberative procedures beneficial, and if Elster's views about the effect of size are correct, we can expect good "bang for the buck" in legislative chambers and committee rooms. While I don't believe that appropriate deliberative procedures have quite the magical qualities that some advocates discover there,[5] and I am skeptical of both the possibility and point of any widespread dissemination of such procedures among the electorate, my reservations have limits. I worked for a legislative committee in the General Court of Massachusetts long enough to be convinced that appropriate deliberation can be quite useful both in improving bills and cooling nerves. And contrary to the position of some advocates, I believe (partly for the reasons set forth by Sherman Clark and discussed earlier) that useful legislative mechanisms can include logrolling and other sorts of bargaining as well as searches for consensus. But a requirement for ample deliberation before moving on to vote trading will sometimes make the latter unnecessary. In the words of the deliberation skeptic, Ian Shapiro, "The point of democratic participation . . . is more to manufacture the common good than to discover it." In a word, "if people talk for long enough in the right circumstances, they will agree more often, and this is a good thing" (2003, 22). So, in answer to Amy Gutmann's question, "What's so great about popular rule if the people do not deliberate?" (1993, 139) we may rejoin "Where there is popular rule, a non-deliberative populace can be expected to benefit greatly from the deliberative activities of their representatives. Such benefits cannot be obtained within either anarchic or autocratic polities."

SEPARATION OF POWERS, REVISITED

The creators of constitutions on the American continent in the eighteen century were (quite sensibly) motivated to a great extent by fear of despotism. They knew at firsthand the terrible things that kings could do to their subjects, and they were equally fearful of the dangers of unrestrained mobs. So, it is quite natural that nearly all of the focus by those considered the wisest men in the country was on security. Most of these men believed in some sort of popular sovereignty and wanted no truck with kings or lords. But they struggled mightily with the puzzle of how to have restful sleep in a democracy. They understood their hold on their property (and even their lives!) given human nature was fragile. They knew that everybody wanted just what they wanted—land, slaves, income, prestige. Why wouldn't they? And, just as a king with few enforceable limitations on his power could take it all from them in a moment, an unrestrained "people" could do so as well. As the New Hampshire Convention of 1781 declared, "The love of Power is so alluring . . . that few have ever been able to resist its bewitching influence." The trick these rule makers devised to prevent such catastrophe was to build into their (extremely hard to amend) constitutions the principle of the separation of powers. If the people are incurably voracious, neither they nor their representatives ought to be entrusted with much authority. As a constitution is no person but rather a document, we may put our faith in *it*, so long as we precisely design it to prevent the feared abuses.

James Madison was the undisputed master of this strategy. He thought long and hard about the sort of governmental machinery that, in a vast country like the United States, could be depended upon to protect not just him and his cohort, but *everyone* within its borders (or at any rate every white man) from that rapacity natural to mortals. His meditations convinced him that a parliament is not to be trusted: combining legislative and executive functions seemed to him to give too much power to the same individuals. And having judiciary functions within the House of Lords similarly offended any sound sense of security. As the prime desideratum of security was clear, it made obvious sense to Madison to cast about for anything that worked to constrict power in other current or former governments, and to try to create a republic that magnifies and solidifies those restrictions.

Reaching this goal would be difficult, not only at the national level but throughout the confederation, because even among the elite, those who would be building the constitutions, there were differences of opinion. Then, as always, one could find arguments about cost, efficiency, the reach of suffrage, and the meaning of "liberty for all." But the primary means of power limitation via constitutional separations was immediately agreed upon almost everywhere in the American colonies of the eighteenth century. The moral seemed clear: deny the lawmakers sufficient power to control the people in any unpleasant manner, while at the same time providing this elite with enough authority to resist control by the citizenry. One component necessary to the attainment of this goal was to both balkanize and limit the authority of all the traditional sectors of government: those who make the laws, those who carry out the laws made, and those who are charged with interpreting those laws. Three seemed to be the magic number of constituents (executive, legislative, and judicial) essential to citizen security, so long as no admixture of those elements would be allowed. There were, of course, other tools too: limitations on suffrage via gender, race, property or other characteristics, for instance. And federalism would provide protections as well. For example, the Electoral College and the requirement for an equal number of Senators for each state would help prevent power-grabs by the most populous regions. But as proposals along those lines tended to be more controversial it was quite fortunate that those federal strategies seemed less essential to the achievement of complete safety from despotism than constitutional limitation of powers. For suppose the worst and most rapacious individuals do somehow get the vote—women, workmen, even slaves!—and imagine further that some states manage to procure many more representatives than others. Not all will be lost if we keep the powers inescapably hampered. If government is appropriately shackled via constitutional restrictions and divisions of its powers, the gravest dangers to person and property will be averted. Of course, the most important security device of all was to place these manacles in an extremely hard-to-amend constitution. With that alone, it seemed that a republican polity could be made safe from the worst forms of despotism.

For good or ill, however, the three powers actually *can't* be separated entirely. And the Rube Goldberg relations that have grown up between them have not done much to preserve the Madisonian illusions. In the United States, legislatures appropriate the money for the salaries for all the three branches of government, and Congress is supposed to have sole authority to declare war. These are not strictly legislative functions. In many jurisdictions, governors appoint various judges, who may or may not need to be confirmed by a legislature, or at least one branch of it. Executives or their appointees veto bills, issue executive orders, and promulgate regulations. Those are not entirely executive functions. Finally, judiciaries write consent decrees and can invalidate laws, regulations, and executive orders. The violations of Madisonianism are numerous, complicated, and inevitable. But it is hard to deny that, even if there is no literal separation behind the curtain and the intent to preserve this illusion has created considerable dysfunction, the division idea is sacrosanct in the United States. No doubt the illusion alone does manage to have considerable effect, for good or ill. If the idea was to avoid the sort of governmental efficiency and speed that might have been provided by a more parliamentary system, surely it has worked swimmingly.

I suggested earlier that the two pillars of constitutionalism and separation were agreed upon *almost* everywhere. There were exceptions, and one, which I'll take a moment to describe now, was particularly interesting. A radical party in Pennsylvania came to power in 1776 that, while friendly to constitutionalism and natural rights, was quite cynical about the true purposes of the (now anti-English) Whigs. Benjamin Rush, an early supporter of the radicals, at first enthused about the marvelous democracy they would bring, writing that "The proprietary gentry have retired to their country seats, and honest men have taken the seats they abused so much in the government of our state."[6] What happened is that a small group of the firebrands concocted a constitution for the state that went well beyond what was considered safe by the men usually entrusted to governance in that era. Early reviews of the document were mixed. Brisot de Warville wrote from France that it was "the closest approach to political perfection ever devised by mankind." Paine wrote that it would be the "pride of ages to come." Quite soon, however, Rush reversed his field and declared the new constitution "absurd in its principles and incapable of execution without the most alarming influence upon liberty."

In a somewhat hagiographic work on James Wilson (Seed 1978), the man perhaps most responsible for drafting the much more conservative 1790 Pennsylvania Constitution that replaced this "pride of ages," Geoffrey Seed (1978, 123) writes that the 1776 document needed to be entirely scrapped because "a system of government so much at variance with sound principles could hardly be ameliorated by mere amendment." And, as will be seen, even Paine, whose writings on governmental structure had been one of the main inspirations for the Pennsylvania radicals who drafted the 1776 Constitution (men branded as "numsculs" by the Whiggish gentry whose seats they had taken), eventually had second thoughts himself.

What were the offending items in this "most detestable constitution that was ever formed"?[7] They were numerous, but before going into the details, I think it is important to understand just what it was that made the drafters of the 1776 Constitution in Pennsylvania "radicals." These men, Thomas Young, James Cannon, George Bryan, and Timothy Matlack—as well as later supporters such as William Findley—were animated by the populist spirit I attempted to describe in my opening chapter. Their motivation, as Wood (1969, 400–401) explains, mostly resulted from an aversion to what they considered artificial distinctions among men. The writers among this party "scoffed at the 'academical education' of their aristocratic enemies and boasted that they were 'plain, unlettered' men better able to communicate with the people." They attacked "overgrown wealth," the professionaliza- tion of various careers, even the jargon beginning to be utilized by doctors. They didn't believe they had any "social superiors" and attacked privilege wherever they found it. And they knew, too, that the "unequal or partial distribution of public benefits within a state, creates distinctions of interest, influence and power"—an aristocracy. William Findley was concerned that Pennsylvanians were "too unequal in wealth to render a perfect democracy suitable to our circumstances" (Wood 1969, 402) and was ready to act to ensure that wealth did not concentrate in few hands because "wealth in many hands operates as many checks." These men insisted, as Randy Newman's "redneck" did nearly two centuries afterward, that their state be run by "little folks like you and me."

Their means of effecting this were indeed sweeping: a powerful unicameral legislature[8] of representatives who had one-year terms and who could serve no more than four years in any seven. Instead of a governor, there would be a twelve-person, executive council lacking a veto, and each member of this council could serve no more than three years. All property qualifications for voting or holding office were eliminated, and all legislation would have to be submitted to the people before taking effect. In addition, the radicals required the election of justices of the peace and restrictions on the sizes of bails and fines; they even incorporated a provision for free public schools (something which, however, was never funded). The whole thing was audacious, and was also obviously the creation of a very anxious group. Besides emasculating the executive, the constitutionalists (as these radicals were called) opposed the creation of a Bank of Pennsylvania as a dangerous monopoly, even while Paine was plumping for the success of that institution by insisting that it would surely make loans to all and only those farmers who needed them. There was no attempt to hide the extreme anxieties of the drafters in the lan- guage of the document. For example, the point of the three-year rotation of councilors was explicitly said to "effectually prevent the danger of establish- ing an inconvenient aristocracy." If the benefits of "separation" were illusory, other means would have to be found to protect people from despotism—not of the rapacious poor, but of the insatiable rich.

The annually elected legislature, facing no veto, was a problem almost immediately, however—especially as the submissions to the people were not generally made. As James Wilson's biographer puts it, the constitution seemed clearly damnable for "vesting the supreme legislative authority in a unicameral legislature which, being unchecked, could enact unjust and tyrannical laws and could usurp both the executive and the judicial author- ity" (Seed 1978, 126). As mentioned earlier, even Paine eventually began to worry about the way Pennsylvania's government had been structured (to the point of fibbing about whether he'd *ever* approved of it). He began to see reason in the view that while the agility of a unicameral legislature might make sense during a war, in peacetime, a more leisurely Madisonian conception might be preferable. And some of the roguery practiced by the single-branch Pennsylvania assembly during its decade or so in existence had convinced him that,

> [A] single legislature, into the hands of whatever party it may fall, is capable of being made a compleat aristocracy for the time it exists. . . . [O]n account of the superabundance of its power, and the uncontrouled rapidity of its execution, [it] becomes as dangerous to the principles of liberty as that of a despotic monarchy. . . . At the commencement of the revolution, it was supposed that what is called the executive part of a government was the only dangerous part; but we now see that quite as much mischief, if not more, may be done, and as much arbitrary conduct acted, by a legislature. . . . By the whole legislative power being entrusted to a single body of men, and that body expiring all at once, the state is subject to the perpetual convulsions of imperfect measures and rash proceedings; as by this means it may happen (as it has happened already) that a number of men, suddenly collected, unexperienced in business; and unacquainted with the grounds, reasons and principles, which former assemblies proceeded on in passing certain acts, and without seeking to inform themselves thereof, may precipitate the state into disorder by a confused medley of doing and undoing. (Paine 1786)[9]

The Whigs, with Wilson at their head, used similar arguments while trying to eliminate this perceived monstrosity. But as the 1776 constitution had been sold as the friend of the common man, these self-described "reformers" knew what they had to do: demonstrate from their Whiggish angle that a much more conventional text would actually be *even more democratic*! Pulling off such a trick is not as hard it may seem: those with sufficient energy and cunning can always put over the claim that they can do a better job than anybody else getting the people what they *really* want. The Councilors under the 1776 rules were required to be elected by voters in the various counties, so the conservatives got the word out that "Only election of the governor by the people at large could render the executive authority properly independent of the legislature" (Wood 1969, 452). Constitutional provisions limiting the reelection of Assemblymen and Councilors were made out to be contrary to any real democracy (which must of course let the people be governed by whomever they want). The lack of an executive veto was claimed to disable the government from stopping dangerous legislative encroachments on the people's power. Even the mechanism for calling the convention that eventually laid the radical constitution to rest was pitched as an important improvement on the democracy front. The 1776 Constitution provided for a Counsel of Censors to convene every seven years to review the work of the government and consider the advisability of amending the constitution by calling a convention. While the people had approved that constitution, including its manner of overhaul, how could it not be even *more* empowering for the people simply to insist that the whole thing be blown up whenever they wanted—without the need to wait for the assessment of any counsel? Here was the paradox of democracy in the flesh—the demos putting the axe to what was supposed to be an extremely democratic provision![10]

HOW MANY CHAMBERS?

And what of unicamerality? While it may have seemed strange to the farmers and artisans to be told that it was now somehow in their interest for their government to ape Lords and Commons by having two chambers, even though in Pennsylvania each branch would be elected by precisely the same people, they were given reasons of a kind they could be expected to swallow. Bicamerality would provide one more protection against tyranny. After all, the point of any "upper branch" (like that of the executive veto) is to be a "check" on improvident or greedy uses of "mob" authority. Indeed, it was felt that multicamerality must be good, since it was found not just in Britain, but in many other countries as well. Indeed, if it was safer to have legislatures with two (or even three) chambers,[11] it should be no surprise to see those necessarily more expensive arrangements used in various jurisdictions. In any case, Pennsylvania's short-lived experiment with populism ended with a whimper. Even Findley, who remained a bitter opponent of the Federal Constitution because of what he took to be its usurpation of states' rights, offered few amendments to the 1790 document and eventually signed on to it.

When Pennsylvania moved to bicamerality, that left only Georgia and Vermont with single-chamber legislatures, and by 1830, those two states had given way as well. The Federal Congress, with its sham Lords and Commons, was mirrored everywhere. This continued until 1935, when Nebraska decided to reduce its legislature to a one-chamber body—what it came to call its "Unicameral." This was fine with SCOTUS. When *Reynolds v. Sims* was decided in 1964, Justice Warren made it quite clear that there were no grounds whatever for requiring bicamerality on the state level.[12] But of course the court did not suggest that there is any defect in the two-branch national arrangement either. It is important to note that when Warren made his list of non-electors in the United States (trees, acres, farms, cities, economic interests) he did not mention *states*. Clearly, in the court's view, since the United States has a federal structure, created via a compromise among a group of autonomous polities concerned to retain a measure of their own sovereignty, states *are* to be separately represented. So, what could make more sense on the national level than a partitioned legislature, with one body representing the totality of the people and the other the various individual states? Let the number of chambers desired in Pennsylvania or Nebraska be a mere matter of utility, a good subject for experiment within our "laboratories of democracy." On the national level, the situation seemed different. No case for efficiency or deliberative efficacy that pushes a specific number of legislative branches could be appropriate for the United States as a whole because of the nation's origin as a collection of sovereign states that agreed to participate in the new arrangement only if each one got its equal piece of the senate. Indeed, this matter was so fundamental to the drafters of the Constitution that they made the provision stating it subject to an even more difficult amendment procedure than any other text in the document. A deal is a deal: a state would have to agree to its loss of equal suffrage in the upper house for such a change to take effect.[13]

Perhaps the most eloquent critic of the Senate is a man who served in the House for almost sixty years, the late Representative John Dingell:

> The Great Compromise, as it was called when it was adopted by the Constitution's Framers, required that all states, big and small, have two senators. The idea that Rhode Island needed two U.S. senators to protect itself from being bullied by Massachusetts emerged under a system that governed only 4 million Americans. Today, in a nation of more than 325 million and 37 additional states, not only is that structure antiquated, it's downright dangerous. California has almost 40 million people, while the 20 smallest states have a combined population totaling less than that. Yet because of an 18th-century political deal, those 20 states have 40 senators, while California has just two. These sparsely populated, usually conservative states can block legislation supported by a majority of the American people. . . . The math is even starker when you look at places like Wyoming and Vermont, each of which has fewer people in the entire state (575,000 and 625,000, respectively) than does the Twelfth Congressional District of Michigan . . . whose more than 700,000 residents are now in the hands of my wife, Debbie. . . . [E]ven should a good bill make it through the hyper-partisan House, it will die a quiet death in the Senate because of the disproportionate influence of small states. . . . There is a solution, however, that could gain immediate popular support: Abolish the Senate. At a minimum, combine the two chambers into one, and the problem will be solved. (Dingell 2018)

Of course, my interest here is in what distilled populism requires, not whether a prudent deal was made or how on earth one is to get out of this agreement today—whether well or poorly made. In prior chapters, I have recommended an approach to the election of state-wide representatives that is bipartite, including both (i) AV members who are there to represent *everyone* in their states and (ii) SNTV members to represent groups of people in the states who have congenial interests and want these members to represent them. So, while there is no reason to separate these representatives into separate chambers, one can certainly construe them as voting on behalf of two somewhat different groups of electors.[14]

Let us now leave for a moment the historico-practical considerations of what it would take to change so entrenched a provision in our Constitution because of what is owed to the Founding Fathers from Rhode Island and other small states, and take a quick look at whether it actually would be preferable to have only one legislative branch. As Frances E. Lee notes in her contribution to the *Oxford Handbook of the American Congress*, "Contemporary bicamerality theory is intuitive. It is easy to see how two chambers rather than one can . . . institutionalize additional veto points so as to make legislating more difficult" (Lee, Ch. 12, 5). It is unsurprising that having two chambers dampens lawmaking, and that nearly half of the legislation passed in each chamber never gets through the other one. Some take that expected effect to be a very good thing. William Riker (1992) argues that without support in both chambers for a proposal there can be no real (or "multidimensional") majority in favor of it, and passage of any measure in spite of the opposition of one or more other majority is nothing but tyranny. Miller, Hammond et al. (1996, 83) likewise insist that "Simple majority rule is . . . prone to instability: once any policy proposal is passed, there will usually be a majority of voters who find that they prefer something different." And they add that, "by requiring that a decisive coalition include a majority of each chamber, bicameralism has made it impossible for some policy proposals to be upset by any decisive coalition" (1996, 90).

Again, this is entirely unsurprising. If we have two chambers: one of the representatives of all the voters at t1, another of all such voters at t2, if the distance between t1 and t2 is great enough, there may well be differences in the sentiments of the representatives. But time is not all that may cause differences. Suppose we have three chambers all elected the same day, each with slightly different requirements for suffrage. Say one requires property ownership, one the recent payment of taxes, and one at least three years of residency. We may again have quite different sentiments among the three sets of representatives. As discussed earlier, in the United States, each of the two pairs of senators represent their state as a whole, while in the House the views of each House member in the various states must be aggregated, since each Congressperson was sent by a distinct (perhaps gerrymandered) constituency. Naturally, there will be disagreements between the two chambers. But the multiplication of chambers (why stop even at two or three?) to discover the "real majority" view is an expensive, inefficient, and, extremely conservative way to discover what the people want. The sensible way to do this would be to utilize a correct manner of aggregating popular sentiment *once*, and, with the use of AV, eliminate the power of legislative agenda setters to rig outcomes through the order in which they allow amendments to be offered. If the goal of multi-cameralism is to prevent the passage of impetuous, poorly drafted, or reckless legislation, it is much more reasonable to require additional readings, the use of AV, minimum deliberation times, or even the support of consecutive legislative sessions than to split legislatures into separate chambers.[15] But in any case, the idea that a governmental structure is better precisely to the extent that it is regularly thwarted in its attempts to enact laws is both antithetical to democracy and bound to the timorous doctrine that whatever happens to be the current arrangement must be preferable to any conceivable alternative.

It is worth noting here that the executive veto is also an effective tool on the anti-recklessness front. And it is one that a populist can support so long as the term of the executive is not too prolonged, the supermajority required for override is not too large (3/5 should be enough), and the recall of an executive does not require proof of criminality. If we assume that both the legislature and the executive have been fairly and appropriately elected, only a bare majority of the legislature wants X, and an executive subject to recall, opposes X, it will seem reasonable even to the most democratic among us that X does not become the law of the land. But if a piece of legislation is stopped because two chambers cannot agree, it makes sense to wonder which chamber is the problem. Surely, Representative Dingell was correct to point his finger at the Senate.[16]

TERM LIMITS

On the question of whether the number of terms a representative, executive, or judge ought to be limited I think we may be quite brief. I have suggested two-year terms for SNTV legislators, four to six-year terms for at-large representatives, and twelve-year terms for judges—all renewable, and I see no problem with indefinitely renewable four- or five-year terms for governors and presidents. However, many have complained that incumbents are so difficult to dislodge that it would be a marked improvement if strict limitations were placed on the number of terms one can serve (as has been done with respect to the U.S. presidency). In that way, it is argued, a more Athenian, lot-style democracy might be attained. More and different people would have the opportunity to be involved in the administration of government, and in addition to all of the other merits of this change, there would be educational benefits. For all who serve will come to understand more of what government is all about.

It should be clear that the view of democracy here pushed by the term-limiter is contrary to that espoused in this book. On the naturalized view, the goal should always be to determine what the people actually want and to attempt to memorialize that in legislation and executive action. Restrictions on reelection are thus no more or less than a limitation on democracy. To say that term limits would "make democracy better" is to confuse outcomes one wants with appropriate procedures. I do not deny the danger of incumbency power. It is real and must not be ignored. The appropriate solution to it is not to be found in limiting the number of terms, however, but in improving the administration of elections, mostly via campaign finance reform. At present, sitting members of the U.S. Congress spend much of their terms raising money for their reelection. And, of course, few non-incumbents have the ability to raise money enjoyed by each sitting Congressperson. I don't deny that this money problem could be at least partially addressed simply by prohibiting reelection runs, but I don't see that this indirect method is the best solution—particularly as it may deprive voters of precisely the representation they want most. I will make my suggestions for the reform of campaign finance laws in the next chapter.

JUDICIAL REVIEW OF LEGISLATIVE PROCEDURES

In the previous sections, I have made several suggestions for the revision of governmental structure, and have made my apologies for the scant attention I have given to political feasibility. I hope the reader will allow me to continue to muse in the same vein by supposing that these changes have somehow all been made. Assume that all over the country, "upper chambers" have been eliminated, voting methodology has been changed, constitutionally or statutorily required deliberation procedures have been improved based on the best science, and so on—all, quite miraculously, just as proposed herein.[17] Suppose also, however, that in spite of this highly unlikely apotheosis, various legislative leaders are able to thwart the majority's will by instituting on their own authority such legislative rules as those regarding quorums, the offering of amendments, filibuster, and cloture that clearly allow a minority of (even correctly apportioned) legislative authority to hold up—or kill—bills having majority support. For example, even if having only one chamber would make it more difficult for a legislative leader to hold up a judicial confirmation vote on a candidate nominated by a president, as Senate Majority Leader Mitch McConnell recently did with President Obama's nomination of Judge Merrick Garland, the same sorts of mischief could be practiced. What then? Would all of our structural enhancements be powerless to produce a distilled populism? Would newly magic doctrines akin to "the separation of powers" and the "respect due to coequal branches" again foil any chance that the people get what they want?

One suggested solution to this is that the courts be authorized to enforce specific democratic procedures within legislative chambers; that is, that there be judicial review of legislative processes. One advocate of such review, Ittai Bar-Siman-Tov (2011), has noted an irony in the fact that Jeremey Waldron and others who, in the name of the right of all citizens to get the government they want, have been among the foremost defenders of legislative independence from the courts, while failing to see that legislative indiscretions may themselves imperil democracy.[18] And Bar-Siman-Tov (2010) points out that future elections may be no disincentive to those who will use unscrupulous means to get laws enacted. It may be, for example, that their constituents (or the activists among them) very much want those laws—even if no more widespread majority supports them. Bar-Siman-Tov warns that the absence of oversight by courts (something available in several other countries) actually helps turn "lawmakers into lawbreakers."

Bar-Siman-Tov has a point, but there is more irony here than he seems to see himself, for the overturning of the old (1892 but still standing) cases of *Marshall Field v. Clark* and *United States v. Ballin* would surely, as the justices at that time understood, make the country less, not more, democratic. Both of those cases were brought by interests disgruntled by the passage of the McKinley Tariff Act. In *Field*, the complaint, renewed by a student loan company as recently as 2007[19] was that the two chambers didn't actually pass the same legislation—something that seems to be required by Section 7 of *Article 1* of the Constitution—but the president and legislative leaders conspired to have some similar measure enacted anyhow. In *Ballin* the plaintiff noted that the majority quorum required by Section 5 of *Article 1* was apparently not met in the House, but the Speaker had the bill engrossed anyways. Presumably, Bar-Siman-Tov and others who want to make legislatures transparently utilize legitimate democratic procedures would want cases like *Field* and *Ballin* overturned in the name of the people's right to *real democracy*. But the second-order irony here is that such a move would simply provide another veto point, that is, make it even harder to get legislation passed.

A bona fide solution to the problem of those sorts of legislative shenanigans (a few of which I witnessed myself during my time as a committee staffer on the House side of the Great and General Court of Massachusetts) cannot be found via the sort of legalistic means that advocates of judicial review may have in mind for such problems. First, courts should not be thought to have a better understanding of internal operations or the facts of legislative undertakings than the legislative bodies themselves have. Why think that a court's determination of a legislature's sense of what the people really want is better than that of the legislative leaders and rank-and-file members themselves? This need not be seen as a matter of "respect" or "separation": it is a simple point about paternalism and the avoidance of an inappropriate substitution of a third-party judgment. Second, the result of the lawyerly change sought by these advocates of procedural review could operate in one direction only. All courts would be able to do is strike down laws if they deem that their passage was procedurally incompetent. They would not be empowered to consider as enacted some measure that, perhaps, would likely have passed but for the requirement of a 2/3 majority vote for the bill to move in some committee or the body as a whole. How can such asymmetrical advice from the courts do anything but make the people's will even less likely to prevail?

What is actually needed is not that various precedents involving the "political question doctrine" or the "enrolled bill rule" be overturned. Rather, we must have clear constitutional requirements regarding appropriate legislative procedures, including those that would preclude most supermajority votes regarding matters within legislative purview.[20] This would not keep the courts out entirely. Interested parties—both representatives and their constituents—must have the right to object to a court of competent jurisdiction when these constitutional provisions have been ignored or violated, and non-performance should be seen as a good reason for recall of the officials involved. With such constitutional necessities in place, there would, I think, be little further need for the judiciary to determine what is a "political question" and is thus beyond their purview, or whether the language in some edition of a *House Journal* ought to be preferred to other sources of evidence. The rules adopted by the deliberative bodies empowered to enact our laws would be required to be revised in a manner that comports with the new constitutional requirements. The independence of the judiciary need not depend on a myth of the separation of powers in the United States any more than it does in other countries.[21] It may even be the case that additional constitutional provisions regarding legislative procedures could serve to reinforce independence: if the constitution in question clearly sets forth the requirements of appropriate democratic procedures, there would be less incentive for courts to impose upon legislatures and their constituencies the "better ideas" that they believe they've come up with on their own.

NOTES

1. See, e.g., Gutmann and Thompson (2006), Macedo (1999), and Bohman (1997).
2. I do not agree, however, with her repeated emphasis on deliberation at what seems to me the expense of populism. I take this to be backward, and to follow from her distinction between "a correct policy, on its merits" (p. 131) and what the people want. It is my view that a correct analysis of these matters requires the naturalization of democracy. If one retains the view that there are Platonistic, entirely external standards of "correctness" for what is good for the people of some group, one will not get this issue right.
3. See Habermas (2006).
4. According to Bell (1999), transparency in public debate may help filter out distinctly bad ideas.
5. See, e.g., Ackerman and Fishkin (2005).
6. This quotation along with the Warville and Rush remarks that follow are taken from Rutland (1983), 45.
7. James Wilson, quoted in Seed: 125.
8. It is worth remembering here that the central government that had been created by the Articles of Confederation was run exclusively by the unicameral Continental Congress. It was too weak to be effective, but was extremely democratic in structure.
9. Paine gives as his main example of mischief the Assembly's hostility to the Bank of Pennsylvania.
10. As I write this, in March 2019, the same sorts of discussions are taking place over a second referendum on Brexit. "How can you ignore the voice of the people?" each side complains—and with equal plausibility. Democratic theory cannot give a definite answer to the question of how long a vote is "good for" any more than philosophy can set specific limits on the "specious present." But as with recommendations about the optimal size of legislatures, the results of empirical studies regarding outcomes of deliberative activities of different sizes and lengths may be instructive. E.g., if we come to learn that repeat votes are extremely likely to produce the same results if taken within 6 months in any group containing over 1,000 likely voters, but that is not the case after 18 months, we will then know something relevant about the workings of the general will. The same is true if we know that different sorts or lengths of deliberation are more or less likely to produce changes of heart. Another lesson that may be learned from what is happening in England is that the initiative process is not dependable. While the Brexit vote that took place in 2016 was called a referendum, it was incorrectly so called, at least as that term is used in this work: to designate voter indications of agreement or disagreement with some position a government has previously taken or enacted. Here, the British Parliament had said, roughly, "You tell

us: Stay or Leave?" I have argued that referendums are salutary (though, perhaps, less necessary in parliamentary democracies like the U.K.), but have also suggested that voter initiatives are not. This is not only because there is too much to know for the average voter to make an intelligent choice, but also because there's a good chance that what they'll be voting on will be something incomplete (like "Stay or Leave?"). Worse, the measure might be crafty, biased, ambiguous, befuddling, or simply stupid. Brexit does show the usefulness, when a polity is dealing with matters of fundamental structure or process, of utilizing delayed, iterative polling. That is the reason that legislatures generally require multiple readings, even of the most trivial bills.

11. Smith (1907, Ch. 1) points out that two Scandinavian countries had utilized tetracameral legislatures and that the split into king, lords, and commons was largely accidental.

> Instead of this double check upon the King there might conceivably have been more than two, or there might, as originally was the case, have been only one. Two distinct elements, the secular nobility and the dignitaries of the church, combined to form the House of Lords. The House of Commons was also made up of two distinct constituencies, one urban and the other rural.

12. The idea was that, while states are sovereign and so require separate representation, cities, towns, counties, etc., are not. Thus, there can be no good argument that, on the state level, if one branch of the legislature represents the people, other branches are needed to represent various towns or municipalities.

13. I believe that in a democracy, political rights must always take precedence over considerations of "how we got here": too much weight placed on a country's "glorious history" will make any hope of a worthy democracy forever impossible to realize. As both those who dismissed the Council of Censors in Pennsylvania and those who have second thoughts on Brexit have argued, to the extent that a prior decision is irreversible— even one on how reversions may be accomplished—there is no democracy. Expressions of the people's will cannot be construed as eternally fixed—except on [F] matters.

14. As indicated earlier, equality of all long-term residents must be guaranteed by the electoral system, so apportionment in a distilled, populistic state must reflect population sizes of districts and/or "yea voters." Clearly, however, my proposal is manifestly inconsistent with the SCOTUS's bi-polarity on apportionment, which has involved both acute concern with voter equality in the House and absolute opposition to that principle in the Senate.

15. According to Twombly (2012, 15)

> Nebraskans appear quite satisfied with the performance of their Unicameral. . . . One example of note is that during the 1990s, more than 75% of Nebraska's citizens disagreed with the statement that Nebraska should return to a bicameral legislature. On nearly all other measures, citizens indicated strong support for their unique style of government and even supported the idea of raising the salaries of the Unicameral's members.

16. It could be added here that the abolition of the senate would also allow for the elimination of the office of the vice president, which itself has costs but serves no obvious purpose other than that of breaking ties in the senate. The concern that

something may happen to a president during incumbency—death, impeachment, resignation—is legitimate, but surely it is more democratic to have an independently elected individual, such as the House Speaker, fill in until the next election is scheduled. For nothing prevents a very popular president from choosing a very unpopular vice president. Obviously, the same point may be made regarding the office of lieutenant governor around the country.

17. For a sketch of a proposal according to which the courts police democracy without the need for constitutional amendment, see Ely, *Democracy and Distrust.* I believe that Ely's scheme is just as utopian as my own, however. While creation of distilled populism in the United States would require the passage of very improbable amendments, Ely relies not only on a quite sanguinary understanding of the Constitution in its current state, but also on the existence both of a SCOTUS whose majority sees the document as he does (and as he suggests Justice Warren did), and a Congress that is willing to acquiesce in that democracy enlarging interpretation.

18. See, e.g., Waldron (2006).

19. *OneSimpleLoan v. Sec'y of Education*, 496 F.3d, 197 (cert. denied).

20. As indicated earlier, this prohibition would not extend to votes on veto overrides or other items involving differences of opinion with the executive branch.

21. Bar-Siman-Tov mentions Germany and Israel as two countries where this sort of judicial review is commonplace, yet the judiciary remains independent in essential respects.

Chapter 11

A Stouter, but More Minimalistic Constitution

Other Teachings of Naturalized Democratic Theory

In the preceding chapters I have attempted to make a case for the supremacy, indeed even the exclusivity, of political rights, based on their intimate connection with group autonomy—*self-government*. Having no recourse to that with which "the creator" may have endowed his/her creations, I have not suggested that governmental protection is required by any "natural" or "essential" characteristic of human beings, except to the extent that such protection is somehow necessary for deciphering or endeavoring to obtain what people want. But it will be urged that surely the right to life (or, say, to air, water and food) is necessary for us to decipher or obtain anything! So it is clear that I need to explain more completely what I mean by "political rights," why I think there are no other rights, and why I am less concerned than many other observers have been about the dangers thought to surely follow from the removal of such allegedly God-given protections as the rights to life, to worshiping as one will, to ownership of property, to the bearing of arms, and so on.

To begin, how can my attempt to simultaneously naturalize democratic theory and elevate political rights not be self-contradictory? For if there are political rights that are in some sense fundamental, there must be fundamental rights. And what is naturalistic about *any* commitment to fundamental rights? William Cobbett (1829), who also placed the right to participate in government at the top of the heap, at least conceded that it was founded upon "natural law":

> Our rights in society are numerous; the right of enjoying life and property; the right of exerting our physical and mental powers in an innocent manner; but, the great right of all, and without which there is, in fact, no right, is, the right of

taking a part in the making of the laws by which we are governed. This right is founded in that law of Nature spoken of above; it springs out of the very principle of civil society; for what compact, what agreement, what common assent, can possibly be imagined by which men would give up all the rights of nature, all the free enjoyment of their bodies and their minds, in order to subject themselves to rules and laws, in the making of which they should have nothing to say, and which should be enforced upon them without their assent? The great right, therefore, of every man, the right of rights, is the right of having a share in the making of the laws, to which the good of the whole makes it his duty to submit.

Of course, once we start down the path of accepting any "natural right" there's no end to the number of items we're likely to come up with. John Ireton made this point to the rights-hungry John Lilburne way back in the 1647 Putney Debates:

[B]y that same right of nature (whatever it be) that you pretend, by which you can say, one man hath an equal right with another to the choosing of him that shall govern him—by the same right of nature, he hath the same [equal] right in any goods he sees—meat, drink, clothes—to take and use them for his sustenance. He hath a freedom to the land, [to take] the ground, to exercise it, till it; he hath the [same] freedom to anything that any one doth account himself to have any propriety in. . . . If you do . . . hold up this Law of Nature, I would fain have any man show me their bounds, where you will end, and [why you should not] take away all property.

So, if we cannot do without at least one "natural right," what case can be made for stopping just there?

WHERE DO RIGHTS COME FROM?

Jeremy Bentham is well known for having called the doctrine of natural rights "nonsense upon stilts." He was more than calmly dismissive of claims involving such supposed rights because he thought that the very mention of these chimeras unnecessarily inflames "the selfish and dissocial passions" of individuals who must be stolidly prepared to make sacrifices if their governments are to provide the public goods they desired from them. "What," he asks, "has been the . . . perpetual and palpable object of this declaration of pretended rights? To add as much force as possible to these passions, already but too strong" (Bentham 1796).

We need not share his impatience or disgust. Instead, we may dispassionately ask ourselves such questions as these: "What 'fundamental human rights' did the Sioux have in the U.S. during the 1860s and 1870s?" "What rights did those brought to America from Africa on slave ships have until the Emancipation Proclamation?" "What rights did female spouses have until the enactments of various Married Women's Property Acts?" Shall we say that all these people actually did have (because they were endowed by their Creator with) a basket of natural rights that were unjustly left unprotected? Or should we not rather say that married women had no right to own property or be to be safe from spousal beatings or rape, and that the Sioux and the black slaves had no rights whatever until those guarantees or protections were *won*—on the battlefield, the halls of Congress, or some court of competent jurisdiction? The same questions may be asked today: Is there a right to a third semester abortion? Is there a right of all fetuses to be born? May we marry one of any gender that attracts us? The answers given to these questions seem to vary by region, and are themselves the result of numerous hard-fought battles. Some may say that the lovers, women, or fetuses surely *ought* to have such rights secured to them. But perhaps there are countless others, many as yet unthought of. If we listen to campaign rhetoric we may come to wonder whether there is a "fundamental human right" to the availability of "good jobs at good wages," to decent housing, to health care for all. But what of sexual relations between adults and children, or between human beings and animals of other species? As Ireton pointed out in the seventeenth century, there is no end to the possible "rights" that may be suggested. Could there exist the (perhaps hitherto unnoticed) rights to live in a home of one's own, to assisted suicide, to free potable water, to own and fire bazookas and rocket launchers, to dump one's garbage wherever one wants, to smoke cigars in schools, to walk any shoreline that looks appealing?

Unless it is conceded that there will never be agreement on what these supposedly preexisting rights *are* until the enactment of relevant laws, it seems highly doubtful that specific rights of the sort enumerated actually precede the laws making for their enforcement. Thus, even if rights are "objective," it is quite hard to believe that they are *natural* properties that we may *discover* quite coincidentally at just the moment when we manage to get a law on the books to protect them. It rather seems the case that, if we want to know what rights we have, we need lawbooks to consult. And even if found therein, without the governmental power and will sufficient to enforce them, no asserted "natural law" will be worth much—unless one happens to be "endowed" with enough wealth or other sort of power to enforce the protection of whatever rights one favors.[1]

While I have criticized the "endowment" claim, it is not hard to understand the intuition that there must be something that protects one's ability to at least *seek* any of the specific "rights" mentioned earlier and any number of others.

It seems we must have a general shield such as the one Jefferson called upon to protect "liberty and the pursuit of happiness." It may be noticed that our own naturalized democracy began in much that same place when it exalted liberty and autonomy and claimed their value to be axiomatic. That we cannot really be prevented from wanting whatever we want may underwrite the widespread support for a claimed natural right to "freedom of conscience."[2] And that sentiment is reflected in the priority given by CHOICE to autonomy: no one may dismiss or deny as false or mistaken our choices of approvable items, either on personal or group levels. On those matters our judgments cannot be subject to substitution by those who claim to know better. On the view propounded here, liberty and autonomy are required for any increases in the intrinsic prudential value produced by human activities. And if one wants to express that point by calling human liberty and autonomy "natural rights," so be it. But if they are, they are the only ones. We might even say that freedom and autonomy should not themselves be counted among even the most fundamental of our rights because they actually *explain* them.

After memorializing the generative importance of liberty and autonomy, I used them to elevate the strictly "political rights" which, as necessary to self-government, are the most fundamental of the (nonnatural) "rights." And protecting the political rights may get us others: as correctly understood, these will arise (i.e., be won) only through the power of those in charge. And they *should* arise if and only if the people want them. That is, if these additional, subsidiary "rights" are appropriate in the sense of reflecting what is actually wanted, they (prudentially) should ensue from the accurate determinations of what we want and the faithful attempts by those in power to obtain all and only those items. This is to say that the bare possibility of *winning* rights involves these prerequisites, just as Cobbett points out in the quote earlier. So, while what I call political rights are no more guaranteed by heaven than the right to good jobs at good wages, naturalized democratic theory nevertheless makes them importantly different from other items commonly called rights.[3]

It is easy to see how other generative civil rights that may be thought to be of lesser stature require the "existence" of the more fundamental political rights in order that they may be enacted and produce still others. Therein lies the necessity of equal access to ballots and right to unfettered expression (and access to) the sort of information that is useful to voters. In this way, political rights—both as traditionally enumerated and as I understand them, deserve primacy over all others. And this is in spite of the fact that even they are products of human choices.

Assuming that something like this picture is correct, how do I think such rights differ from those currently set forth in the Bill of Rights? In my view all of the following should be included within the sphere of political rights:

- Each person and each person's choices must be treated with equal respect.
- The people must be free to disseminate as widely as possible plentiful, accurate information relevant both to the individual and joint choices of the people, as well as to their representatives' (if they have them) deliberations and other activities.[4]
- The populace has a right to expect that best-practice deliberative procedures, conducted publicly, will be utilized by their representatives, and that those empowered to bring what has been chosen by voters in fair, frequent elections will faithfully endeavor to do so.

Although these look different from what we are familiar with (and will be further refined later), it might be suggested that they require something like the traditional rights of speech, press, assembly, association, and religion. That is not quite right, however. The political rights in our Constitution, and their supposed derivation from "liberty and the pursuit of happiness," have long been defended on grounds involving "robust exchange in a free marketplace of diverse ideas." And such argument, in turn, has resulted in a largely negative construal of these rights, one that has been endorsed by such thinkers as Mill, Popper, and Hayek, as well as any number of anarchists and libertarians from the right and left. For its part, distilled populism takes the somewhat different position that political activities should be constitutionally protected where and only where fair democracy requires it. In other words, to be ensconced as an [F] principle, a provision must be demonstrated to be intimately connected with our concept of fair, non-paternalistic, individual, and aggregative decision making, since only such principles are essential to freedom and autonomy. And it is evident that the traditional constitutional protections are both too much and too little.

Clearly our own [F] provisions cannot be of quite the same form as, for example, "Congress shall make no law abridging the freedom of speech or assembly." Not only would they need to be more expansive, calling also upon nongovernmental entities, such as private individuals and corporations, to both act and refrain from acting in certain ways; but they would also be more limited, since they would not extend to every sort of speech or assembly. For example, we should not need a high court to declare that a law prohibiting the mischievous yelling of "Fire!" in a crowded theater is permissible. (Of course, if the populace wants such pranks allowed, they should be able to have that as well.) All the traditionally construed rights should be reimagined in the same way. Governments should face only such constraints in doing what their citizens want that are required by authentic democracy. But private actors must also face such constraints. In the area of, for example, allowing or restricting gun ownership or religious practices, so long as they are not inconsistent with any universal democratic principles and are what the relevant electorate wants, they must be allowed or proscribed, just as desired by the electorate. But where actions or constraints *are* required by democracy, constitutional provisions must apply to both public and private entities. The so-called horizontal protections against obstacles to freedom erected by nongovernmental actors are clearly necessary if a polity is to be prevented from descending into such practices as apartheid, employer demands for the forfeiture of (political) speech rights as a condition of employment, or even the return of chattel slavery, since no act of government is required for any of those sorts of institutions to arise.[5] Again, it is not any moral revulsion of these practices that makes their constitutional prohibition obligatory; it is the recognition that they are incompatible with authentic self-government.

Getting the [F] provisions right in our naturalized constitution is no easy task and would likely require careful deliberation by a number of wise drafters, but as a first pass, one might expect provisions resembling the following:

- This polity is and shall always remain a self-governed democracy, a country where, with the few restrictions stated herein, the entire populace can demand by fair plebiscite what they want from their government and have a reasonable expectation that that government will do its utmost to provide all and only what has been demanded.
- Impairments or restrictions of political speech, assembly or association may be imposed only where they are consistent with a recognition of the paramount importance to democracy of activities that foster self-government, such as (i) facilitating access to reliable political information, (ii) making voting easier or fairer, and (iii) creating opportunities to attain political office or interact with governmental officers and agencies.
- No discrimination based on race, creed, gender, orientation, or other such characteristic shall be allowed, and all long-term residents having reached sixteen years of age shall receive an equal vote, have equal access to ballots and candidacy for government offices, and have abundant, reliable, cost-free information relevant to such ballots and offices available to them. Governmental elections shall be frequent throughout this polity and all of its subdivisions.
- Consistent with the principles set forth earlier, within the country as a whole and within each state, approvals by the plurality of those voting on each ballot item shall determine which candidate is to be the chief executive of such jurisdiction, based on the fair and accurate count of such approvals. Exactly one Congressperson shall also be elected in that fashion in each

state. But every significant subdivision of the people shall also have its proportionate say in the administration of government through the election of additional members of Congress, where (i) such subdivisions are mutually exclusive subsets of the populace determined by asking voters whom they would most like to represent them, and (ii) significance is determined solely on the basis of group size. In no state shall the number of significant subdivisions ever drop below three.

- The amount of ultimate authority to make government policy wielded by each representative shall always be a strict function of the total number of voters that have approved of that representative. But individuals chosen to represent either an entire populace or a significant subdivision therein shall each be provided with fair and equal opportunity to speak and equally weighted votes in committees. Deliberation and bargaining among representatives shall always proceed according to the best current science regarding what deliberative procedures are most likely and efficiently to produce concord; provided, however, that such procedures shall require that simultaneous approval votes on all alternatives—including no change to the status quo—must always be used in lieu of successive individual votes on amendments and final votes on enactment.

- As specified elsewhere herein, certain governmental officers shall be subject to recall, certain enacted laws shall be subject to repeal by referendum, and certain judicial decisions shall be subject to reversal.

To note only that these are imperfect would be extremely charitable. Each is fuzzy and the entire group is likely both incomplete in some ways and overbroad in others. Some may be found unworkable. And there is little doubt that they would engender problematic disputes requiring judicial intervention. In a word, their obvious shortcomings make clear that better principles (and more competent drafters) are needed. But they at least make a start, and we need to make a start.

SPEECH, MONEY, AND POLITICAL CAMPAIGNS

Now that we have tried to demarcate a few democratic rights, it is necessary to inquire as to the precise nature and entailments of a couple of them. Campaign finance provides a good example of how agreement on political rights is not sufficient to achieve harmony regarding what a polity should actually *do* to protect democracy. In his thoughtful and illuminating Tanner Lectures of 2014, Robert Post makes a plea for what he calls "discursive democracy," which largely consists in an appreciation for appropriate "communicative chains" between the people and their representatives. Post takes such chains to be appropriate when they are healthy enough to produce confidence that these representatives are really doing their constituents' bidding, rather than concentrating on their own or anybody else's desires. Post is sympathetic to the views of progressives according to which corporate money in elections is to be distrusted, because the goal of democracy is an "unobstructed and undistorted representation of majority will." He believes, however, that the early-twentieth-century progressives never quite grasped discursive democracy, because they were "primarily interested in a democracy organized for action," while Post's own vision concentrates on the creation of a steady back and forth between public opinion and representative behavior, via an extensive modern media. Professor Post is, I think, on the right track here.

The main focus of Post's lectures is the *Citizens United* decision, to which he devotes considerable space and acute analysis. The court was right, he thinks, to have given short shrift to both *Buckley v. Valeo*, which equated campaign money with political speech only on the expenditure side and to *Austin v. Mich. Chamber of Comm.*, which upheld a law limiting corporate donations based on fear of the "corrosive and distorting effects of immense aggregations of wealth . . . that have little or no correlation to the public's support [for various political ideas]." Post agrees with *Buckley* that it is neither proper nor feasible to have a goal of *equal* participation, and he sympathizes with the goal of *Austin* to root out the distorting and possibly corrupting influence of corporate involvement in politics. But, in his view, the *Buckley* distinction between contributions and expenditures is too fragile to depend upon. And while *Austin*

> adopted the plausible view that corporate expenditures are not correlated with the judgment and opinion of actual people . . . [t]here is . . . no "baseline" from which "distortion" can be assessed. . . . The First Amendment would undoubtedly prohibit legislation capping the budgets of feature films to prevent runaway blockbusters from "distorting" public opinion. (Post 2014, 52)

Thus, rather than returning to a First Amendment jurisprudence along the lines of Justice Marshall's *Austin* decision, Post calls for a reinterpretation of the entire point of political speech. It is not that equality must be obtained or distortion or corruption must be prevented, it is that institutions must be established that are "designed to make government continuously responsive to public opinion [so that] the people might come to develop a 'sense of ownership' of 'their' government" (2014, 36).

I generally sympathize with Post's sentiments, but perhaps I join with the old progressives in being "primarily interested in a democracy organized for action," because I find one aspect of his approach oddly passive. He notes with approval the decision (*Red Lion v. FCC*) that declared the "Fairness Doctrine" constitutional, yet neither he, nor any of the four commentaries on his lecture that have been included in its published version stops to consider whether (and to what extent) the obvious damage to fair elections wrought by *Buckley* and *Citizens United*, might be mitigated by the FCC's reinstitution and firm enforcement of something like that Doctrine. Even with the adoption of all the constitutional changes I have proposed, given the importance of speech rights, we could not put the corporate campaign money toothpaste back in the tube, and Post seems to me quite right that any walls envisaged by the *Buckley* Court between expenditures and donations must eventually collapse. I therefore think that the goal should be to address distortions created by corporate (or union, etc.) money that the *Austin* Court sensibly feared by coming up with a feasible campaign finance policy that is consistent with the principles I have set forth earlier.

This goal of getting "big money" out of politics has been elusive for a long time. There are two main approaches to the problem today. The first is public funding of campaigns, according to which candidates who agree can voluntarily limit their fundraising to some relatively small amount per donor in return for the receipt of matching (or greater) public funds.[6] The second is a Constitutional amendment specifically exempting certain types of political expenditures from First Amendment protections so that Congress can pass donation and spending limitations that will not be struck down. There are several well-known objections to the first route. Forgoing large private donations has seemed to candidates in high-visibility races to be as senseless as tossing away one's weapons before engaging in a battle with an unknown assailant. It is also an expensive solution: a great deal of public money would need to be spent on (often wasteful) items that may not really be "informative" at all. Think of all the disposable buttons, bumper stickers, palm cards, and misleading attack propaganda that would have to be funded by taxpayers. Finally, it is difficult to fashion public financing laws in a way that could safely curtail the "speech" (i.e., commercial buys) by "independent" interest groups in the form of "infomercials" or other misrepresentations.

The second route, based on the proposals I have seen, is somewhat better (if much more difficult to accomplish), but it is also likely to be expensive, since it would put the FCC or some other government agency in the position of having to be a watchdog—not only over all the broadcast and cable channels but, presumably, over substantial portions of the internet as well—to ensure that no person or group is advocating for or against some candidate or ballot initiative—or is doing so within allowable financial constraints. As that seems hardly feasible, I would recommend a third approach.

Several SCOTUS decisions[7] have proclaimed that nothing prevents Congress from placing substantial restrictions on non-print media. Unfortunately, not only has the limited-channel environment that produced the Fairness Doctrine changed dramatically since 1949, but the doctrine itself, which required broadcast radio and television stations to (i) provide informative political material and (ii) do it in a balanced way, was never really enforceable and, arguably, had a significantly chilling effect on broadcasters. There was, however, one aspect of broadcast fairness that I think could be resurrected with immense benefit. That is what was called "The Zapple Doctrine." Section 315(a) of the Communications Act of 1934 guarantees candidates for high office that if their opponents receive airtime on a broadcast station, they will be offered equal and equivalent airtime (though subsequent Commission rulings indicated they would have to pay for it). The Zapple doctrine of the FCC (named for Senate Commerce Committee Counsel Nicholas Zapple who sent the Commission a letter urging its adoption) extended equal-time requirements to those doing electioneering other than the candidates themselves. The Zapple requirement died, either in 1987 when the significantly broader Fairness Doctrine was dropped by Reagan's FCC, or in 2014, when that Commission specifically addressed the matter in letters involving two separate cases. I believe, however, that its reintroduction and strict enforcement would not only be legal, but would also be much more sensible and much less expensive than any approach involving public financing.

Of course, the Fairness Doctrine applied only to broadcast stations (not to cable, the internet or print media), and, as indicated earlier, any partial reintroduction—even in broadcast media alone—would be fiercely opposed on First Amendment grounds. Indeed, *Red Lion* specifically indicated that the Fairness Doctrine should be reconsidered if it turned out that it is resulting in the dissemination of *less* information to voters.[8]

Libertarians (and corporation-backers generally) have pointed to the substantial increase in talk radio stations following the demise of the Fairness Doctrine, and warn of the chilling effect of any reinstitution of any part of it anywhere (and, of course, would object violently to any imposition beyond broadcast licensees). The response to this is that, in spite of any marketplace metaphors or Millian proclamations, quantity of speech guarantees neither the quality nor the diversity of it. And if a reintroduction of Zapple results in a reduction in quantity, it would almost certainly produce an increase in quality and diversity. No multiplication of blogs or videos urging that 2 + 2 = 5 can make it more likely to be the case that that equation is true. And 20,000 talk radio stations all saying the same thing isn't even quantity—it's just loudness. No doubt, a requirement to provide equal (and equivalently valued) time to opponent campaigns—and perhaps even equal space in print media with wide circulation—whenever opposing campaigns buy time for commercials or send candidates or their spokespeople to electioneer in their place, would result in increased rates for political advertising (especially if the equal-time responses were required to be free, as I would recommend).

Furthermore, this approach would certainly result in additional expenditures for the FCC, since it is reasonable to expect complaints of non-compliance to be brought before that agency. But the public costs connected with such a procedure would be much less than if the FCC were required to do all the policing on its own (as is required by the Constitutional proposals I have seen). If providing free time for opponents would be a financial burden to any outlet, they might indeed stop including as many stump speeches in their published material as they do now. But the libertarian claim that to see campaign ads or listen to wildly spinning press secretaries without rejoinder is to gain useful information is utterly absurd. The reduction of such material would be an example in which less would actually be more. And again, under this proposal the Zapple doctrine would not extend to any matter of public interest besides the promotion of qualified candidates.[9]

This single change would go a long way toward leveling the electioneering playing field without harming a single talk radio station that is not largely funded by political campaigns or their corporate sponsors, since nothing in the proposal would require any media outlet to run election ads or push specific candidates at all if they don't want to have to provide free equal time to others. Obviously, there is no embedded goal here of "informing the public." Rather, the point is specifically to reduce the effect of large imbalances in the money available for spreading what everyone knows is mostly *dis*information— whether or not such a change would produce a net chilling effect on electioneering speech. The amount of useless noise has grown at an alarming rate over the last generation and any reduction in it would be valuable. The blogs, talk radio, and television shows can continue to push their views without being subjected to any other content regulation—they would simply not be able to take ads or other content from campaigns or campaign proxies without the obligation to provide cost-free response time. I will not attempt to produce the exact parameters of the regulation envisaged here: I'm not sure I could do so, and concede that it might be complicated. The space of social media outlets alone is both vast and diverse. But the goal, as Professor Post's lectures make plain, is too important for us to be daunted by the complexities. Since *Citizens United*, the situation is very dire in the United States.

While I believe the extension of Zapple as set forth earlier would be extremely beneficial, attention must also be paid by populists to the steadily increasing concentration of media ownership as well as the dangers connected with the loss of net neutrality. In these areas too, great gains in the quality and availability of diverse information can be made without the expenditure of large sums of public money. All that is needed is an increased will to prevent oligopolies in this area. Here, there is not even the hint of a reasonable First Amendment claim against moving forward as quickly as possible. If it is thought to be ironic that while I call for the elevation of political rights

I simultaneously press for changes that could conceivably chill political speech, no such complaint can be leveled against advocacy for net neutrality or the wide and diverse ownership of media outlets.

THE ALLEGED DANGERS OF RESTRICTING FUNDAMENTAL RIGHTS TO CHOICE RIGHTS

While there continues to be interest in expanding or contracting constitutional rights (think ERA and NRA), there has perhaps been less thought given to questions involving whether it makes sense for a number of other constitutional provisions to be taking up space in our founding document at all. For example, except for the prohibition of poll taxes, levies that would clearly constrain fair democratic procedures, it seems to me odd to have constitutional provisions involving how and what the Federal government may tax. And while I am happy that no soldiers have been or are likely ever to be quartered in my house, I can imagine situations in which that sort of unpleasantness might be required to be imposed upon me for the preservation of the nation. In general, the U.S. Constitution contains a mish-mash of items, including those that are neither [F] nor [E] propositions. Naturally, most of us want to be secure in our persons and property—not only from encroachments by our government, but from dangers arising from everybody and everything (including loud neighbors and catastrophic weather). As terrible things do happen, some may want to be sure they may have lots of guns to protect them, while others may wish to calm themselves by owning the entire water supply or prohibiting eminent domain.

But *constitutional* protections of life and property seem to me appropriate only where they are necessary to defend fundamental democratic principles, that is, where they follow from axioms of democracy. As previously discussed, McClosky (1949) takes a similar position and was forcefully attacked in Kendall (1950). McClosky had written (in words obviously congenial to the present author) that "[t]he principle of majority rule recognizes no limitations on the power of the majority except those that are essential to the attainment of freely-arrived-at majorities and to the maintenance of political consent and accountability" (1949, 646). Kendall wanted no reader to ignore McCloskey's clear intent to deprive us of the constitutionally protected rights to life, property and freedom of religion, so he ridicules McClosky's populist program (as he likely would my own) with heavy sarcasm:

> On these trivial matters . . . we can trust the majority to delimit itself, and so can leave it free inter alia to set up extermination camps for Jewish children (not Jewish adults, because that would evidently prevent majorities from being

freely-arrived-at by silencing some electors)—and, presumably, to obligate the minority to pay tax-monies with which to defray their expenses. We end up, in short, with a standard that assigns a unique and exclusive value to the preservation of majority rule. (Kendall 1950, 712)

I hope it is obvious by now that singling out any religious or ethnic group for special treatment—even if restricted to their young—would be violative of equal protection/anti-discrimination provisions that I believe populists like McClosky would strenuously defend. Clearly, unequal treatment of the children is also unequal treatment of their parents. But other ominous situations may be hypothesized that do not seem to require any sort of unfair discrimination, and I shall offer a couple myself later.[10]

These quite intuitive sorts of objections should not be given short shrift: we must not ignore the fact that numerous supposed natural rights have seemed to many to take precedence over both democratically determined wishes and reasonably estimated likelihoods of future successful activities. Let me therefore provide two science-fiction scenarios that I believe may further inflame those sharing Kendall's sentiments, but which may also shed some light. One involves a supposed natural right to life, and the other a supposed natural right to procreate and move about as one pleases.[11] I base the first of these on the 1967 *Star Trek* episode "A Taste of Armageddon," while the second involves hypothesizing different facts in the 1927 SCOTUS case, *Buck v. Bell*.

"YOU MUST WAIT IN LINE TO DIE"

In an early episode of *Star Trek* (Hamner and Coon 1967) the *Enterprise*, hoping to sign up a new member for the Federation of Planets, learns that the planet that it is heading for, Eminar Seven, has been fighting a high-casualty but "bloodless" war with a neighboring planet. The "battles" in this war are conducted exclusively by using computer simulations to determine which people would die in an attack. This has been going on for 500 years. Connected computers on each planet calculate the effectiveness of simulated attacks given defense capabilities and notify both adversaries of the results. These outcomes are often very unpleasant. On Eminar Seven about three million people each year walk into "disintegration chambers" in accordance with provisions of their ancient treaty with Vendikar, the nearby planet with which they are at war. These innocents simply do their duty and go uncomplainingly to their death rooms, where they are killed painlessly without collateral damage. Scanners on each world can reveal any cheating, for which the penalty would be resumption of the conventional warfare that would presumably doom each civilization entirely.

The leaders of both worlds are Hobbesians: they believe that all people are, at bottom, savages who can never learn to completely suppress their barbaric impulses. They also agree that a traditional war would destroy everything on both planets, and do so with the utmost pain. It is unsurprising that the swashbuckling Captain Kirk would urge Eminar Seven to violate this treaty. It seems to him much more cruel and "inhuman" (of course, no actual *humans* are involved in this war—in spite of all the participants looking and sounding like 1960s Americans) than continuing with their own quiet conflict. In Kirk's view, it is precisely the noise, the pain and risk of utter obliteration, that makes people do all they can to stay clear of open warfare. The sterility and relative "safety" of Eminar's conflict is exactly what he believes to have caused it to go on for centuries.

This is an interesting story for our purposes, because unlike Kendall's hypothesis involving Jewish babies, the applicable treaty requires no discrimination based on color, gender, religion, ethnic background, sexual orientation, creed, etc. on either planet. There is nothing even to suggest that those who die first will be the old, infirm, or weak. The victims may be in particular (geographical) places where the defenses are calculated via the simulations to be unsuccessful, but there's no reason to believe that it is possible for planetary leaders to tell where such places are in advance so that various disliked, disdained or ostensibly unneeded subgroups might be sent there before the "battle." If there were a right to life that the residents of Eminar and Vendikar believed in, we would expect them to have recourse to something like Lilburne's plea in *An Agreement of the Free Peoples of England* (1649):

> That it shall not be in [the government's] power to make or continue any law for taking away any man's life except for murder or other . . . heinous offences destructive to humane society . . . but shall use their uttermost endeavor to appoint punishments equal to offenses so that men's lives, limbs, liberties, and estates may not be liable to be taken away upon trivial or slight occasions as they have been.[12]

In the fictional interplanetary struggle, one need neither commit some alleged offense against society nor exemplify any claimed personal defect in order to be picked to die. In those worlds it might be said that *no lives matter*.

The *Star Trek* story may sound familiar to those who remember disputes about the appropriateness of the development of a neutron bomb during the administration of President Jimmy Carter. That weapon, like the simulations on Eminar Seven and Vendikar, was said to do its work by enhancing the deadliness (through intensification of the emission of radiation) while reducing the other destructive aspects we associate with bombardment. It is horrible to think about choices of this kind. Which is worse?—more dead or lower chances of continued life and culture? Which is better?—slow, painful deaths among fewer people or higher quantities of quicker expiry? Whether one agrees with Kirk or with the combatants, it is clear that both sides are relying on empirical premises. One side says that unleashed ferocity is more likely to shorten or curtail hostilities, the other that it is more likely to eventually result in complete mutual destruction. My own view is that only psychological and sociological science can settle that dispute. But the value questions (*Which is better, which is worse?*) the people must be allowed to decide by plebiscite. As the Eminarian "solution" (which let us here assume has been and is continued to be approved by the citizenry) involves no impermissible violations of equal protection, it cannot be ruled out because it violates an alleged "natural right to life." In a sense, the planetary solution is no different from many decisions currently made by every country involving war and diplomacy. It is an extreme case, certainly, but it differs in no essential respect from declaring a war or staying out of one. Such decisions should be made by the people, always with an eye to the best science available on deterrence, cooperation, mutual advantage, likely casualties, and the rest. If there is war, there will almost surely be deaths, whether they be in disintegration chambers, on battlefields, or as a result of drone attacks on an apartment complex. What we can learn from this story is that any perceived right to life must actually be less fundamental than the authentic political rights.

"YOU MUST BE STERILIZED"

In *Buck v. Bell,* Justice Holmes famously proclaimed that "Three generations of imbeciles is enough" and affirmed the right to sterilize certain inmates of various Virginia institutions based on the likelihood that any children they have will be mentally deficient, liable to criminality, and a burden on society. He argued first that the sterilization procedure was safe and painless, and that Carrie Buck, the plaintiff, was provided with ample process. Then, he likened the forced cutting of fallopian tubes to compulsory vaccination. Finally, he appealed to a sense of patriotic sacrifice:

> We have seen more than once that the public welfare may call upon the best citizens for their lives. It would be strange if it could not call upon those who already sap the strength of the State for these lesser sacrifices . . . in order to prevent our being swamped with incompetence. It is better for all the world if, instead of waiting to execute degenerate offspring for crime or to let them starve for their imbecility, society can prevent those who are manifestly unfit from continuing their kind.[13]

While *Buck v. Bell* has never been overturned, the "facts" on which the decision was based have been shown to be illusory. In his "Three Generations, No Imbeciles: New Light on *Buck v. Bell*," Paul Lombardo (1985) concludes not only that Ms. Buck was neither insane, idiotic, imbecilic, feeble-minded, nor epileptic (as was required for compulsory sterilization by the Virginia statute), but that her mother and daughter also had no such "defects." Carrie was, in his view, simply a victim of a eugenics obsession not much different from the one that played its part in Hitler's Holocaust. The procedure was, Lombardo tells us, "a landmark in the endorsement of intrusive medical procedures as tools to be used for state ends" (1985, 33). In his words, "*Buck* does not merely represent the popular triumph of eugenical theory, but also the success of a small group of professionals who were able to use the specious 'scientific' tenets of eugenics to legitimate their private prejudices."

Lombardo is surely right about this. The "facts" in this case were nearly all "fake" and the results horrific. Yet, as indicated, the decision has never been overturned. Let us therefore consider a science-fiction alternative to see what, under our proposed view of rights, a *real* societal danger might allow. The situation here will be somewhat different from "Armageddon," where there was no distinguishing characteristic used to determine which citizens must be put to death. The treaty there simply required putting all the names in a computer so it could spit out the "suicide victims" based on where they happen to be at a particular moment. No weight was given to any individual characteristics. This case is different. We will hypothesize for our new scenario the (scientifically absurd) existence of a heritable, widespread, and highly communicable disease (call it "Tribbies Syndrome") that, once contracted, always causes a painful death that takes about six months in the case of newborns entering the world with it and about one year for anyone who catches it from them. Those whose babies will almost certainly contract Tribbies need not themselves have the disease, and they cannot catch it from their own children, although they can spread it from their children to others. The spread of Tribbies from person to person seems to be airborne, but no bacterium or virus has been found, and nothing but quarantine has yet been discovered that can ensure the safety of anyone who goes near a Tribbies sufferer or their parents (except the parents themselves, who never get it from their own children). Let us suppose finally, that there is a highly accurate test that can be performed on women and men of childbearing age to determine whether their offspring will have Tribbies. A positive result on this test for either parent is sufficient to guarantee that his or her baby will be born with the disease.

Let us now ask whether, in such an environment, it would be acceptable to sterilize those whose children will have Tribbies, and whether we could, in good conscience, allow quarantining of the sick babies for their few months of life and of their parents forever. In this scenario, the Kendall-style critic cannot be put off with arguments either about equal protection (which is clearly violated in the Jewish children example) or factual errors (as occurred in the procedure leading to *Buck*). Here, it is not *all* but only *certain* lives with bona fide characteristics that are made not to matter, and, by hypothesis, it is no cultish eugenics but rather the best (albeit imaginary) pathology and epidemiology that is to be relied on. We have scientific confirmation of a relevant distinction that is of the utmost importance to every human being on the planet.

It cannot be denied that some lives will be diminished if the government acts in the proposed ways. Some adults will never get to enjoy the wonders of parenthood if they are forcibly sterilized; some babies and their parents will have their freedom of movement strictly curtailed. The CHOICE standard instructs us to consider what course of action will be conducive to the largest future quantity of successful choices. If Tribbies is as virulent as our story hypothesizes, failing to constrain the pursuit of happiness of certain adults and children could result in the extinction of humans via pandemic. Perhaps again some natural rights enthusiasts or highly religious individuals (or Kirkian swashbucklers) will say that, even in the face of imminent extinction, the right to the pursuit of happiness in the face of Tribbies absolutely precludes anyone's quarantine or sterilization. In my own view, the empathy we feel for the harmed innocents does not make the undeniable damage either gratuitous or cruel. As Holmes suggested, equal treatment must have limits. But I don't believe that where these are found should be up to me or even Holmes. I think the demos must have its way on such matters. It is better science, not the consulting of Platonic verities or the enumeration of alleged natural rights that is needed to handle this crisis. In the meantime, the people must be allowed to choose which awful horn of the dilemma to accept.

Before moving on to a pressing non-hypothetical issue, I want to consider Amy Gutmann's worry about how one can handle flag-burning in a populist democracy that countenances all and only purely political rights as fundamental.[14] In her example, Gutmann (1993) distinguishes the publication of pornography, something she takes to be clearly nonpolitical, with flag-burning, an activity which seems to her to be essentially tinged with political intent and so, in her view, not subject to limitation by the populist. Several of her claims are not obvious to me, however. Perhaps a political party or movement has arisen that, because of its celebration of non-reproductive sex, depends on easy access to pornography. Or, again, perhaps there has come to be a raft of flag-burning strictly because of some aesthetic thrill that the activity has been found to engender, and political associations with "Old Glory" have all died out. It may sometimes be quite hard to determine precisely what speech is political. But if, for example, a society seems to want to be able to restrict the burning of flags that emit pollutants for environmental reasons, they should have a way of being sure precisely what restriction is actually wanted.[15] Such questions will no doubt be subject to dispute, and their final resolution may require judicial intervention. But when some activity is determined to be political, it may be restricted only if doing so will prevent larger losses of democratic rights. And when an activity is not strictly political, it must be open to the populace to regulate it in any manner it chooses.

CHOICE SHOULD NOT BE EXPECTED TO PRODUCE CONCORD

I must admit that there are creditable objections to my use of science-fiction examples earlier. First, both scenarios seem particularly extreme. Since one involves the complete destruction of a planet and the other the possibility of genocide, there is reason to suppose that they may be limiting cases only. We are likely all familiar with arguments including such challenges as "Would you even provide due process to a mad man with a machine gun?" First, the fact that we might want to restrict protection of apparent rights in some extreme cases may not constitute a plausible reason for denying that those rights exist at all. Second, it will likely be urged that I have again given too short shrift to emotional intensities. When we exercise our empathy, really put ourselves in the shoes of Ms. Buck or those asked to sacrifice their very lives for some abstract greater good, if we do not come to feel we have made a terrible mistake by calling for bloodless deaths, sterilizations, or quarantines, it will seem to some that we are little better than unfeeling demons. In this respect, CHOICE, for all of its claimed sophistication, will be accused of simply rehearsing Bentham. After all, it seems subject to many of the same criticisms long brought against utilitarian sentiments regarding compulsory organ donations, lifeboat alternatives, and trolley-track nudges. Based on feelings of righteous indignation and disgust, it may simply be concluded that the position I am advocating is neither more nor less than monstrous.

I think it will be helpful to try to reply to these objections in connection with the real-world controversy of abortion rights. Perhaps there is no more intense locus for rights-talk in the United States today than that surrounding whether a woman may terminate a pregnancy without interference. The philosophical discussion of this matter has largely focused on two areas: first, the alleged obligations of mothers to keep something else alive, especially when their own life or liberty is at stake (or a perceived right of theirs has been previously violated), and second, the supposed natural right to life which, according to some, inheres in prenates either at conception or at some later point prior to birth. CHOICE approaches from a somewhat different angle, although it may seem familiar because it shares some features with more traditional consequentialist tactics. According to CHOICE, what matters most are the counts and probability estimates, given various environments, of successful choices of mothers, their possible future babies, and other members of the community. In that light, it seems that certain societal conditions will result in the sanctioning of more births while other environs will call for fewer. Estimates of the counts of possible future desires connected with these conditions will also vary—each (discounted) future possible desire coming with its own probability of being satisfied. Societies may be richer or poorer, and potential for adoption higher or lower, depending on legal requirements, religious proscriptions, the amount of interest, and so on. We might expect that in an impoverished community where abortions are not available and adoptions are rare, the likelihood of satisfactions of the prospective desires of future children whose mothers don't want them would be quite low. On the CHOICE theory, these and other variables would affect whether or not abortions should (prudentially) be easily available, indeed whether pregnancies and births should be encouraged or discouraged generally. Perhaps, where impoverishment is severe and the birth rate is high, all the lives will be quite short and unfulfilled, births or no births, while in affluent societies where many families want to adopt, it may only be the unwilling mothers whose lives would be negatively affected by having to bring their pregnancies to term. Thus, CHOICE calculations may not only suggest more or fewer abortions, but more or fewer children, generally. And such suggestions could inform policies regarding the availability of fertility treatments as well as of abortions.

Again, CHOICE theorists differ from traditional utilitarians and orthodox desire-satisfaction theorists alike by disdaining both estimates of intensity and preference orderings, and by taking autonomy rather than pleasure to be fundamental. The idea that either a fetus's desire to live (should such desires actually exist) or a woman's desire for "bodily integrity" have measurable, comparable intensities would be entirely abandoned by CHOICE practitioners, if not by other theorists. But there is no doubt that the dispute over abortion rights is unlikely to be resolved by *any* consequentialist calculations—no matter their type or how carefully they are performed.

While it would be wonderful indeed if some political theory could magically overcome this controversy in a single stroke, I hope it will be unsurprising to discover that CHOICE cannot do so any better than its predecessors. On the contrary, it is much more likely that those on both sides of the abortion debate would use any intervention of CHOICE in this arena as an additional reason to press the objections to that theory that we have already heard: (1) it is exceedingly difficult (if not utterly impossible) to calculate and implement; (2) it is monstrous because it ignores both morality and how much more important some choices are to some than to others; and (3) even if we accept the CHOICE theory of what makes a society better off, nothing requires the electorate to vote in ways that will maximize—or even increase—ultimate net prudential value. Let me take these up in turn.

I think (1) will have to be conceded. CHOICE provides a theory of what is best for people's lives, and takes the position (roughly) that what is best for a society will be that which is best for most of the people in it. But it provides no assurances that its prescriptions will be easy to discern or that there will be widespread agreement on either (i) the prudentially best states of affairs now or in the future, or (ii) the appropriate methods to obtain any sought-after conditions. Such differences of opinion are inevitable. But at least this theory allows us to dispense with pointless contests of intrinsic importance between a prenate's "call to life" and a woman's desire to have no interference with what she does with her body. A policy based on CHOICE would attempt to quantify the difference between the *actual* autonomy of an adult woman (with her *actual* desires) and the *mere potentiality* of the autonomy and future successes of the prenate. And such discounting of future (possible) choices may provide an argument for abortion rights advocates. But it would never be dispositive evidence, since, besides including controversial calculations, the undiscounted choices of the pregnant women seeking abortions might be swamped even by discounted potential desires.[16] So, vehement arguments— even gridlock—would as likely ensue under CHOICE as under any competing theory. Given populism, these would be settled by vote. But why should there be no chance of near gridlock where there are strong differences of opinion among lots of people? It seems to me at any rate, that where there are divisive, deeply held opinions, "solutions" ought to be viewed with suspicion.

The second objection requires repetition of the point (and it will not be the last time) that prudential values are not moral values. Many believe the latter are more important than what does or does not make one or more persons *better off*. While I have made a case for the (human-made) objectivity of prudential values, I have been quite willing to admit that I have no particular insight into moral values: certainly nothing worth sharing. Furthermore, in spite of CHOICE's apparent wildness in calling for probability assessments of what must seem no more than misty potentialities, it does not make any simple quantification of the "importance of a life" and attempt to contrast that with anybody else's autonomy. In any case, as I have said, I do not insist that moral intuitions must be ignored or that they may not even be required to take precedence over prudential valuations. If one takes the view, either on the personal level, the group level, or both, that, where there is a clear conflict, morality *simply must* be given priority over what will make the life of a person or a society better off, I have no contrary argument to make, and the parties to this argument may continue to fight about what is "right." I insist only that there be an acknowledgement of this prioritizing of morality over the goal of better (off) lives and societies. And I think it is important to note that there is often considerable resistance to any such public concession. It seems to me quite rare when those ostensibly pushing for "the high road" will admit that their proposals may make more people worse off, not just at present, but over the long term.

Perhaps there are proponents of either "the right to choose" or "the right to life" who have no problem acknowledging that standing with them on moral grounds could make their societies worse off. Such advocates may be quite content to make judgments regarding what constitutes justice or gratuitous cruelty, and, unlike myself, may harbor few doubts regarding the moral implications of the relevant activities. They may simply see any governmental interference with a woman's autonomy or its non-interference with the possible destruction of a living prenate as obviously and impermissibly wicked behavior. I have nothing to say that is likely to change their minds.

On the other hand, those who join me in finding moral issues murky at best may be more sympathetic to the idea of leaving matters at the level of prudential values. This problem of integrating "positive law" (what the government commands) with "positive morality" (what we ought to do independently of laws) has dogged many observers, including that most melancholy and socially awkward of political philosophers, John Austin. He believed that his version of rule utilitarianism was the only thing we could be certain to have derived from God's moral code, since a perfectly benevolent being should be expected to care most about making the most people happy. But Austin (1869, Vol. I, 115–116) knew it was reasonable to think that others would disagree with him.

> If utility be our only index to the tacit commands of the Deity, it is idle to object to its imperfections. We must make the most of it. If we were endowed with a moral sense, or with a common sense, or with a practical reason, we scarcely should construe his commands by the principle of general utility. If our souls were furnished out with innate practical principles . . . man would be gifted with a peculiar organ for acquiring a knowledge of his duties. The duties imposed by the Deity would be subjects of immediate consciousness, and completely exempted from the jurisdiction of observation and induction. . . . But, if we are not gifted with that peculiar organ . . . [w]e must gather our duties as we can, from the tendencies of human actions; or remain, at our own peril, in ignorance of our duties. We must pick our scabrous way with the help of a glimmering light, or wander in profound darkness.

Perhaps I ought to be even more troubled than Austin, for I am no more sanguine about our ability to derive morality from utility than I am in thinking that we can reach what is right through any "moral sense." But if there is to be an ineliminable insistence that morality take precedence over prudence, so be it. Populist principles and election results will simply have to take their seat below the high table of ethics. At least when the arguments have somehow been settled over what is "obligatory" or "impermissible," in the area of abortion and prenate rights, we can proceed to arguments that take their (nonethical) positions on the desirability of access to abortions as functions of equally weighted choices, not only of mothers and prenates (whenever the latter can make them—a question for scientists), but also on estimates of the probability-weighted occurrences of otherwise equally weighted approvals expected to issue from newborns, their parents, possible adopters, and all the other "villagers" that it may take to provide for children whose mothers might have preferred to have abortions. And if there is no agreement, we can proceed to the voting booth.

The point of objection (3) is to press that if successes cannot be guaranteed even to those having perfect empirical knowledge reflecting both an infinitude of information and a perfect use of scientific method, it is highly unlikely that average voters will happen to match maximally advantageous items with their own approvals. But consider the following:

• X is a successful choice.
• X will be more or less productive of net prudential value than Y over the long term.

While the second bulleted item is a matter involving scientific assessment, the first is—and can only be—determined by what people approve of. Obviously, a large majority of people may choose X over Y even though a choice of Y would have been more productive of net prudential value. But while this might be said to make X an "incorrect" choice, it does not follow that choosing Y would have been a successful pick. CHOICE requires that both of its two conditions be satisfied for a choice to be intrinsically valuable: the successful getting *and* the net gain over the long term. Neither one alone can make a choice a good one.

Naturalizing democracy makes the matter of abortion rights a fitting subject for determination by "the general will," the vote. Does it follow from this sort of "solution" that each state should be able do what it wants with respect to these matters? That is, does the populist thus suggest that a pregnant woman seeking a legal abortion may well have to travel a thousand miles get to state that allows them? Not necessarily: there is nothing in the theory that prohibits a Federal law from legalizing (or prohibiting) these procedures everywhere.[17] While neither an embryo's right to life nor a woman's right to choose is either an [E] or an [F] proposition and should therefore not be found in any nation's Constitution, no prohibition of the national (statutory) treatment of the issue ought to be found there either. Just as our congressional representatives may impose a national speed limit, they may allow (or prohibit) abortions throughout the land or in certain areas only. Whether the determinations are local or national should be largely based on efficiency and may be handled statutorily, but a constitution could also generally designate geographical divisions for specific purposes via [E] provisions. However handled, the deep-rooted nature of such issues as abortion/prenate rights should make obvious the pressing need for inclusion into our Constitution provisions making for all of these: referendum, reversal, recall, unicamerality, reform of campaign finance, and authorization of the judicial review of legislative procedures. At present, both sides of the abortion issue can only look to the courts for support. That is not how democracy should work.

NOTES

1. This seems particularly clear with respect to freedom of religion, as anyone who has followed legal disputes in that area will know. There have long been restrictions applied to purported "religious freedoms," say to the deprivation of children's necessary medical care based on the belief that as God is perfectly good, pain and illnesses must be illusory. See, e.g., *Reynolds v. U.S.* (1878), *Sherbert v Verner* (1963), and *Employment Division v Smith* (1990).

2. This precedence may explain Spinoza's remark in his *Tractatus Theologico-Politicus* (1670) that "Tyranny is most violent where individual beliefs, which are an inalienable right, are regarded as criminal."

3. We have seen that they are not exactly coextensive with what are traditionally characterized as political rights (speech, press, assembly, and association) either. For example, equal protection/treatment must be included, as well as whatever one might call that which would have prevented the sort of partisan gerrymandering SCOTUS recently allowed in *Rucho v. Common Cause.* Other differences will be discussed later.

4. One might wish to add that the dissemination of relevant misinformation as truth should be restricted to the extent consistent with meeting the goals of worthy democracy, but, if a restriction of that type is feasible without endangering political rights, it seems it must be a matter for statutory rather than constitutional law. For obvious reasons, it would be a quite difficult provision to draft without creating more harm than good.

5. For an overview of why and how the spectrum of constitutional rights should be broadened to include horizontal rights, see Andras and Uitz (2005) and Gardbaum (2006).

6. At least one municipality (Seattle) has even eliminated all requirements for initial private donations by simply giving several $25 vouchers to every voter that may be distributed to candidates at will.

7. Most notably, *Red Lion Broadcasting Co., Inc. v. FCC*, 395 U.S. 367 (1969).

8. I note that such attacks generally depend on an entirely negative interpretation of free speech rights, an interpretation which is itself based on the theory that an unregulated "marketplace of ideas" is uniquely efficacious in the hunt for truth.

9. As I have proposed earlier the desirability of having most elections be for individuals rather than for initiative petitions, I would restrict the applicability of Zapple to instances of statements of support for candidacies by qualified candidates,

their staff, or their supporters during campaign seasons. The outlets could continue to spend the rest of their time saying or printing whatever they want on any matter with no equal-time consequences and, during off-seasons, could engage in unlimited electioneering as well.

10. To Kendall's concern that a limitation of rights to the purely political is dangerous to life and property, we may add Amy Gutmann's warning that it may be productive of opacity. She has suggested (1993, 131–132) that one who takes political rights to be fundamental will likely see no reason to allow pornography but will be faced with a democratic paradox when attempting to determine what to do about flag-burning. I will discuss this concern later.

11. I do not wish to spend too much time here on property rights, partly because the numerous well-known limitations and aberrations provided by centuries of common and statutory law make such an examination seem unnecessary. However, I should say something about the fear of wholesale "expropriation" often associated with radical populism. In his savage attacks on "bourgeois parliamentarism" and "pure democracy," V. I. Lenin (1918) made quite clear that his ultimate goal was not getting the people of Russia precisely what they want, but rather destroying capitalism and ending forever what he took to be the obvious exploitation of the working class. While no authentic democrat can agree with the substitution of any particular Marx/Engels aspiration for the accurately determined wants of the entire relevant populace, it is also crucial that real democracy not be considered inconsistent with the *possible* attainment of Leninist ends. For this reason alone, no property rights can be baked into an authentically democratic constitution. Consideration of Marxist goals (whether we agree with them or not) also makes clear that electioneering cannot be allowed to be dominated by financial or corporate interests. You and I (and the stockholders of IBM) may fear there will be egregious assaults on "what is justly owned" because charismatic Bolshevist leaders insist, e.g., that working class assemblies must be allowed to take place in the "best mansions and manorhouses," but no authentic democracy can create lawful prohibitions based solely on what you or I (or even an entire economic class) happen to fear.

12. I have updated Lilburne's spelling and grammar.

13. *Buck v. Bell*, 274 U.S. 200 (1927).

14. I write "purely political" here because the most narrowly specified political rights entail a number of subsidiary principles, like those involving equal protection, due process, habeas corpus, criminal procedure, bails, warrants, etc. If, for example, one is to have a fair chance of attaining an elective office, one cannot lawfully be subject to discrimination because of race, orientation, gender, etc., or face the danger of being carted away by police in the middle of the night without due process of law.

15. That difficulty is one of the main reasons why it is such an arduous business to correctly put the [F] provisions I have tentatively set forth earlier.

16. CHOICE, an ERA friendly theory, makes no distinction between the desires of adult women and those of adult males. But, in spite of rejecting any such equality for prenates of either sex, both by denying them voting rights and by the discounting (via probability weighting) of any possible future successes, distilled democracy cannot decisively tip the scale toward a women's right to choose for the reasons mentioned earlier.

17. I am grateful to Carol Calliotte for helpful comments on this matter.

Chapter 12

Last Words on Distilled Populism

Objections and Replies

It is no doubt oxymoronic (if not terribly unusual) to brag about one's humility. And the critics of distilled populism may scoff at my modesty claims since they will likely consider the position's modesty to be a good reason to condemn it. To see what I mean, consider the work of two men who are perhaps the deans of twentieth-century Anglophone political philosophy and democratic theory, respectively: John Rawls and Robert Dahl. Rawls's work might be considered a precursor of naturalized democratic theory in that it also calls for a replacement of the grasping of alleged Platonic truths about well-being with a procedure that indicates how and why humans can create the principles that support just societies.[1] Dahl's advocacy of what he called "polyarchy" likewise eschews Platonism and any calls for guardianship that may be supposed to follow from it.[2] (It may also be noted that Dahl's 2015 list of six criteria[3] for "large-scale democracies" and for polyarchies in Dahl 1989 is quite similar to any list that I would give in answer to the question of what is required of "worthy democracies.") However, like the works of Rawls, Dahl's books and articles are replete with discussions of justice, rightness, goodness, decency, and fairness. The present work provides a stark contrast by either pleading ignorance of those spheres or avoiding them entirely. That is a form of "modesty" that it is difficult to brag about. This difference in outlook is likely at least in part a function of the fact that neither Rawls nor Dahl was careful about demarcation lines between ethical and prudential valuations—between what is (ethically) better and what makes one better *off*.[4] But it is unlikely that either philosopher would have relied on that distinction to do much work in their theories in any case. Surely, if Rawls were to have been pressed to tell us whether it was moral or prudential values that are to be determined "behind the veil of ignorance," he'd have unhesitatingly responded, "Both." In spite of the fact that I believe my attempt to justify democratic principles provides something that eluded Dahl throughout his long and illustrious career, and that would only have been of tangential interest to Rawls, there is also a clear sense in which I fail even to attempt to understand what not only Rawls and Dahl, but countless others of less stature have at least made credible runs at—the nature of justice. This may seem unforgivable, because, since the *Republic* at least a cursory discussion of justice has seemed required of any comprehensive work either in political philosophy or democratic theory. In any case, my reluctance to engage in that matter here is unlikely to be considered a virtue by many observers: it will rather be seen as a clear mark of incompleteness. I have but two meager responses to this. First, as the concept of justice seems to me largely incoherent, it is my view that any analysis of it is bound to be either itself incoherent or wrong. Second, I rely on the plea that one ought not to be expected to do more than one can.

IS "MODEST" REALLY JUST A CHARITABLE TRANSLATION OF "HEARTLESS"?

It would be difficult to deny that the sort of modesty claimed for distilled populism is consistent with dastardly consequences. Any position that, like mine, compares societies solely based upon which residents have the most (equally ranked) successes must seem unsympathetic to those who are not well off. For, by the lights of our "maximinless" theory, it seems like we are permitted to rearrange existing goods by accumulating various greatly enjoyed possessions of the 10,000 most impoverished people and divvying them up among any five really rich people, so long as the recipients get a fleeting smile's worth of satisfaction from each of their newly obtained items. While traditional act-utilitarianism—with all of its own apparent blindness to the requirements of justice—recognizes marginal decreases in the value of obtaining additional goods once a certain level of satiety has been reached, CHOICE doesn't even seem to manage *that* basic insight, since it deems every success, no matter how paltry, to be equal to every other success. And if preference-based systems have foundered on the shoals of Arrow's Impossibility Theorem and Sen's Lewd/Prude Paradox, at least such systems have attempted (and continue to attempt) to remedy these defects in ways that take justice, minimal well-being, and non-maleficence seriously. Have I simply forgotten that human beings are known sometimes to derive pleasure from hurting others? As already conceded, if we are looking for ways to distinguish either individuals or polities on the basis of ethics or comparative justice, CHOICE cannot help. Given such explicit limitations, it would be surprising if there were no complaints to the effect that there is no point whatever to a theory *that* modest.

It should be clear, however, that unless one can really succeed in one's own attempt to naturalize moral values, calling CHOICE fatally incomplete because of its amorality requires dependence on an "external" criterion for goodness. In other words, where no "outside" ethical verities are appealed to, moralistic criticism must rely on a successful reduction of ethical values to natural items. Just as CHOICE offers a restatement of prudential values in terms of successful choices, any alternative reduction of ethics must be able to restate all supposed moral truths in its own naturalist language.

I do not mean to suggest here that neither Platonistic arguments nor any attempt to derive ethical conclusions can possibly be successful—whether the latter rely on aggregations of pleasure, considered judgments made behind a "veil of ignorance," what regular people ordinarily say about moral matters, or any other arguably amoral constituents. Although such reductions have been and are bound to remain controversial, perhaps one or more of them is correct. It may well be that good public policy determinations in the face of progress and poverty require the admixture of calculations of prudential goods with moral truths regarding their equitable distribution. Such determinations may even call for estimates of our responsibility to strangers in strange lands suffering from Ebola. I do not want to suggest either that these ethical considerations cannot be folded into (or made separately from) CHOICE estimations that are calculated by some polity, or that the determination of obligations in these areas is not of the highest importance. I claim only that a modest theory of democracy and social goods may be devised that leaves the ethical elements of public policy to moralists, theologians, and philosophers (who no doubt will resolve them any minute).[5] Surely separation of these matters is possible, and the failure to distinguish them will only import age-old perplexities regarding justice, goodness, and the supererogatory into what at least *might* otherwise be a bit easier (though still no day at the beach). I will here suggest (perhaps contentiously) that treating considerations of equity or distinctions between what is obligatory and what is beyond the call of duty as if they were additional items that expert calculations may either include or churn out seems to me a fool's errand. But again, although I personally take such endeavors to be hopeless quests, I do not say that they cannot or ought not to be undertaken by those with talents greater than my own. My point here is only that they *need not* be an element of every species of political theory.[6] Let those who can provide plausible moral theories do so, and if they can successfully integrate them into democratic practices, so much the better. But let us not throw out a theory plausibly based on prudential value only because someone has shouted "Evil!" at us. Let us rather note that, whether consistent with our moral intuitions or not, nonempirical principles, including my own democratic axioms of equality and autonomy, will, in the end, require the assent of the people or be largely ignored. And while my axioms exalt democracy, it seems likely that moral doctrines can only constrict it. Thus, where there is no consensus (and there surely is none in the area of ethical principles), it may be better to let the people decide than to rely on either the wisdom of sages or the markings on golden tablets.

A LIBERTARIAN CRITIQUE OF DEMOCRACY

Libertarian writers have had an uncomfortable relationship with democracy. Obviously, anti-government anarchists like Albert Nock (and, perhaps, Murray Rothbard)[7] have had little truck with it at all, but the attitude has been somewhat different among those who faced Hitlerism or Stalinism at first hand. Ludwig von Mises had no particular faith that democracy would produce the best leaders,[8] but the fact that Russian Marxists hated it was almost enough for that libertarian champion to give it his wholehearted endorsement. "Democracy is self-government of the people; it is autonomy," he wrote. And, in his view, democracy is peace-producing: the actions of the state are unlikely to be peacefully coordinated with the desires of the people without it. But there is no need either for direct democracy or for a randomly picked ordinary citizen to have any role in administration:

> To achieve the ends for which democratic institutions strive it is only necessary that legislation and administration shall be guided according to the will of the popular majority. . . . The essence of democracy is not that everyone makes and administers laws but that lawgivers and rulers should be dependent on the people's will in such a way that they may be peaceably changed if conflict occurs. (1922, 63)

F. A. Hayek, another libertarian hero, took a similar tack when he wrote, in *The Constitution of Liberty*, that conservatives were wrong to attack democracy rather than big government.

> [I]t is not democracy but unlimited government that is objectionable. . . . I can have no sympathy with the anti-democratic strain of conservatism. It is not who governs but what government is entitled to do that seems to me the essential problem. (1960, 348)

Hayek (1944) had made a similar point in *The Road to Serfdom* when he applauded Tocqueville for understanding that, because democracy is essentially individualistic, it is irrevocably opposed to socialism. I don't mean to suggest that either Mises or Hayek would be any more sympathetic to the populism espoused in this book than I am to the government limitations proposed in theirs. The only "democracies" they could support were republics that would be even more limited than Madisonian ones. But neither man was opposed to the very idea of majority rule.

The most popular libertarianism of our own day is somewhat more hostile. In his lucid and engaging book, *Against Democracy*, contemporary libertarian Jason Brennan writes,

> In modern democracies, rather than having a one-headed incompetent king, we have a many-headed incompetent king. In a democracy, the incompetent, irresponsible ruler isn't some bearded fellow in a castle but rather almost everyone else I see. . . . Few voters consciously think, "I really hope this politician will hurt others." There's an important sense, however, in which most politically active citizens do desire to harm or impose unjustified risk of harm on their fellow citizens. (2016, 243)

Brennan makes his objections to the "equal vote" aspect of democracy from a standpoint that he denies requires any libertarian premises. I myself think that much of his work, both in that book and elsewhere, can appropriately be called a libertarian critique of populism. It cannot be denied, however, that his view seems somewhat friendlier to paternalism than to those positions that exalt the individual autonomy of each citizen—something one might expect libertarians to do. In any case, he uniformly pushes the sentiment that since stupid ideas can hurt us, we should do whatever we can to keep stupid people from having any power over us.

Brennan's argument in *Against Democracy* is simple, forcefully made, and intuitively compelling. I think it can be fairly summarized this way:

1. Citizens don't have any basic right to vote or run for office (as he believes they do to freedom of speech, religion and association). And there is nothing intrinsically good about democratic methods of distributing power.
2. While individuals should be allowed to make bad, imprudent or irrational decisions that only harm themselves, they should not be allowed to make bad, imprudent or irrational decisions that make the lives of those around them worse off.
3. Thus, citizens should be entitled to vote generally and to equal voting in particular only if such entitlement(s) (and their effect on government) are unlikely to make the lives of the citizens worse off than other sorts of procedure.
4. At least some political questions have *right* or *true* answers that, if found, will make the lives of citizens better off, and if missed, will make the lives of the citizens worse off.

5. Thus, citizens should be entitled to equal votes only if this entitlement is truth-tracking, that is, likely produce right or true answers to those political questions that must be answered.
6. A truth-tracking procedure for public policy requires knowledge, absence of bias, and virtue or consideration for others.
7. Considerable empirical research demonstrates that the average citizen is neither sufficiently knowledgeable, sufficiently impartial, nor sufficiently virtuous to make votes that are truth-tracking.
8. Thus, the average citizen should not be given an equal vote.

Brennan has several suggestions regarding how to incorporate this conclusion into (what's left of) a democracy that does not require equal votes. For example, there might be tests one needs to pass in order to be allowed to vote, or those who are more knowledgeable and can demonstrate their impartiality might be given extra votes.

Brennan makes a good case for the importance of expertise in his book, and my reaction to his argument should not be thought to suggest that I think there are no political or economic propositions of the kind he's referring to (say, "Unilateral disarmament will make war more/less likely"). I hope it is clear from the preceding chapters that distilled populism encourages polities to avail themselves of experts. But I do think he makes several mistakes here. We have seen that it is confusing to consider popular elections epistemic: they must not be thought (as Brennan obviously believes democracy supporters do think) to provide insight into, for example, the policy that will produce the smallest trade deficit or the least chance of war with China. In reality, the information that polls can and do provide is no more nor less than what the voters want. Brennan assigns information of that kind no value whatever: like Lenin, he knows what the people *should* want. Indeed, it seems clear that reaching his goal of elevating the importance of epistocratic judgments is achieved precisely via the utter disdain he has for the significance of what the citizenry actually does desire. And he takes this degradation of voter preferences to be implied by another sort of degradation. Suppose, he asks us, that the people vote to allow adults to rape children and "they also vote to have the police ensure that no one stops adults from raping children" (2016, 12). He then asks us: Can we all not at least agree that it is disgusting that "pure proceduralists" (those who think—as I do—that democratic procedures must be given the highest priority) could suggest to us that we bestow such a vote with significance for public policy?

I believe we can see the confusion embedded in this challenge from the fact that one might ask precisely the same question of the results of any epistocratically altered election on this matter of restraining the police in pedophilia cases. If Brennan thinks that a child's right not to be raped trumps the outcomes of democratic procedures (and he clearly does), then those rights would prevail however the democracy is set up. Of course, one could guarantee certain results by baking in "virtue" requirements for voters that require the replication of Brennan's views regarding what is morally permissible. But that is something he does not suggest. As I have said, I believe that, optimally, elections would be restricted to candidates for office, so that the people may select who they believe will best represent their interests, rather than opine on initiative petitions, possibly involving criminal laws and appropriate police procedures.

Voters may like protectionists or free-traders, doves or hawks, even, I suppose, child-raping libertines, and, in my view, they must be allowed to vote for them (assuming the latter are not in prison and so unable to provide the required representation). If Brennan wants to insist on moral constraints governing what laws the legislature may pass or what orders the executive may implement (or even what activities the police must not allow) so be it. But no such constraints would get one any closer to epistocracy anyhow, because the desired limitations would affect *any* democracy, epistocratic or otherwise. Constraints of that type would limit (inappropriately, in my view) what (or preferably *who*) may be voted for or against, not who may vote or how much their votes should count.

Just as one need not understand Ricardo's law to support one's favorite candidate, one need not know whether child rape is a permissible human activity to vote (perhaps unwittingly) for a representative who might try to decriminalize child rape. If Ricardo was right, his law will have its effects—whether those who voted approve of those effects or not. If, as seems extremely likely (and, I hasten to add, as reflects my own preference), child rape will always be a crime in accordance with the attitudes of a vast majority, anyone who is included in that majority but nevertheless votes for a candidate who is a complete libertine on this matter, may come to be sorry for her vote. That is the price of democracy (and, perhaps, a good reason for allowing recall elections). But moral revulsion provides no justification for restrictions on who may vote, and it is absurd to suggest that available political outcomes and well-being choices may only be made in accordance with Brennan's own set of ethical views.[9]

It can be seen from this discussion that libertarians may join others in pressing for the discarding of certain choices based on their own—or some elite's— determination that some types of choices are beyond the pale. They may argue that the result of fulfillment of certain desires would simply be too harmful either to the choosers or to some other group. But those items that purportedly evil or stupid people approve of are no less ex ante successes when they are chosen than what is desired by the elite of whom Brennan approves—even if some of the successes achieved by "inferiors" do not increase net prudential values for the society. No doubt estimates of net prudential values are difficult and bound to be controversial, but elites are often wrong about such matters too.

I repeat that Brennan's interest in obtaining expertise—both inside and outside government—seems to me quite reasonable. Our shared view on that matter seems to me to support, for example, requiring civil service tests for bureaucrats, legislative aides and other government employees. But that agreement provides no basis for discarding or devaluing any particular vote or voter. No one knows what people want better than they do themselves, and neither their choices nor the platforms of the candidates who'd like to represent them should be required to meet eligibility criteria imposed by tests that Brennan sanctions or by moral empathies that he shares. As Randy Newman sang of Huey Long, some candidate *may be a fool, but he's our fool.*[10]

In addition to the misplaced moral indignation that does nothing to support epistocratic notions, Brennan conflates these three aspects of choices: *What?, Why?,* and *Is it a good idea?* Jones and Smith want a new bridge to be built. Robinson does not. Jones wants this bridge because the old one is ugly; Smith thinks the old one is crumbling; Robinson wants people to walk more. But perhaps the old bridge is *not* actually crumbling and the absence of a bridge will actually *not* result in people walking more. Furthermore, whether more walking or a prettier bridge is likely to produce a net increase in successful choices over the long term is very difficult to determine, partly because to do so one must estimate what will in the future be deemed successes by the relevant public. All of these are separable matters: some are best made by representatives; others likely need consultants with special expertise. But neither seasoned legislators nor structural engineers ought to be allowed to substitute their judgments for Smith's, Jones's, or Robinson's ex ante take on what would be a happy outcome. And we cannot get any better insight into the wishes of the entire constituency by declaring some subset of that group better or wiser than the rest.

A epistocrat of Brennan's type can be expected to respond to this populist attack in the following way: "Surely you admit yourself that voting for a tax rate above some level cannot produce a favorable result for a society. If we know those would be bad votes, why in the world would we let people make them?" Let us agree to call any vote that is violative of either of the two constituents of the CHOICE definition a "bad vote." That is, if the vote is either for (i) something of which the voter does not herself approve ex ante or (ii) something that cannot reasonably be expected (according to the best available information and science) to increase prudential value over the long term, we may agree that it is not a "good vote." The epistocrat here suggests that where a vote is "bad" for failing to meet the second criterion, it ought to be eliminated—or worse, replaced by one that may well fail even to meet the first criterion! We must, according to this theorist, either ignore the fact that this voter wants X or substitute a Y vote for her X vote.

One should recognize an important flaw in the argument here: while it is quite difficult to reasonably estimate the number of future successes, it is quite easy to determine what some voter currently approves of. Generally, all one need do is ask her. For, as we have seen, no terribly high level of cognitive ability is required to know what one wants. Even if we are absolutely certain that a tax rate of 100 percent will be bad for the economy, perhaps the voters who support so high a rate want the economy to fail or are predicting a future in which the populace will cease to care about the meeting of material needs. The fact that such motives are possible ought to give pause to all those who, based on impressions of their own great wisdom, are inclined to devalue the ballots of everybody who votes in ways that they wouldn't. The inclusion of the second criterion within CHOICE does not require either the replacement or the discarding of votes that may be unwise. But it does lend support to the claim that providing the best available relevant information to voters is useful to a worthy democracy. What makes up *that* information is *not* a matter of voter views regarding what constitutes good evidence, but must be determined by bona fide expertise. It is important, however, to render unto each criterion within CHOICE only that which is due it.

No doubt, when one looks at an apparently democratic jurisdiction whose public policies seem to have contributed significantly to mass starvation, widespread bloodshed, or unsanitary living conditions, one may be quite hostile to the idea that it is a good thing that the people there have the right to control their destiny at the ballot box. After all, why shouldn't sustaining that form of government lead to continued, or even additional, tragedy? But that way of looking at the matter entirely ignores the fact that self-determination is an intrinsic good, even when it produces harm. In common with experience machines, despotism has the characteristic that there is no amount of "happiness" producible by it that can wash away the fact that, where it is in effect, people are not allowed to freely choose what they want and get precisely *that*. Just as one cannot coherently sign away one's individual freedom in perpetuity, we cannot let even a wise and benevolent guardian be the judge of what we want, Thus, we must retain the right to recall our great and powerful Oz and pick a new one as soon as we decide we no longer like what is being provided. And by "we" in the previous sentence, I mean *all* of us, with each treated equally.

Another argument that has become quite popular with anti-democratic libertarians is the well-known "It doesn't matter if you vote, anyhow" attack. Brennan writes,

> [F]or any individual voter, it makes no difference whether they vote or abstain. The probability that our votes will make a difference is vanishingly small. It is not as though the government will help you just in case you vote or ignore you just in case you abstain. As individuals, our single votes do not influence whether our elected leaders decide to help, ignore, or hurt us. (2016, 86)

This concern is understandable and is part of the reason that I believe moving to SNTV or another form of minority representation is so important. It

is also why I believe that campaign financing must be reformed. Voter interest requires vigilance in ensuring not only that everyone has the equal right
to vote—and can do so without much trouble or legitimate concern about
fraud—but that everyone's vote *matters*.

A good way to look at this issue is to ponder the following analogy.
Consider a village society in which the central council provides a large feast
for all the citizens each week. The way the feast has been arranged is that the
council cooks a giant stew. All the ingredients are in the pot except that which
will give it flavor: the seasoning is supplied by the villagers. Each person in
this community may donate one equal-sized packet of either salt, pepper,
cardamom, cilantro, oregano, garlic, basil or something entirely tasteless that
still takes up the same amount of volume. So those who like salty food will
bring salt, those who like garlic will bring that, and so on. Those who like
bland food will bring the tasteless seasoning, and those who don't care one
way or the other will likely abstain (or come with whatever their families
or friends urge them to bring). Since the villagers' participation or non-
participation doesn't make the stew larger or smaller, there can be no free-
rider complaint directed toward those not bringing anything but getting to eat
anyhow.[11] Given this arrangement, if you like the taste of garlic, it is foolish
not to bring some—even if your failure to do so is unlikely to make any
appreciable difference in the taste of the stew because of the small size of the
packet you are allowed. You may need there to be 100 packets of garlic in all
for the stew to take on a bit of that flavor, but if you put your packet in, only
99 others will be needed. Encouragement of other garlic lovers may help—so
you must be free to do that; and it must be the case that the council won't just
throw out the garlic packets because one of the elders doesn't like the stuff.
On the view urged in this book, to vote is to make your own contribution to
the "taste" of the society you will have. While it ought not to be required of
you, it will be the case that a failure to add your own fragment to the people's
will—however small—is just self-harm—unless you really don't care one
way or the other. If you *do* care about the result, voting is made easy (i.e.,
nearly cost-free), and you have good reason to believe that your vote will be
fairly counted and the electoral results will be appropriately constitutive of
government actions, it seems almost irrational *not* to insert your own packet
of policy seasoning.[12]

In America today—with our Electoral College and Senate, our single-
member, gerrymandered districts,[13] our attempts to deny access to voters
in certain groups, absurdly undemocratic legislative procedures, the vast,
insulated power of the courts, and our election-day polling booth and chad-
counting mishaps (or intentional interference)—there seems little hope even
that the tiny morsels we are allowed will count for anything at all. So, an
attitude of despair or indifference is entirely understandable. But it should be

noted that as I write this (Spring 2019) several of the democratic presidential candidates have opined on issues mentioned herein. A couple have indicated their support for the abolition of the (antidemocratic) Electoral College, and (sadly) a few others have indicated their lack of concern about the (also antidemocratic) Senate filibuster. So, votes for or against these candidates— as well as contacts with campaigns—just might make a difference.

ESTLUND'S EPISTEMIC DILEMMA

It is interesting to note that the non-libertarian John Estlund, in his 2008 book *Democratic Authority: A Philosophical Framework*, makes some of the same missteps as Brennan.[14] First, Estlund hunts around for democratic procedures that can bring a polity *justice*—a hope I myself consider a pipe dream. As I take democracy's goal not to be justice, but group autonomy (and, perhaps, high levels of well-being in accordance with what people freely want), it seems to me no theoretical strike against when a purportedly unjust result emerges from a proper democratic procedure. Estlund wants *moral permissibility* to be productive of legitimacy, but I believe that what makes a public policy legitimate is its being a result of a faithful attempt to figure out what equally treated people want and give it to them. Correct procedures enable us to discover what autonomous people would actually like their governments to do, because with groups, unlike with individuals, what is desired is not obvious before a fair election is held. Estlund agrees with me that political authority cannot arise from expertise, but he does not seem to see that such authority has nothing to do with whether this or that view is "qualified" where he takes that to mean *worthy of respect.*

Like Brennan, Estlund plays what might be called "the degradation card." Instead of using child rape to attempt to show that some votes ought not to be counted, Estlund returns to the Nazi motif favored by Kendall.[15] He writes,

> People who believe that their own race has a right to rule other races . . . will not accept certain principles about moral and political equality. But objections stemming from [such a point] of view [are] morally weightless. (Estlund 2008, 4)

And he (somewhat strangely) continues by saying that that if one thinks restricting "qualified" views to those that seem to him justified is elitist, one must think that justifications need to be acceptable to everyone, including Nazis, before being assigned any value. That Paretian inference seems wrong to me, because removing the restrictions Estlund proposes on what it is to be "qualified" could just as easily suggest that value justifications need only seem compelling to *somebody,* rather than to *everybody.* In that case, there would be no need to have all the groups—angels and Nazis both—approve any value claim for it to have "force."[16]

Estlund's main departure from what I take to be an apt picture of this matter again involves the expectation that good democratic procedures might produce *just* results. He writes,

> We are supposing that some things are unjust, some right, some things vicious, and so on, regardless of what anyone thinks about them. Then we say that some people have erroneous views about these matters, some other people less so. . . . This way of talking about truth makes it pretty hard to deny truth in political matters or to deny that some know it better than others. . . . I have proposed to avoid [the move from expertise to authority] by denying that there is expertise that is generally acceptable in the right way even if it is genuine. But having acknowledged that there are truths about the high-stakes matters that are present in politics, we must ask whether its discovery plays any role in the best account of how political authority and coercion would be justified. . . . Why not understand democracy as a way of giving every (adult) person an equal chance to influence the outcome of the decision? (2008, 5–6)

While a populist will likely answer the question concluding this paragraph in the affirmative, the passage as a whole will seem wrongheaded because of its failure to recognize that the point of democracy is not to find out what would be "just" outcomes, even if there *are* such things.

Of course, the people (or preferably their representatives) may vote on a tax law that incorporates some particular conception of justice. But it is not the democratic procedures that can either make some distributive outcome of a policy just, or determine whether it is. Votes cannot even provide *evidence* that justice is likely to be produced through the enactment of some particular policy. For even if *everybody* likes some proposal, that only makes it (weirdly) popular, not *just*. Even a confirmed Benthamite who is quite willing to reduce justice to pleasure will recognize that the ex ante sentiments of a group of people toward some public policy may turn out to be mistaken regarding that policy's ultimate generation of (for Bentham, justice-creating) utiles.

I have conceded earlier that there is a sense in which what the majority of voters want may be said to be "incorrect," that votes may be "bad." This is a sense according to which "correct" (and "good") imply a prudential-value increase, and which recognizes that the second prong of CHOICE involves an empirical proposition about which voters may certainly make erroneous judgments. But, as I have stressed, there is no sense of "correct" that can simply ignore what the voters want, because both prongs involve the largely conative (Estlund would say "Active") requirement of "approval." He writes that there is an important (indeed, he says, ancient) tension between (i) the belief that "the general mass of people is in no position to make good decisions" and (ii) the view that governments have authority and legitimacy only when their actions are a function of collective determination by all the citizens. (2005, 205) Populism obviously takes care of (ii), but Estlund is concerned about (i) because he believes that, without truth-tracking power, elections are little better than producing policies via a random decision generator. While I have allowed for "bad" decisions to be democratically arrived at, it seems to me absurd to suggest that only "good" ones can have been fairly made.

In my view, "good decision" should be understood in one of only three ways: (i) something reflecting what the decider actually wants (i.e., something that satisfies the first conjunction of CHOICE); (ii) something reflecting an increase in net prudential values in the jurisdiction over the long haul (i.e., it satisfies the second conjunct); or (iii) something reflecting satisfaction of both conjuncts. It is clear that voters cannot be expected to know what will increase net prudential values over the long term (partly because that would require knowledge of what future societal members want). I think, therefore, that if we plan to make "good decisions" a criterion for legitimate government, we must be utilizing (i). For surely fair democracy cannot require electoral omniscience.

Estlund recognizes that elections might not be the best epistemic device available to produce what he takes to be "true" outcomes. But, as I have said, even a fairly conducted election is epistemic only in a confused sense. The voter-supplied information is of necessity quite limited; it does not include truths about, for example, what course of action is just, informed, reasonable, likely to produce the most prudentially valuable outcomes, or "true" (whatever that would mean). In fact, votes need not even be "sincere," and may well not be if voters think an "insincere" ballot is more likely to get them what they want.[17]

All this talk of voter ignorance and incompetence leads me to briefly consider another matter that might be brought up by critics of CHOICE or democracy, or both. It is certainly true that a person may have conflicting desires and make conflicting choices. Indeed, not only may someone make choices that are not known by her to be contradictory, she may also be unable to stanch desires she knows to conflict with one another. Suppose Helen wants Hal to be elected U.S. president this November, but also (perhaps because she just bought him a particular kind of birthday card) wants Hal to be thirty years old on his birthday this Sunday—something inconsistent with his becoming president under the Constitution (as Helen knows). It may also be that Helen is unsure whether what she *really* wants is for Hal to be commander in chief or for him to just be out of town for a while. Such uncertainties, while undeniable, show the epistemic limitations faced by any theory that attempts to grasp the complete meaning of—to *fully understand*—election results. It seems to me that the hope that we can learn the *truth* of this or that policy proposal by coming to "understand voter desires" through a close examination of election outcomes is preposterous. Any serious attempt to reach a comprehensive understanding of Helen's thought processes when she votes for Hal will surely lead us rather to the view that we will never be able to assess election results in any manner that would enable us to determine the *evidence* for (never mind the *truth* or *goodness* of) much besides the fact that ballot option X received N approvals, ballot option Y received M approvals, and so on. Fortunately, legitimacy-generating elections require results no more complicated than that.

ARNESON'S INSTRUMENTALIST
CRITIQUE OF DEMOCRACY

Like Estlund, Richard Arneson is no libertarian. In his view,

> [A]long with substantial guarantees of freedom of speech, privacy, and individual liberty . . . fundamental rights include egalitarian rights to material resources such as are implied by John Rawls's difference principle regulating the shares of primary social goods or by Ronald Dworkin's principle of equality of resources or by some other principle in this family. (Arneson 2003b, 9)

But if he seems comfortable with governmental redistributions of wealth, Arneson does agree with libertarians that democracy is supportable only if it has instrumental value: for, in his view, it surely has no other. (One might think that such basic disagreements among highly educated philosophers might give epistocrats pause, but alas—.) Arneson's views are consequentialist generally, and he shares with Brennan the expectation that "enforcing severe competency requirements . . . that would disenfranchise some or even many currently eligible to vote . . . would generate morally better consequences over the long haul than would the alternative of sticking with one-person-one vote" (2003a, 130). According to Arneson, in order to get to democracy—whether epistocratic or not—one would have to take something like the following trip:

(1) All competent persons share an equal basic moral status.
(2) Whenever one chooses an act or a policy conscientiously, one expresses the idea that the act or choice is morally right so far as one can tell.
(3) Alternative actions can generally be assessed as morally better or worse based on their consequences, but not their decision procedures, so that

which is the morally best is that which, over the long haul, produces the morally best results.

(4) The morally best results are those which may be identified with maximal fulfillment of significant individual moral rights.

(5) Rights may be divided into those that are fundamental and those derivative rights that give power over others.[18]

(6) Democratic rights are a species of rights that give power over others.

(7) Those rights that give power over others are derivative and nonfundamental.

(8) The derivative, nonfundamental rights may be justified only by their maximal production of fundamental rights.[19]

(9) There's good reason to believe that democratic rights are maximally productive of rights that are fundamental.

(10) Therefore, democratic rights ought to be protected.

Arneson is supportive of (1)–(8), but, predictably, repudiates (9) and so denies that one can get to (10), even if all the rest are granted. But, equally predictably, the distilled populist will reject entirely this Arnesonian road to democracy. For my own part, I have no particular problem with (1) so long as it is derivable from notions of fair assessments of group will, and as an occasional ethical consequentialist myself (during some of those times when I think moral values make any sense at all), I would consent to (3) and (4). It seems to me hard to deny (6), and I am willing to concede that (8) would be reasonable so long as "rights" are placed in scare quotes and the list of fundamental ones being proposed is correct. I will also grant that (10) seems to follow from the premises above it.

But my half-hearted sanction should not be seen as a terribly strong showing for this argument. First, even supposing that there are clear moral principles that we can agree upon, (2) seems much too broad: most of our actions are, on all plausible theories, morally neutral. If the "conscientiously" in that premise is taken to rule out all activities but those with "ethically positive" results, it not only makes the premise tautologous, it makes it irrelevant to many—if not most—actions, whether individual or social, private or public. (5) seems false for the reasons brought forth in Griffin 2003: *all* rights imply some sort of power over others in the sense of being correlative with obligations in them. That makes (7) false too. And, as there is no reason to think that rights may be divided in the sense that Arneson requires, (8) also needs work.[20] Worst of all, (9) seems too confused even to require comment. Remember, in my view, democratic rights *are* the only fundamental ones. Finally, I disagree with this entire program: I deny that (10) needs the support of the material above it in the first place.

The differences between Arneson and me on these issues are thus probably too numerous and deep to be resolved or even fruitfully discussed. He is certain—if not always of particular moral principles or fundamental rights that must be guarded—at least of what their existence would entail and the moral requirement that we do what can be done to maximize them. Like Brennan, he is instrumentalist with respect to democratic procedures, but while Brennan seems to want the system set up so that economists, actuaries and social scientists will get to determine what is most productive of the well-being of citizens, Arneson is interested in maximizing moral goods/justice rather than prudential value. And to maximize "the good," it would seem that only the approbation of philosopher kings will fit the bill. Distilled populism, on the other hand, rejects the entire idea that fair democratic procedures must be either defensible on moral grounds or be most productive of "good" outcomes (considered either morally or prudentially) when compared with all other conceivable mechanisms.

On the theory espoused in this book, democratic procedures must be fair so that people's wishes can be known and appropriate action can be taken to obtain what they want. The outcomes arising from those procedures, whether (correctly or incorrectly) deemed good or bad (morally or prudentially) by this or that philosopher or other pundit—or even by the people of that polity at large—will only then be products of autonomous activity—an intrinsic prudential good. In other words, true self-government is the sum and substance of what is required of every worthy democracy. And whether some entity is actually self-governing may well be entirely orthogonal to whether or not its *results* are (or are thought by this or that philosopher, moralist, politician, demagogue, or saint to be) good or bad, prudent or ill-conceived.

In *Federalist 15,* Alexander Hamilton asks, "Why has government been instituted at all?" He gives us this answer: "Because the passions of men will not conform to the dictates of reason and justice without constraint." Hamilton and his fellow Founders believed that freedom (mainly of white male adults to obtain and retain property) requires careful protection, and they felt sure that the key to accomplishing that goal was to restrain groups (or "factions") from getting up to mischief. Although Hamilton took factions to be nothing but bundles of individuals who each have fundamental rights, he believed that restricting the allowable activities of the factions themselves (conceived as whole units) was absolutely crucial to the preservation of personal liberties. Was it that Hamilton denied that factions might have their own desires, so that they, unlike real persons, do not require protection of (the merely metaphorical) "freedom to pursue their own happiness"? Not at all. Indeed, his view that groups are infected with "a poison of spirit" that causes them to act with less "rectitude and disinterestedness" than individual persons, surely requires the existence of corporate purposes, strategies and wills. But if there *are* general wills, what has them must resemble individual persons in being more or less free, more or less autonomous. Now, it is hard to deny that, all else equal, more liberty and autonomy, more opportunities for successful free choices, is an unalloyed prudential good. (*The more good, the better!*) But an understanding of that fact will move one to recognize that the main point of government is not, as Hamilton thought, to constrain the passions of men (or factions), but rather to maximize successful choices. Such maximization requires the precise deciphering of what is wanted by both persons and factions so that the utmost can be done to bring those states of affairs into existence. In the case of social choices, let us call the methods for such precise deciphering and subsequent faithful endeavors to obtain what is wanted "fair democratic procedures." It will follow that the only restraints that are absolutely fundamental to a praiseworthy polity are those that are necessary to limit any activity—by person, institution, faction, or the government itself—that might serve to restrict or pervert the operation of fair democratic procedures.

NOTES

1. This feature of his work is highlighted in Taschetto (2015) and Chan (2005).

2. Consider Dahl (1989, 82–83): "If the general good were composed only of individual interests, and if we could also agree on a satisfactory principle for aggregating individual interests—a majority principle, perhaps—then just as paternalism would be unnecessary and undesirable in private life, so too guardianship would be unnecessary and undesirable in public life."

3. (1) Elected officials; (2) free, fair, and frequent elections; (3) freedom of expression; (4) alternative sources of information; (5) associational autonomy; and (6) inclusive citizenship.

4. Thomas Scanlon (1991, 18) put it that "Not all judgments of relative well-being are made with morality in mind. . . . We can ask, quite apart from any question of right or justice, how well a person's life is going and whether that person is better off than another, or better off than he or she was a year ago." And that alone is what I consider here. See also the quote in chapter 2 from Jackson (1991).

5. Given my predilections in this area, I can't plausibly deny that my Kelsenianism (at least sometimes) extends to moral relativism. Perhaps this concession will help explain my insistence that those who wish to subordinate prudential value assessments to moral principles explicitly acknowledge when they call for activities that may well make both the relevant individuals and their societies worse off for time everlasting.

6. Recognizing the possibility of separating calculations of individual utilities from assessments of justice or "what is right" is nothing new. Amartya Sen (1980, 464–466) defines the following two theories:

> *Act Consequentialism*: An action a is right if and only if the state of affairs x resulting from it is at least as good as each of the alternative states of affairs that would have resulted respectively from the alternative feasible acts.

> *Outcome Utilitarianism*: Any state of affairs x is at least as good as an alternative state of affairs y if and only if the sum total of individual utilities in x is at least as large as the sum total of individual utilities in y.

He then notes that it "could be asked whether outcome utilitarianism is a moral principle at all [since] on its own it asserts nothing about rightness of actions" and adds that "intertemporal comparisons of 'social welfare' based on, say, real national income, are primarily judgments of states of affairs and not of [the rightness of] actions."

7. See Nock (1943). Rothbard's main critique of democracy can be found in his *Man, Economy and State* which originally appeared in 1962.

8. "On this point the enemies and the friends of democracy will never agree" Von Mises (1922, 63).

9. One wonders precisely where Brennan would place such a constraint. For example, would *consensual* relations between adults and adolescents pass muster? And if so, must everyone agree with Brennan's take on the age of consent in order to gain the franchise?

10. I want to stress that my objections to epistocracy fade to the extent that exaltation of expertise is not made to be inconsistent with egalitarian democracy. Landa and Pevnick (2019) for example, make a strong case that representative democracy is itself essentially epistocratic. My concerns don't *entirely* disappear, however, since I think it is quite difficult to reconcile what I take to be the necessity of recall, reversal and referendum with epistocratic conceptions of trusteeship.

11. That suggests that there is no good reason for making participation compulsory. On this matter I agree with Brennan. See, in particular, Brennan (2012). As I have said earlier, the expression of indifference also transmits information.

12. This stew analogy is looser without the plentiful use of something like SNTV—both to select at least some representatives and perhaps to pick finalists for AV elections as well. The AV votes are uniquely capable of amalgamating the desired ingredients into a skeletal general will, but cannot do much more than that.

13. While I was writing this paragraph, SCOTUS issued *Rucho v. Common Cause*. As obnoxious as I find the facts of blatant partisan gerrymandering that were the basis for the appeals decided therein, it is hard not to agree with Justice Roberts that there is little in the U.S. Constitution that can be relied on to stop it. In 1911, Congress passed a reapportionment act that contained the requirement that "the Fifty-eighth and each subsequent Congress shall be elected by districts composed of contiguous and compact territory and containing as nearly as practicable an equal number of inhabitants. The said districts shall be equal to the number of the Representatives to which such State may be entitled in Congress." But, alas, the compactness requirement was not retained. And, of course, the unfortunate requirement for single-member districts does remain.

14. Before commencing my critique I want to emphasize that I find much of Estlund's work on democracy important and instructive. In particular, his three constraints on votes—aggregability, advocacy, and activity-seem to me to nicely demarcate a CHOICE construal, and I agree with his critique of voting-as-preference-expression (Estlund 1990). I note, however, that Estlund (1990) describes what he

thinks votes (essentially) *are*, and I disagree with his insistence that they may not just *be* choices in the sense of ex ante approvals. In addition, his critique of "fair proceduralism" in Estlund (1997) seems to me to morph into a criticism of rule by coin-flip only because it improperly overlooks all the requirements for fair democratic decision making besides impartiality.

15. Michael Huemer, another libertarian, settles on a less extreme example of ostensible awfulness with his "Bar Tab argument," in which democracy is castigated for allegedly allowing majority-vote determinations of who should have to pay tavern bills (Huemer 2012, 76–77). But it is not any *should pay* that matters here, but only a *must pay*. If democracy were actually to result in statute or case law that allowed (or even required) coercion of that sort among revelers, my sense is that people would make pre-drink agreements or pick their pub buddies quite carefully. Huemer clearly joins the vast majority (including me) in preferring current societal norms for determining and enforcing such cost allocations. But it should be clear that laws do not allow what Huemer fears here, not only because of (in my view inappropriate) constitutional property protections, but because majorities in no country in the world actually *want* to allow the coercion of those sorts of cost allocations, at bars or elsewhere. However, if I am wrong about this or if present preferences should change, Huemer's current predilections (and my own) should still not be allowed to take precedence over general wills. For more on this matter, see endnote 11 of chapter 11.

16. In my own view, when it comes to public actions, unanimity behind such an assertion as that a new bridge is wanted has only practical repercussions. We can know there isn't likely to be a lot of public turbulence if building commences. It cannot make a position more or less "correct."

17. A similar misconception seems to me to mar Carlo Invernizzi-Accetti (2017), an otherwise laudable critique of Estlund. I am quite sympathetic with the author's Kelsenian defense of majority rule (roughly, that any other standard will provide autonomy/freedom to fewer people in at least some circumstances). But in addition to his apparent assumption that simple majoritarianism (i.e., without minority representation) is the best democratic procedure, Invernizzi-Accetti seems to buy the epistemic democrats' view that votes are the sorts of things that at least *might* be true or "get things right."

18. Griffin (2003) makes a very solid case that no coherent distinction can actually be made between rights that do and do not give power over others, so that classifying some as fundamental based on that characteristic is inapt. In his response, Arneson (2003a) gives what seems to me to be precious little argument, for his dismissive responses to that and every other point suggested in Griffin's quite cogent paper.

19. Arneson joins Brennan in being less convinced than Mill or Hayek of the salutary effects of fair democracy on voter education. I have no opinion on that matter myself.

20. Furthermore, though it may be that some rights need to be productive of other rights in order to have a claim to reasonable protection themselves, that thesis at the very least requires more support than Arneson provides for it in either his 2003 or his 2009 study.

References

Ackerman, Bruce A., and James S. Fishkin. 2005. *Deliberation Day*. New Haven, CT: Yale University Press.

Adams, Robert Merrihew. 1999. *Finite and Infinite Goods*. Oxford: Oxford University Press.

Altman, David. 2014. "Strengthening Democratic Quality: Reactive Deliberation in the Context of Direct Democracy." *Working Paper: Kellogg Institute for International Studies*, no. 400: 1–31.

Anon. 1969. "Equal Representation and the Weighted Voting Alternative." *Yale Law Journal* 79, no. 2: 311–321.

Arneson, Richard. 1999. "Human Flourishing Versus Desire Satisfaction." *Social Philosophy and Policy* 16: 113–142.

———. 2003a. "Defending the Purely Instrumental Account of Democratic Legitimacy." *The Journal of Political Philosophy* 11, no. 1: 122–132.

———. 2003b. "An Argument for Democratic Equality." In *Philosophy and Democracy: An Anthology*, edited by Thomas Christiano: 95–115. Oxford: Oxford University Press.

Arrow, Kenneth. 1951. *Social Choice and Individual Values*. New York: Wiley & Sons.

Auriol, Emmanuelle, and Robert J. Gary-Bobo. 2012. "On the Optimal Number of Representatives." *Public Choice* 153, no. 3/4: 419–445.

Austin, John. 1869. *Lectures on Jurisprudence*, edited by John Campbell. London: John Murray.

Austin, J. L. 1957. "A Plea for Excuses: The Presidential Address." *Proceedings of the Aristotelian Society* 57, no. 1: 1–30.

Banzhaf, John F. 1967–1968. "One Man,? Votes: Mathematical Analysis of Voting Power and Effective Representation." *George Washington Law Review* 36: 808–823.

Barry, Brian. 1973. "Liberalism and Want Satisfaction: A Critique of John Rawls." *Political Theory* 1, no. 2: 134–153.

———. 1979. "Is Democracy Special?" In *Philosophy, Politics and Society, Fifth Series: A Collection*, edited by Peter Laslett and James S. Fishkin: 156–171. New Haven: Yale University Press.

Bar-Siman-Tov, Ittai. 2010. "Lawmakers as Lawbreakers." *William and Mary Law Review* 52: 805–871.

———. 2011. "The Puzzling Resistance to Judicial Review of the Legislative Process." Columbia Public Law & Legal Theory Working Papers. Paper 9198. http://lsr.nellco.org/columbia_pllt/9198.

Beard, Charles A. 1912. *The Supreme Court and the Constitution*. New York: MacMillan.

———. 1913. *An Economic Interpretation of the Constitution of the United States*. New York: MacMillan.

Beard, Charles A., and Mary R. Beard. 1921. *History of the United States*. New York: MacMillan.

Beckman, Ludvig. 2019. "Deciding the Demos: Three Conceptions of Democratic Legitimacy." *Critical Review of International Social and Political Philosophy* 22, no. 4: 412–431.

Bell, Daniel A. 1999. "Democratic Deliberation: The Problem of Implementation." In *Deliberative Politics: Essays on Democracy and Disagreement*, edited by Stephen Macedo: 70–87. Oxford: Oxford University Press.

Bentham, Jeremy. 1796. "Anarchical Fallacies." In *The Works of Jeremy Bentham*, Vol. 2 (1843), edited by John Bowring. Edinburgh: Tait.

———. 1825. *Leading Principles of a Constitutional Code, for Any State*. London: A. J. Valpy.

Bohman, James, and William Rehg, eds. 1997. *Deliberative Democracy: Essays on Reason and Politics*. Cambridge, MA: MIT Press.

Borda, Jean-Charles. 1784. "On Elections by Ballot." In *Classics of Social Choice* (1995), edited by Iain McLean, Arnold B. Urken, et al.: 81–89. Ann Arbor: University of Michigan.

Bowler, Sean, David M. Farrell, et al. 2005. "Expert Opinion on Electoral Systems: So Which Electoral System Is 'Best'?" *Journal of Elections, Public Opinion and Parties* 15, no. 1: 3–19.

Bradley, Ben. 2007. "A Paradox for Some Theories of Welfare." *Philosophical Studies* 133, no. 1: 45–53.

Brams, Steven J., and Peter C. Fishburn. 2005. "Going from Theory to Practice: The Mixed Success of Approval Voting." *Social Choice and Welfare* 25, no. 2/3: 457–474.

———. 2007. *Approval Voting*. New York: Springer.

Brennan, Jason. 2012. *The Ethics of Voting*. Princeton, NJ: Princeton University Press.

———. 2017. *Against Democracy*. Princeton, NJ: Princeton University Press.

Brighouse, Harry, and Marc Fleurbaey. 2010. "Democracy and Proportionality." *Journal of Political Philosophy* 18, no. 2: 137–155.

Brock, Dan. 1973. "Recent Work in Utilitarianism." *American Philosophical Quarterly* 10, no. 4: 241–276.

Bronsteen, John, Christopher Buccafusco, et al. 2010. "Welfare As Happiness." *Georgetown Law Journal* 98: 1583–1641.

Broome, John. 1978. "Choice and Value in Economics." *Oxford Economic Papers* 30, no. 3: 313–333.

Browdy, Michelle H. 1990. "Simulated Annealing: An Improved Computer Model for Political Redistricting." *Yale Law & Policy Review* 8, no. 1: 163–179.

Butler, Joseph. 1827. *Fifteen Sermons Preached at the Rolls Chapel*. Boston: Hilliard, Gray, Little, and Wilkins.

Canovan, Margaret. 1981. *Populism*. New York: Harcourt.

Chan, Ho Mun. 2005. "'Rawls' Theory of Justice: A Naturalistic Evaluation." *Journal of Medicine and Philosophy* 30: 449–465.

Chan, Tak Wing, and Matthew Clayton. 2006. "Should the Voting Age Be Lowered to Sixteen? Normative and Empirical Considerations." *Political Studies* 54, no. 3: 533–558.

Clark, Sherman J. 1998. "A Populist Critique of Direct Democracy." *Harvard Law Review* 112, no. 2: 434–482.

Cogan, Jacob Katz. 1997. "The Look Within: Property, Capacity, and Suffrage in Nineteenth-Century America." *The Yale Law Journal* 107, no. 2: 473–498.

Cohen, Joshua. 1986. "An Epistemic Conception of Democracy." *Ethics* 97, no. 1: 26–38.

———. 1997. "Deliberation and Democratic Legitimacy." In *Deliberative Democracy: Essays on Reason and Politics*, edited by James Bohman and William Rehg: 66–91. Cambridge, MA: MIT Press.

Coleman, Jules, and John Ferejohn. 1986. "Democracy and Social Choice." *Ethics* 97, no. 1: 6–25.

Cox, G. W. 1996. "Is the Single Nontransferable Vote Superproportional? Evidence from Japan and Taiwan." *American Journal of Political Science* 40, no. 3: 740–755.

Crisp, Roger. "Hedonism Reconsidered." *Philosophy and Phenomenological Research* 73, no. 3: 619–645.

Croly, Herbert. 1914. *Progressive Democracy*. New York: MacMillan.

Cudworth, Erika. 2007. *The Modern State: Theories and Ideologies*. Edinburgh: Edinburgh University Press.

Culp, Maurice S. 1929. "A Survey of the Proposals to Limit or Deny the Power of Judicial Review by the Supreme Court of the United States." *Indiana Law Journal* 4, no. 6: 386–490.

Dahl, Robert A. 1989. *Democracy and Its Critics*. New Haven: Yale University Press.

Dahl, Robert A., and Ian Shapiro. 2015. *On Democracy*. New Haven: Yale University Press.

DeSilver, Drew. 2017. "U.S. Trails Most Developed Countries in Voter Turnout." *Pew Research Center*, May 15, 2017: http://www.pewresearch.org/fact-tank/201 7/05/15/u-s-voter-turnout-trails-most-developed-countries/. Retrieved 6/9/2017.

Dingell, John D. 2018. "I Served in Congress Longer Than Anyone. Here's How to Fix It." *The Atlantic*, Apr. 12, 2018.

Dorsey, Dale. 2011. "The Hedonist's Dilemma." *Journal of Moral Philosophy* 8, no. 2: 173–196.

———. 2012. "Subjectivism Without Desire." *Philosophical Review* 121, no. 3: 407–442.

Downs, Anthony. 1957. *An Economic Theory of Democracy*. New York: Harper.

Dummett, Michael. 1997. *Principles of Electoral Reform*. Oxford: Oxford University Press.

Dworkin, Ronald. 2013. *Justice for Hedgehogs*. Cambridge, MA: Belknap of Harvard University Press.

Eckstein, Harry. 1980. "Theoretical Approaches to Explaining Collective Political Violence." In *Handbook of Political Conflict*, edited by Ted R. Gurr: 135–166. New York: The Free Press.

———. 1991. "Rationality and Frustration in Political Behavior." In *The Economic Approach to Politics: A Critical Reassessment of the Theory of Rational Action*, edited by Kristen Renwick Monroe: 74–93. New York: HarperCollins.

Elster, Jon. 1998. "Deliberation and Constitution Making." In *Deliberative Democracy*, edited by Jon Elster: 97–122. Cambridge: Cambridge University Press.

Ely, John Hart. 1980. *Democracy and Distrust: A Theory of Judicial Review*. Cambridge, MA: Harvard University Press.

Enoch, David. 2005. "Why Idealize?" *Ethics* 115, no. 4: 759–787.

Estlund, David M. 1990. "Democracy Without Preference." *Philosophical Review* 99, no. 3: 397–423.

———. 1997. "Beyond Fairness and Deliberation." In *Deliberative Democracy: Essays on Reason and Politics*, edited by James Bohman and William Rehg: 173–204. Cambridge, MA: MIT Press.

———. 2005. "What's So Rickety? Richardson's Non-Epistemic Democracy." *Philosophy and Phenomenological Research* 71, no. 1: 204–210.

———. 2008. *Democratic Authority: A Philosophical Framework*. Princeton, NJ: Princeton University Press.

Ewing, A. C. 1948. *The Definition of Good*. London: Routledge and Kegan Paul.

Feldman, Fred. 2006. *Pleasure and the Good Life: Concerning the Nature, Varieties and Plausibility of Hedonism*. Oxford: Clarendon Press.

Frank, Thomas. 2018. "The People, No." *The Baffler*, no. 42: 6–7.

Galston, William A. 2018. *Anti-Pluralism: The Populist Threat to Liberal Democracy*. New Haven: Yale University Press.

Gardbaum, Stephen. 2006. "Where the (State) Action Is." *International Journal of Constitutional Law* 4, no. 4: 760–779.

Gilens, Martin, and Benjamin I. Page. 2014. "Testing Theories of American Politics: Elites, Interest Groups, and Average Citizens." *Perspectives on Politics* 12, no. 3: 564–581.

Goodin, Robert E., and Christian List. 2006. "A Conditional Defense of Plurality Rule: Generalizing May's Theorem in a Restricted Informational Environment." *American Journal of Political Science* 50, no. 4: 940–949.

Goodwyn, Lawrence. 1976. *Democratic Promise: The Populist Moment in America*. New York: Oxford University Press.

Graaf, J. F. 1957. *Theoretical Welfare Economics*. Cambridge: Cambridge University Press.

Green, Jeffrey E. 2011. *The Eyes of the People: Democracy in an Age of Spectatorship*. Oxford: Oxford University Press.

Grether, David M., and Charles R. Plott. 1979. "Economic Theory of Choice and the Preference-Reversal Phenomenon." *American Economic Review* 69, no. 4: 623–638.

Griffin, Christopher G. 2003. "Democracy As a Non-Instrumentally Just Procedure." *The Journal of Political Philosophy* 11, no. 1: 111–121.

Grofman, Bernard. 1999. "SNTV: An Inventory of Theoretically Derived Propositions and a Brief Review of the Evidence from Japan, Korea, Taiwan, and Alabama." In *Elections in Japan, Korea, and Taiwan Under the Single Non-Transferable Vote*, edited by Bernard Grofman, Sung-Chull Lee, et al.: 375–416. Ann Arbor: University of Michigan Press.

Gutmann, Amy. 1993. "Disharmony of Democracy." *Nomos* 35: 126–160.

Gutmann, Amy, and Dennis Thompson. 2006. *Democracy and Disagreement*. Cambridge, MA: Harvard University Press.

Habermas, Jurgen. 2006. "Political Communication in Media Society: Does Democracy Still Enjoy an Epistemic Dimension? The Impact of Normative Theory on Empirical Research." *Communication Theory* 16: 411–426.

Hall, Everett W. 1943. "An Ethics for Today." *American Journal of Ethics and Sociology* 2, no. 4: 433–452.

———. 1945. *The Road to Freedom: An Ethics for Today*. Unpublished manuscript at the Everett Hall Archive, Southern Illinois University.

———. 1947. "A Categorial Analysis of Value." *Philosophy of Science* 14, no. 4: 333–344.

———. 1949. "The 'Proof' of Utility in Bentham and Mill." *Ethics* 60, no. 1: 1–18.

———. 1952. *What Is Value?* New York: Humanities Press.

———. 1961. *Our Knowledge of Fact and Value*. Chapel Hill: University of North Carolina. Print.

Hamid, Shadi. 2016. "Everyone Says the Libya Intervention Was a Failure: They're Wrong." *Vox*, Apr. 5, 2016: https://www.vox.com/2016/4/5/11363288/libya-intervention-success. Retrieved 6/9/2017.

Hamilton, Vivian E. 2011. "The Age of Electoral Majority." *ExpressO:* http://works.bepress.com/vivian_hamilton/3/.

Hamner, Robert, and Gene L. Coon. 1967. *Star Trek*: "A Taste of Armageddon." Directed by Joseph Pevney and first broadcast on Feb. 23, 1967.

Hampton, Jean. 1997. *Political Philosophy*. Boulder, CO: Westview Press.

Hanna, Jason. 2018. *In Our Best Interest: A Defense of Paternalism*. New York: Oxford University Press.

Hare, R. M. 1963. "Some Confusions About Subjectivity." In *Freedom and Morality*, edited by John Bricke: 191–208. Lawrence: University of Kansas.

Harsanyi, John C. 1985. "Does Reason Tell Us What Moral Code to Follow and, Indeed, to Follow Any Moral Code at All?" *Ethics* 96, no. 1: 42–55.

Hausman, Daniel M. 2000. "Revealed Preference, Belief, and Game Theory." *Economics and Philosophy* 16: 99–115.

———. 2011. *Preference, Value, Choice and Welfare*. Cambridge: Cambridge University Press.

Hayden, Greg M. 2003. "The False Promise of One Person One Vote." *Michigan Law Review* 102, no. 2: 213–267.

Hayek, F. A. 1944. *The Road to Serfdom*. London: Routledge.

———. 1960. *The Constitution of Liberty*. London: Routledge & Kegan Paul.

Heathwood, Christopher. 2006. "Desire Satisfaction and Hedonism." *Philosophical Studies* 128, no. 3: 539–563.

———. 2014. "Subjective Theories of Well-Being." In *The Cambridge Companion to Utilitarianism*, edited by Ben Eggleston and Dale Miller: 199–219. Cambridge: Cambridge University Press.

Hobbes, Thomas. 1651. *Leviathan*. London: Andrew Crooke.

Horn, Walter. 2013. "Metaphysical Realism and the Various Cognitive Predicaments of Everett W. Hall." In *The Roots of Representationism: An Introduction to Everett Hall*, edited by Walter Horn: 259–297. Saarbrucken: Lap-Lambert Academic.

———. 2015. "Tonality, Musical Form, and Aesthetic Value." *Perspectives of New Music* 53, no. 2: 201–235.

———. 2018. "Epistemic Closure, Home Truths, and Easy Philosophy." *The Journal of Philosophy* 115, no. 1: 34–51.

———. 2019. "CHOICE: An Objective, Voluntaristic Theory of Prudential Value." *Philosophia*: https://doi.org/10.1007/s11406-019-00117-0.

Huemer, Michael. 2012. *The Problem of Political Authority: An Examination of the Right to Coerce and the Duty to Obey*. New York: Palgrave-Macmillan.

Huntington, Samuel Phillips. 1991. *The Third Wave: Democratization in the Late Twentieth Century*. Norman, OK: University of Oklahoma.

Hurme, Sally Balch, and Paul S. Appelbaum. 2007. "Defining and Assessing Capacity to Vote: The Effect of Mental Impairment on the Rights of Voters." *McGeorge Law Review* 38: 931–979.

Hyland, James L. 1995. *Democratic Theory: The Philosophical Foundations*. Manchester: Manchester University Press.

Invernizzi-Accetti, Carlo. 2017. "Does Democratic Theory *Need* Epistemic Standards?" *Democratic Theory* 4, no. 2: 3–26.

Jackson, Frank. 1991. "Decision-Theoretic Consequentialism and the Nearest and Dearest Objection." *Ethics* 101, no. 3: 461–482.

James, William. 1917. *The Varieties of Religious Experience: A Study in Human Nature*. New York: Longmans, Green.

Jevons, W. Stanley. 1888. *The Theory of Political Economy*. London: MacMillan.

Kazin, Michael. 2017. *The Populist Persuasion: An American History*. Ithaca: Cornell University Press.

Keller, Simon. 2009. "Welfare as Success." *Noûs* 43, no. 4: 656–683.

Kelsen, Hans. 1949. *General Theory of Law and the State*, translated by Anders Wedberg. Cambridge, MA: Harvard University Press.

Kendall, Willmoore. 1950. "Prolegomena to Any Future Work on Majority Rule." *The Journal of Politics* 12, no. 4: 694–713.

Kendall, Willmoore, and George W. Carey. 1968. "The 'Intensity' Problem and Democratic Theory." *American Political Science Review* 62, no. 1: 5–24.

Kraut, Richard. 2007. *What is Good and Why*. Cambridge, MA: Harvard University Press.

Kubala, Robbie. 2017. "Valuing and Believing Valuable." *Analysis* 17, no. 1: 59–65.

Kurland, Philip B. 1987. *The Founders' Constitution.* Chicago: University of Chicago.

Laclau, Ernesto. 2005. *On Populist Reason.* London: Verso.

Lamont, W. D. 1946. *The Principles of Moral Judgement.* Oxford: Clarendon.

———. 1955. *The Value Judgement.* Edinburgh: University of Edinburgh.

Landa, Dimitri, and Ryan Pevnick. 2019. "Representative Democracy As Defensible Epistocracy." *American Political Science Review*: 1–13. doi:10.1017/S0003055419000509.

Lee, Frances E. 2011. "Bicameral Representation." In *The Oxford Handbook of the American Congress*, edited by George C. Edwards III and Frances E. Lee: Part IV, Ch. 12. Oxford: Oxford University Press.

Lenin, V. I. 1918. *The Proletarian Revolution and the Renegade Kautsky*, translated by Jim Riordin. Moscow: Kommunist Publishers.

Levinson, Sanford. 2002. "One Person, One Vote: A Mantra in Need of Meaning." *North Carolina Law Review* 80, no. 4: 1269–1297.

Lewis, David. 1989. "Dispositional Theories of Value." *Proceedings of the Aristotelian Society Supplementary Volume* 63, no. 1: 113–137.

Lijphart, Arend, Rafael Lopez Pintor, et al. 2003. "The Limited Vote and the Single Nontransferable Vote: Lessons from the Japanese and Spanish Examples." In *Electoral Laws and Their Political Consequences*, edited by Bernard Grofman and Arend Lijphart: 154–169. New York: Agathon Press.

Lilburne, John. 1649. *An Agreement of the Free People of England. Tendered as a Peace-Offering to This Distressed Nation.* Oxford: Bodleian Library. Trascribed by H. Antonn. Published by Tony Gosling, 10 Highwood Close Orpington, Kent.

Lindsay, A. D. 1929. *The Essentials of Democracy.* Oxford: Oxford University Press.

———. 1947. *The Modern Democratic State.* Oxford: Oxford University Press.

List, Christian. 2014. "Three Kinds of Collective Attitudes." *Erkenntnis* 79, no. 9: 1601–1622.

Locke, John. 1680. "Second Treatise of Government." In *The Works of John Locke in Ten Volumes* (1823), edited by John Locke. London: Tegg, Sharpe, Offor and Robinson, Evans.

Lombardo, Paul. 1985. "Three Generations, No Imbeciles: New Light on Buck v. Bell." *New York University Law Review* 60: 30–62.

Lundberg, Thomas Carl. 2007. *Proportional Representation and the Constituency Role in Britain.* New York: Palgrave/MacMillan.

Macedo, Stephen, ed. 1999. *Deliberative Politics: Essays on Democracy and Disagreement.* Oxford: Oxford University Press.

MacKenzie, Debora. 2019. "Partition Mentality." *New Scientist*, May 25, 2019.

Mackie, Gerry. 2003. *Democracy Defended.* Cambridge: Cambridge University Press.

Matthews, Dylan. 2018. "The Case for Massively Expanding the US House of Representatives, in One Chart." *Vox*, Apr. 6, 2018.

May, Kenneth O. 1954. "Intransitivity, Utility, and the Aggregation of Preference Patterns." *Econometrica* 22, no. 1: 1–13.

McClosky, Herbert. 1949. "The Fallacy of Absolute Majority Rule." *The Journal of Politics* 11, no. 4: 637–654.

Mill, John Stuart. 1861. *Considerations on Representative Government*. New York: Henry Holt.

Miller, David. 2009. "Democracy's Domain." *Philosophy & Public Affairs* 37, no. 3: 201–228.

Miller, Gary J., Thomas H. Hammond, et al. 1996. "Bicameralism and the Core: An Experimental Test." *Legislative Studies Quarterly* 21, no. 1: 83–103.

Millgram, Elijah. 2000. "Mill's Proof of the Principle of Utility." *Ethics* 110, no. 2: 282–310.

Mises, Ludwig Von. 1922. *Socialism: An Economic and Sociological Analysis*, translated by J. Kahane. London: Jonathan Cape.

Mishan, E. J. 1960. "A Survey of Welfare Economics, 1939–1959." *The Economic Journal* 70, no. 278: 197–265.

Moore, G. E. 1903. *Principia Ethica*. Cambridge: Cambridge University Press.

Mounk, Yascha. 2019. "A Russia Scandal Even Populists Couldn't Stomach." *Atlantic Monthly*, May 21, 2019.

Mueller, Dennis C., Robert D. Tollison, et al. 1975. "Solving the Intensity Problem in Representative Democracy." In *The Public Choice Approach to Politics*, edited by Dennis C. Mueller: 143–183. Aldershot: Edward Elgar. 1993.

Muller, Jan-Werner. 2016. *What Is Populism?* Philadelphia, PA: University of Pennsylvania.

Murphy, Mark C. 1999. "The Simple Desire-Fulfillment Theory." *Noûs* 33, no. 2: 247–272.

Nagel, Jack H. 2007. "The Burr Dilemma in Approval Voting." *Journal of Politics* 69, no. 1: 43–58.

Newman, Randy. 1974a. "Kingfish." In *Good Old Boys*. Warner Brothers.

———. 1974b. "Rednecks." In *Good Old Boys*. Warner Brothers.

Nock, Albert Jay. 1943. *Memoirs of a Superfluous Man*. New York: Harper.

Nozick, Robert. 1974. *Anarchy, State and Utopia*. New York: Basic Books.

———. 1977. "On Austrian Methodology." *Synthese* 36, no. 3: 353–392.

Overvold, Mark. 1982. "Self-Interest and Getting What You Want." In *The Limits of Utilitarianism*, edited by Harlan B. Miller and William H. Williams: 186–194. Minneapolis: University of Minnesota.

Paine, Thomas. 1786. "On the Affairs of Pennsylvania." *Pennsylvania Gazette*, Sept. 26, 1786.

Parfit, Derek.1984. *Reasons and Persons*. Oxford: Oxford University Press, pp. 493–502.

Pecanha, Sergio. 2020. "Are Cows Better Represented in the Senate than People?" *New York Times*, Jan. 16, 2020.

Perry, Ralph Barton. 1926. *General Theory of Value*. Cambridge, MA: Harvard University Press.

———. 1932. "Real and Apparent Value." *Philosophy* 7, no. 35: 62–67.

Peterson, Martin. 2009. *An Introduction to Decision Theory*. Cambridge: Cambridge University Press.

Pildes, Richard H., and Elizabeth S. Anderson. 1990. "Slinging Arrows at Democracy: Social Choice Theory, Value Pluralism, and Democratic Politics." *Columbia Law Review* 90, no. 8: 2121–2214.

Pitkin, Hanna F. 2004. "Representation and Democracy: Uneasy Alliance." *Scandinavian Political Studies* 27, no. 3: 335–342.

Pojman, Louis P. 1997. "On Equal Human Worth: A Critique of Contemporary Egalitarianism." In *Equality: Selected Readings*, edited by Louis P. Pojman and Robert Westmoreland: 282–299. Oxford: Oxford University Press.

Polsby, Daniel D., and Robert D. Popper. 1991. "The Third Criterion: Compactness As a Procedural Safeguard Against Partisan Gerrymandering." *Yale Law & Policy Review* 9, no. 2: 301–353.

Post, Robert. 2014. *Citizens Divided: Campaign Finance Reform and the Constitution*. Cambridge: Harvard University Press.

Radcliff, Benjamin. 1993. "Liberalism, Populism, and Collective Choice." *Political Research Quarterly* 46, no. 1: 127–142.

Rae, Douglas W. 1975. "The Limits of Consensual Decision." *The American Political Science Review* 69, no. 4: 1270–1294.

———. 1981. "Two Contradictory Ideas of (Political) Equality." *Ethics* 91, no. 3: 451–456.

Ransom, William L., and Theodore Roosevelt. 1912. *Majority Rule and the Judiciary*. New York: Scribners.

Rawls, John. 1971. *A Theory of Justice*. Cambridge, MA: Harvard University Press.

Reed, Steven R. 2003a. *Japanese Electoral Politics: Creating a New Party System*. New York: Routledge.

———. 2003b. "What Mechanism Causes the M +1 Rule? A Simple Simulation." *Japanese Journal of Political Science* 4, no. 1: 41–60.

Reiss, Julian. 2013. *Philosophy of Economics: A Contemporary Introduction*. London: Routledge.

Rice, Christopher M. 2013. "Defending the Objective List Theory of Well-Being." *Ratio* 26, no. 2: 196–211.

Rice, Stuart A. 1928. "The Distribution of Individual Political Attitudes." In *Quantitative Methods in Politics*, edited by Stuart A. Rice: 71–91. New York: Appleton-Century-Crofts.

Riker, William H. 1982. *Liberalism Against Populism: A Confrontation Between the Theory of Democracy and the Theory of Social Choice*. Long Grove, IL: Waveland Press.

———. 1992. "The Justification of Bicameralism." *International Political Science Review* 13, no. 1: 101–116.

Riker, William H., and Barry R. Weingast. 1988. "Constitutional Regulation of Legislative Choice: The Political Consequences of Judicial Deference to Legislatures." *Virginia Law Review* 74, no. 2: 373–401.

Riskin, Robert. 1997. "Meet John Doe." In *Six Screen Plays by Robert Riskin*, edited by Pat McGilligan. Berkeley: University of California Press.

Risse, Mathias. 2004. "Arguing for Majority Rule." *Journal of Political Philosophy* 12, no. 1: 41–64.

Roosevelt, Theodore. 1912. "Introduction." In *Majority Rule and the Judiciary*, edited by William L. Ransom and Theodore Roosevelt. New York: Scribners.

Rosberg, Gerald M. 1977. "Aliens and Equal Protection: Why Not the Right to Vote?" *Michigan Law Review* 75, no. 5/6: 1092–1136.

Rothbard, Murray Newton. 1962. *Man, Economy, and State: A Treatise on Economic Principles*. Princeton, NJ: Van Nostrand.

Rousseau, Jean-Jacques. 1762. *The Social Contract*, translated by G. D. H. Cole. London: J. M. Dent & Sons.

Russell, Bertrand. 1917. *Principles of Social Reconstruction*. London: Allen & Unwin.

———. 1955. *Human Society in Ethics and Politics*. New York: Simon & Schuster.

Rutland, Robert Allen. 1983. *The Birth of the Bill of Rights, 1776–1791*. Boston: Northeastern University Press.

Saffon, Maria Paula, and Nadia Urbinati. 2013. "Procedural Democracy, the Bulwark of Equal Liberty." *Political Theory* 41, no. 3: 441–481.

Sajo, Andras, and Renata Uitz, eds. 2005. *The Constitution in Private Relations: Expanding Constitutionalism*. The Hague: Eleven International Publishing.

Samuelson, Paul. 1938. "A Note on the Pure Theory of Consumers' Behavior." *Economica* 5, no. 17: 61–71.

Sanders, Lynn M. 1997. "Against Deliberation." *Political Theory* 25, no. 3: 347–376.

Scanlon, Thomas M. 1975. "Preference and Urgency." *Journal of Philosophy* 72, no. 9: 655–669.

———. 1991. "The Moral Basis of Interpersonal Comparisons." In *Interpersonal Comparisons of Well-Being*, edited by L. J. Elster and J. E. Roemer: 17–44. Cambridge: Cambridge University Press.

Schmitt, Karl. 1932. "Concept of the Political." In *Concept of the Political: Expanded Edition*, translated by George Schwab: 19–79. Chicago: University of Chicago.

Schultz, Bart. 1992. "Bertrand Russell in Ethics and Politics." *Ethics* 102, no. 3: 594–634.

Schumpeter, Joseph. 1942. *Capitalism, Socialism and Democracy*. New York: Harper & Bros.

Schwartz, Barry. 2016. *The Paradox of Choice: Why More Is Less*. New York: HarperCollins.

Seed, Geoffrey. 1978. *James Wilson*. Millwood, NY: KTO Press.

Sen, Amartya. 1970. "Impossibility of a Paretian Liberal." *Journal of Political Economy* 78, no. 1: 152–157.

———. 1973. "Behavior and the Concept of Preference." *Economica* 40, no. 159: 241–259.

———. 1980. "Equality of What?" In *The Tanner Lecture on Human Values I*: 197–220. Cambridge: Cambridge University Press.

Shapiro, Ian. 2003. *The State of Democratic Theory*. Princeton, NJ: Princeton University Press.

Shapiro, Martin. 1985. "Gerrymandering, Fairness, and the Supreme Court." *UCLA Law Review* 33: 227–256.

Sharp, Frank Chapman. 1941. "Voluntarism and Objectivity in Ethics." *Philosophical Review* 50, no. 3: 253–267.

Sidgwick, Henry. 1901. *Methods of Ethics*. London: MacMillan.

Sigler, Mary. 2014. "Sensible Disenfranchisement." *Iowa Law Review* 99: 1725–1744.

Simon, Herbert A. 1985. "Human Nature in Politics: The Dialogue of Psychology with Political Science." *The American Political Science Review* 79, no. 2: 293–304.

Sitaraman, Ganesh. 2019. "How to Rein in an All-Too Powerful Supreme Court." *The Atlantic*, Nov. 16, 2019: https://www.theatlantic.com/ideas/archive/2019/11/congr essional-review-act-court/601924/. Retrieved 21/11/2019.

Smith, John Allen. 1907. *The Spirit of American Government: A Study of the Constitution, Its Origin, Influence and Relation to Democracy*. New York: MacMillan.

Smith, Rogers M. 1988. "The "American Creed" and American Identity: The Limits of Liberal Citizenship in the United States." *The Western Political Quarterly* 41, no. 2: 225–251.

Smith, Warren D. 2005. "Examples of Our Unbiased District-Drawing Algorithm in Action." *Center for Range Voting*: http://www.rangevoting.org/GerryExamples .html. Retrieved 6/9/2017.

Sobel, David. 1997. "On the Subjectivity of Welfare." *Ethics* 107, no. 3: 501–508.

———. 2009. "Subjectivism and Idealization." *Ethics* 119, no. 2: 336–352.

Song, Sarah. 2012. "The Boundary Problem in Democratic Theory: Why the Demos Should Be Bounded by the State." *International Theory* 4, no. 1: 39–68.

Still, Jonathan W. 1981. "Political Equality and Election Systems." *Ethics* 91, no. 3: 375–394.

Sumner, L. W. 1988. "Review of Utilitarianism, Hedonism, and Desert: Essays in Moral Philosophy by Fred Feldman." *Ethics* 109, no. 1: 176–179.

———. 1995. "The Subjectivity of Welfare." *Ethics* 105, no. 4: 764–790.

———. 1996. *Welfare Happiness and Ethics*. Oxford: Oxford University Press.

Taschetto, Diana. 2015. "Justification and Justice: Rawls, Quine and Ethics as Science." *Principia: An International Journal of Epistemology* 19, no. 1: 147–169.

Toplak, Jurij. 2008. "Equal Voting Weight of All: Finally 'One Person, One Vote' from Hawaii to Maine?" *Temple Law Review* 81: 123–176.

Trollope, Anthony. 1862. *North America*. New York: Harper & Brothers.

Tullock, Gordon. 1967. "The General Irrelevance of the General Impossibility Theorem." *The Quarterly Journal of Economics* 81, no. 2: 256–270.

Twombley, Jim. 2012. "The United States of Nebraska: Are Bicameral State Legislatures Necessary and Could Unicameralism Serve Other States Well." Paper presented at the Midwest Political Science Association Annual Meeting, Chicago, IL, Apr. 12–15, 2012.

Urbinati, Nadia. 2000. "Representation As Advocacy." *Political Theory* 28, no. 6: 58–86.

———. 2010. *Representative Democracy: Principles and Genealogy*. Chicago, IL: University of Chicago.

———. 2014. *Democracy Disfigured: Opinion, Truth, and the People*. Cambridge, MA: Harvard University Press.

Waldron, Jeremy. 1995. "The Dignity of Legislation." *Maryland Law Review* 54, no. 2: 633–665.

———. 2006. The Core of the Case Against Judicial Review." *The Yale Law Journal* 115, no. 6: 1346–1406.

———. 2010. "A Majority in the Lifeboat." *Boston University Law Review* 90: 1043–1057.

Walzer, Michael. 2010. *Spheres of Justice: A Defense of Pluralism and Equality.* New York: Basic.

Weaver, Matthew. 2018. "Lower Voting Age to Six to Tackle Bias Against Young, Says Academic." *The Guardian*, Dec. 6, 2018: https://www.theguardian.com/politics /2018/dec/06/give-six-year-olds-the-vote-says-cambridge-university-academic.

Whitt, Matt S. 2017. "Felon Disenfranchisement and Democratic Legitimacy." *Social Theory and Practice* 43, no. 2: 283–311.

Wood, Gordon S. 1969. *The Creation of the American Republic: 1776–1787.* Chapel Hill: University of North Carolina.

Index

About the Author

Walter Horn has published articles in the areas of epistemology, metaphysics, value theory, public policy, and aesthetics, and has edited a book on the early-twentieth-century philosopher Everett Hall, whose work he has championed for over forty years. Horn has provided policy research and expert testimony to both the legislative and executive branches of the Commonwealth of Massachusetts and has been an occasional philosophy professor since 1978, when he received his doctorate from Brown University. He lives with his family in Arlington, Massachusetts.

www.ingramcontent.com/pod-product-compliance
Lightning Source LLC
Chambersburg PA
CBHW050637280326

41932CB00015B/2684